# In the Background

*DEDICATED TO THE MEMORY*
*OF*
*PETER LAVENDER*

# In the Background

## AN EXTRA'S HANDBOOK

•

## Bill Tarling

edited and with additional material by
*Peter Messaline*

Simon & Pierre
Toronto, Ontario

We would like to express our gratitude to the **Canada Council,** the **Ontario Arts Council,** the **Book Publishing Industry Development Program** of the **Department of Communication,** and the **Ontario Publishing Centre** of the **Ministry of Culture, Tourism and Recreation** for their generous assistance and ongoing support.

*Kirk Howard, President*

1 2 3 4 5 • 9 8 7 6

**Canadian Cataloging in Publication Data**

Tarling, Bill, 1960-
       In the background : an extra's handbook

ISBN 0-88924-267-4

1. Motion picture acting - Vocational guidance.
I. Messaline, Peter, 1944- . II. Title.

PN1995.9.A26T37 1995    791.43'028'023   C95-932561-1

**Editor:** Jean Paton
**Designer:** Sebastian Vasile
**Printed and bound in Canada** by Webcom Ltd.

Order from **Simon & Pierre Publishing Company Limited,** care of

| Dundurn Press Limited | Dundurn Distribution | Dundurn Press Limited |
|---|---|---|
| 2181 Queen Street East | 73 Lime Walk | 1823 Maryland Avenue |
| Suite 301 | Headington, Oxford | P.O. Box 1000 |
| Toronto, Canada | England | Niagara Falls, N.Y. |
| M4E 1E5 | 0X3 7AD | U.S.A. 14302-1000 |

# CONTENTS

*Don't worry. This isn't brain surgery.*
*You can go on set and be successful without studying this whole book.*
*Experience says you'll get more work and enjoy it more, if you think about it.*
*This book is full of things to think about.*

*No longer a rookie, you're expected to know the basics, and improve on your earlier performances. Feel you know just enough to be scared about doing another shoot? The chapters in this section are full of specifics about actual working conditions, and some answers to give you back your confidence.*

*This is a graduate course, for those who are in the business for the long term. These chapters are seminars on organizing your office – and your life. Here's some leverage to help you find success in a very special industry.*

*The worksheets and forms in this section are for everyone, beginner to graduate. Use some to decide how the extra's life can work for you, some are to organize your life as an extra, and some self-evaluation forms you could use no matter which career path you choose. Look at them now, but use them with the chapters they belong to.*

MIRROR, MIRROR
*This is fun if you take it seriously. Find out where you are and how you're doing.*

*Here's the jargon you need to baffle outsiders. Be an insider: find out how big an apple is, who's the Best Boy, and why ambience isn't always room tone.*

## WITH SPECIAL THANKS TO:

Donna Dupere, Stephanie Kelly, Eleanor Lavender, Gabrielle Ivaney, Rose Lewis, Jane Rogers-Avigdor, The Kosty Family, Converse/Smith Talent, Claire & Jack Wahl, Peter Messaline, Frenchie Smith, and Elizabeth Dean...

An extra special thanks to my best friend Norm, without whose patience, understanding, and assistance, I would never have had the chance to create this book or even enter into this crazy film industry.

And a final thanks to Extras everywhere, without whom films just wouldn't be the same. You've got a thankless job, but we need you and I wish you all the best of success.

The author and editor are grateful to the staff at Simon & Pierre and Dundurn for their unfailing interest and sympathy. Particularly to Jean Paton, who deserves her retirement, even if it came at the worst time for us, and Kirk Howard, who always seems ready to go out on a limb for a new project.

# FOREWORD

**William McColman Tarling III**, Bill, was one of those serious children who sit in their rooms and take things apart. A self-taught electronic wizard, he started by rigging microphone bugs in soft toys, and will now take your computer apart and put it back together, improved, if you take your eyes off it for a moment.

Almost as soon as he became a fulltime Extra, he took time out to run an Extras agency. By working single-handed an insane number of hours a week, he rescued the failing agency and started building his current reputation among extras on set.

In the last years, he has been a regular background performer on *War of the Worlds*, *Friday's Curse*, *Top Cops*, *Kung-Fu* and *Forever Knight*. His longest Extra job was twenty-two days (250 paid hours) on *Millennium*, his most concentrated work period was four continuous days on three rotating shoots back to back (to back), sleeping only on the bus from set to set.

And people can't understand why he looks so relaxed playing an upgrade or one of his many principal roles.

Bill was an ACTRA Toronto Branch Councillor, and then Chair of the Background Performers' Committee. He continues to take an active part in ACTRA politics.

While he now has Extras agents again, and a principal agent, Bill thinks he is more devoted to his career than anyone he has met, and has no intention of giving up steering the boat.

This book started as a collection of dog-eared notes Bill had made to remind himself of clear answers to common questions. After the questions became requests for the notes, this book became a dream, and then a pile of manuscript and, after editors and computers and too many late nights, this book.

**Peter Messaline**, the Taxpert, trained as an oil geologist, worked as a theatre carpenter, became an actor with the Royal Shakespeare Company, performed on three continents, and came to Canada pursuing Miriam Newhouse. He has worked on stage from Vancouver to Montreal, and from Niagara Falls to Fort McMurray. His media work includes a series lead on *MacPherson,* many educational and industrial videos, radio drama across the country, and Extra, Actor, SOC, principal and Guest Star roles on commercials and episodic television.

As an ACTRA Councillor, he tightened definitions and fought for logic, as the union switched to local autonomy from central control. He remains Chair of the Questionnaire Committee and sits on the ACTRA Co-op Committee.

For Simon & Pierre, he and Miriam Newhouse, with Margaret Bard, edited *"And what are you going to do for us?"* the first book of Canadian audition speeches, and *"And do you have anything else?"* which was the second. Together they wrote *The Actor's Survival Kit,* now in its second edition with a third planned. They produce *The Canadian Performers' Tax Kit*: tax advice and a receipt filing system to minimise tax bills.

Peter is The Taxpert, author of tax and finance articles in the newsletters of both performer unions and Theatre Ontario. Currently, he sits on a working group with both unions and a caucus of entertainment accountants, making sense of new Revenue Canada tax policies.

Bill and he had shared the same side of many Council arguments, and his small Extra experience convinced him that the book was needed. While the expertise in the book is Bill's, Peter contributed the bulk of the tax material and some of his own experience on film shoots. He also read, advised, coaxed and argued, and burned up a modem as the manuscript inched to completion.

10

# FROM THE TOP

Being an extra is easy. Being a professional extra can use as much energy and know-how as you want to give it.

If you are on the outside looking in, wondering about being an extra, worrying about the unknowns, here's insider information so you can enjoy yourself more.

If you're already working as an extra, here are proven tactics to get you more work, real-life up-to-date experience.

If you're an extra on the way to a wider range of performer work, I'll show you how to lay the foundation for your career and grow as an artist.

Everyone dreams of being a movie star. The fame, the money, the admiration.... What a way to make a living. The theatre darkens, a hush falls over the audience, the screen erupts in a blaze of glory and your countless fans scream their applause. You smile and shake your head as you stand to take your bows.

A jolt in the ribs from your companion snaps you back to reality. With some grumbling (and just a touch of blush), you settle in your seat to watch somebody else's film success.

Welcome to real life. Being a professional actor is unprofitable, as well as physically and mentally exhausting. From the latest Canadian figures, the reality is that the average performer makes around $23,000 from all sources, and the average income from union film and television work alone is $9,830. That means you'd better have a day job to survive, and a mate with income if you want to raise a family at more than the poverty level.

Being an Extra is much harder, and much less well-paid. You won't receive star treatment, nor will you enjoy a star's pay cheque or status. You will be ignored, given very minor chores, and you will be broke. It's a thankless job, but somebody has to do it.

And someone had to write this book. I've worked for years as an extra, and in the main cast in Actor and Principal categories. It's all acting, but the practical details are very different. Extras have unique challenges on set and in casting, and no-one has written about that world properly. There are some American books, some *Stay in Red Deer and Be a Star* dream builders and a few slim volumes telling you just enough to get you into major trouble. This is the first book offering you information about the aggressive and successful career strategy that has worked for me. You don't have to use it – but it's here, in detail, for when you need it.

My first problem was what to leave out – I wasn't ready to tackle an encyclopedia! Anyway, I learn something new every time I work, so I could never say, "Okay, now I know all I need for the book." In the end, I threw out all my lists and started to write about the things I am asked about on set.

Even if you know the ropes, don't skip the familiar stuff; it's easy to forget the basics. If you're just starting, prepare for "Extras Boot Camp." You can use the skills you have now to learn more and earn more.

If it's cash you're after, the pay starts at around $40 (cash in hand at the end of the day) to $100 and up (for a union member, by cheque in a couple of weeks).

If you're ready for a challenge or a break from your usual drudgery, the dreams come free. We live in a world of make-believe, and you're invited to join in: become a fireman, a brain surgeon, a comic book hero, a time traveller. One day you relax by a brook in the seventeenth century countryside, the next you're valiantly fighting to save the planet from bug-eyed invaders. Relive your childhood and drink from the fountain of youth.

If you're just beginning an acting career, this book will help you to get the confidence and experience that will make you more useful and get you more work. You want to learn on the best sets possible, but more experienced actors will work for as little as you will on union sets. Non-union work, even as long as you can afford it, can only take you so far. Extra work on union sets can be your foot in the door. With the competition for small roles in union productions, many beginning actors rely on extra work to get experience on set.

If you're an established performer, you needn't be ashamed of adding Extra work to your range. Not every part we play is Lear, but every part deserves all our concentration. And we all have to pay the rent. You're smart enough to do so by working at your craft – what do other performers do between roles?

The reason you're getting into Extra work doesn't matter. The dreams are there if you want them, but this is a job, not the priesthood. If you find you don't like the madhouse, take your energy and make a success of something else. There are rules here but it sometimes seems there are more exceptions. I'll tell you what I've seen work, but only one thing is certain: you'll need all your enthusiasm and self-discipline to have a chance of success.

Self-discipline involves making your own choices, not relying on others. Without the structure a regular nine-to-five job imposes, you can choose to drift along and do the minimum if you like. Of course you don't have to work yourself like a slave-driver; you should have a life outside the business. You're the boss. Just remember, the job you skip today won't be there tomorrow.

"Do you seriously want to be a star? No problem. This is the wonderful world of film, where overnight success is routine and fortunes are yours for the taking."

"There is no way that you will ever get anywhere as an extra. You're at the bottom of the totem pole and that is where you'll stay, with all the other extras who once had ambition. Talent? Forget it: if you had any real talent, you wouldn't be an extra."

You'll hear both these points of view presented as the gospel truth, but let's look at what you can really expect.

It is actually possible to become a star overnight, but you're more likely to be struck by lightning sitting in your house, looking at this year's third winning lottery ticket. And as Rhett Butler nearly said, "Frankly, my dear, being a star isn't worth a damn." Hollywood has created a fantasy world around its stars, building fairy stories about the glamorous lives they lead and ignoring the years they struggled to pay the rent. Even once they make it, they're up before dawn to be on set and it's dark again when they get back to their room to start learning tomorrow's lines. Remember the last minutes before high school English classes, memorizing those poems? How would you like to spend the rest of your life doing that? And stars earn their money by selling themselves to the public twenty-four hours a day. Being approached for your autograph is exciting for a while, but imagine being the celebrity I once saw being asked for his autograph while busy in a public washroom.

All right. So being a star isn't all it's cracked up to be, but what about being an ordinary successful actor? You've got what it takes and you're bound to be discovered, right? Sorry, as a rule of thumb, overnight success takes twenty years. Don't expect instant magic. If you do find it, treat it gently, because magic doesn't last.

In the States, doing Extra work is accepted in the industry as a legitimate way for actors to work. Eventually the same may be true in Canada, if enough extras take their craft seriously. At the moment, though, many people think that background work is strictly for wannabees who weren't good enough to do "real acting," and that "real actors" never work as Extras. This isn't just prejudice: some Extras simply don't have any talent; more often they don't care, or are simply ignorant of professional skills and attitude. Their faults can help you. Their amateur approach will make your professional attitude shine. Your talent will be noticed.

You will hear that people see extras only as extras. Don't believe it. I've been told by many directors that I got the current speaking role thanks to previous Extra work. Actors use their skills to help make the scenes work, and being an Extra is no different. If you learn what's required and provide what's necessary, you are using, and exhibiting, professional skills.

If you're an established performer, your agent may discourage you from doing background work. This may be part of a larger plan, but be sure it isn't just prejudice. My first talent agent confirmed that over sixty per cent of my work in the main cast had been from upgrades and from auditions for directors who knew my work as an extra.

If you are serious about establishing an acting career, working as a background performer can be a solid foundation. You have to learn to use your skills, even if you're hot out of a training course. Extraordinary natural talent doesn't help beginners hit their marks, cheat the shot, find the key light, maintain continuity, all while concentrating on making their dialogue believable. The set can be very intimidating, and worst of all, the director expects you to deliver the goods right now, without time to work into things.

In the main cast, you can't hide away when it's not going right, because you're in the focus of the scene, however small your part. You'd better learn, and you'd better learn quickly.

As an extra, it's your job to blend in with the other background performers: you aren't expected to carry the scene. You can learn the tricks of the trade at your own pace and be paid while learning. Take advantage of the opportunity.

Don't waste your time as an extra plotting to get into the spotlight. Spend your time being a better extra. The Extras Casting Director, the director and ADs will see the quality of your work. Did you look like a faceless nobody who just happened to walk down the street when they were shooting? Good, that's your job, and you obviously did it well. Your skill is to be a part of the unnoticed background to the main action. And it is a real skill. This is a craft you can be proud of, even if you intend to move on to other casting or back to your main career.

There are all sorts of reasons to be an extra, but please don't start if you're already ashamed of it.

Average Extras simply go to set, do what they are told, and go home. You can do that, too. Or you can do more, work more – and make more! It takes effort and time to be a Super Extra: years to build a career, hours each day working to get work. Each set can provide new challenges, each shot can showcase your skills. It's not easy to look fresh and energetic after fifty takes, when you're sick and miserable and all you want is to go home and sleep. It's not easy, but it is the job.

You've been hired as an extra. Hired is the important word – it is a job, like any other. Your regular boss wouldn't put up with lateness or sloppiness. You're being paid to be there, to be ready at any moment, because set delays can cost a production thousands of dollars an hour. Chatting with your buddies may mean missing some important instructions. An amateur attitude can cost you work: directors, crew, and especially casting personnel are famous for remembering those who make their work harder.

If you really want to make it as an extra, you've got a career that can demand attention twenty-four hours a day. Keep your files, résumés, and photos up to date and in stock. Call your industry contacts (agents, casting, other extras).

Clean and maintain your wardrobe and search for more outfits and accessories. Be concerned with anything which might affect your career. What's happening in the industry? What shows are being shot? Watch them on TV to learn what kind of characters they have and how the extras are being used. Read books about the business (including my competition). Read the trade magazines. Save newspaper articles dealing even remotely with the industry. If you have a government channel in your area, watch for debates affecting the entertainment industry. Like most things, the more you put in, the more you get out.

If you do everything perfectly, your chances of making a living are low. Not zero, mind you, just low. If you choose to work at it, you can make the best of your abilities and make the most of your luck. Show business is an artistic dream world, but it often feels like a cruel and unforgiving industry. In fact, the business is more like a tornado: it can kill you, but it doesn't care about you. You can protect yourself, and you can harness the winds.

This is not the French Foreign Legion. You can get out at any time, and never worry about it. Not everybody is suited to the job. Some find Extra work easy and relaxed, others find it boring and tedious. Still others, seeing hundreds of people running around in total chaos, long for their quiet desk job again. If you decide being an extra's not for you, at least you had enough nerve to give it a try – and think of the long boring stories you can tell about your times on set.

This book won't magically make an extra out of you. It won't get you cast, it won't answer all the problems you will encounter in the business. Rather than tell you what to do, I've tried to explain how and why a certain approach works for me. Use the book as a guide. It's meant to be read the way you read a road map: there are all sorts of routes and it's up to you which way you go.

Be brave, run risks, take control. This is not a run-through – this is Live to Tape. Prepare yourself as well as you can, look ahead, and meet the challenges as they appear. You'll make good decisions and bad throughout your career. Don't waste time trying to work out which was which. Play the hand you're dealt.

Enjoy the game. See you on set.

# BACKGROUND ON THE BACKGROUND

# AN EXTRA LIFE TO LIVE

1

BLACK SCREEN
SOUND: A CROWDED RESTAURANT

> BOB (O.S.)
> (He sounds really ticked off, this has not
> been a good day)
> I dunno, I mean, like Jack said it was
> real easy. Besides, I'm only gonna be
> doing it a little while. Thanks for buying
> me the book and all, but it's like school
> again. And you're supposed to be my
> friend, y'know.

A BOOK moves away from the lens. We see that it
is this book.
As it is lowered, we see

INT. THE COPPER KETTLE    DAY
Bob is a regular-looking teenager, seated across
the table from our POV. The Copper Kettle is not
where we expect to see his Docs and his hairstyle.

> JANE (O.S.)
> We told your mother we'd make it as extras
>   both of us. Why not find out as much as
> we can ahead of time? Did you read it?

> BOB
> (Pulling out his copy)
> Yeah, I read it. Some of it... I read the
> first bit, and the guy says I gotta work
> hours an' days an' years. I mean, I'm
> gonna be an actor, so how hard can bein' a
> stupid extra be? You just turn up and wan-
> der around like a bunch of sheep.

                    JANE (O.S.)
That's a very BAAAd attitude.

(Bob looks around, embarrassed.)
I think you should read the book, and then
I suppose you can work at it as hard as
you want.

                    BOB
Well, he does say I need to make all my
own choices... Okay, I'll give it a shot.

                    JANE (O.S.)
Let's see if his way works. If it doesn't,
we can always drop it. Look, I used to run
an office, I know I can do better than be
a sheep. And so can you, Mr. Wolf.

                    BOB
Okay, but if we're ever on a set together,
promise me you won't do any more sheep
impressions?

                    JANE (O.S.)
               (Laughter in her voice)
Baa!

                    BOB
               (Grinning suddenly)
Baa! BAAAAA!

OVER HIS SHOULDER, we see another customer look
up at the sheep noises. As THE SHOT WIDENS, we
see the restaurant amused by the boy and his
grandmother, baa-ing as they refuse to be sheep.

# MIRROR, MIRROR (ON THE WALL...)

Who are you? What are you? What are your problems? How can you deal with them? This chapter makes a start on these questions. Don't try to solve everything as you read: be as honest as you can and the right solutions for you will follow.

Before you read any further, complete the questionnaire, "Tell Me about Myself" in Toolkit at the back of the book. Whether you have Extra experience or not, it's a way to find out what you currently think, about the industry and about yourself. DO IT NOW! Do not pass Go, do not collect $200 ("before taxes")...

There! You've just finished what an industrial consultant or a psychotherapist would have charged you hundreds of dollars for. (You didn't skip the questionnaire, did you?) You have a private snapshot, the first in a series, to look at later and see how you're changing. Another tool in your shoulder bag.

In this chapter there are no rights and wrongs. Just as in the questionnaire, there are no good or bad answers. This is a product assessment: the product is you, what you are and what you can do. Know your product, see its strengths, and you'll be able to sell it more effectively.

You are a salesman and your first client is yourself. You not only have to know your product, you have to believe in it. What are your problems?

*I would do well, but I'm too:*

| | |
|---|---|
| fat | short |
| ugly | skinny |
| tall | good-looking |
| egotistical | ambitious |
| old | self-conscious |
| young | nerdy |
| plain average | |

But are these problems? Think about this:

*I could do well **because** I'm:*

| | |
|---|---|
| fat | short |
| ugly | skinny |
| tall | good-looking |
| egotistical | ambitious |
| old | self-conscious |
| young | nerdy |
| plain average | |

**20**

Everybody is unique, but at the same time everybody belongs to dozens of categories, even if we all hate the categories we put ourselves in. If you are Ms Boring, you complain you have nothing special to make you stand out from the crowd at the audition. If you are Big Hairy Harry, a seven foot tall Yeti speaking only Sanskrit, you don't have Ms B's problem, but you may have others. Everything about you cuts you off from some casting chances, and makes others possible.

If you are of Asian descent you may be asked to play Japanese, Korean or Chinese, ignoring your actual background. Black refers to skin tone and features, regardless of heritage. If you are an exceptionally fair skinned person of African background, then Casting would not usually call you black. Don't confuse politics or accuracy or national pride with castability. Think about the groups you could be used in. You may not like being in a given group, but that doesn't necessarily mean you should avoid playing it. You can either avoid stereotyped roles or you can bring your individuality to them: it's your choice. Slowly, Casting is including visibly different people in the ordinary mix. It's still rare, though, and some groups have real and unfair trouble.

Your real age is your own business, as long as you're an adult. You'll be cast according to what you look like and how you behave. Your birth certificate is a guide, friends may tell you what they think, but your agent and the casting director make the decision for you. If they think you look forty, you're forty.

Look at the "Casting Worksheet" in the back of the book and start thinking about the groups you can claim in casting. Use the worksheet to go into detail, and to ask your friends what they think. (Maybe you look younger than you thought. Perhaps your friends see you as a bouncer, not as a fat slob.)

Don't go overboard trying to find weird types to play. Most casting is looking for the regular guy and the ordinary woman. Look at any crowd and see how few weird people there are. Limiting yourself to extreme characters may give you priority when those characters are needed, but it may also get you stereotyped as weird, and lose you work. I made the decision to concentrate on my specialty characters years ago: I do very well, but it's also meant a lot of days without work when those characters aren't needed.

Whatever you see as your casting limitations, you have choices. You can change yourself, you can make the best of things, or you can treat the problems themselves as advantages. It's all in your attitude.

I am an ugly, scrawny, awkward, long streak of rainwater. I am also a skilled horse-rider and biker, with experience in stunt fighting. Most important, I am confident in my product. People who cast and direct know I can play the meanest oddballs, without being mean or weird off set. I get work.

**21**

Enough soul searching.

People who look down on extras say that we are just warm scenery. Like most insults, it has a grain of truth, but there's more to being an extra than that. Professional extras have a tough job: we need to protect ourselves and look after our health on and off set. Come on, you're thinking, you don't need to go into heavy training to be in a shopping scene in a mall. No? Just try spending eight hours walking up and down, doing it the same every time, being natural and interested and avoiding noise, equipment, technicians, and the stars' eyeline.

How is your general health? Do you suffer from any allergies? Get your doctor to tell you precisely what it is you are allergic to, so you can tell Wardrobe.

Are you on any special medication or do you have any medical conditions the production should know about? You are responsible for yourself, but you are a fool if you don't let someone know what your danger symptoms are. The "Health Worksheet" in the back will help you decide what, precisely, you need to tell people. Remember that your concentration on set might cause you to forget the time and miss the meal or the medication your condition requires.

If you must wear glasses on set make sure they're anti-glare, or else the lights will flash off them, and the set, crew, and cameras will be reflected in them on film. Avoid lenses that change tint according to the light: the production doesn't want the audience to watch your sunglasses change colour.

Everybody has situations they hate. Some years ago, a star admitted that he had once accepted a water rescue scene despite the fact that he hated the water and couldn't swim, relying on being able to beg help from the girl he was to rescue. Out in the harbour at night, clinging to the dinghy, he discovered she too was terrified of water. Our instinct is to say, "I can do that!", but sometimes it can be unpleasant and even dangerous not to think ahead. Grit your teeth and fill in the "Personal Limitations Worksheet."

It may seem odd to include nudity on the worksheet, and it is rare you'll be asked to perform nude. But scanty clothing is a real possibility, and you can feel barer in some costumes than you would fully nude. And how relaxed are you working around other people's bare bodies? Don't duck this by saying, "As long as it's necessary for the production and done in a tasteful way." What was your instinctive first reaction to the thought?

For some people, nudity is a moral problem. Others have moral problems with a production's content: sometimes a production will let you know about a potentially offensive scene, rather than have an embarrassed crowd at the lynching. They don't usually bother; it doesn't occur to them that someone would have a problem. Think about it now, rather than have to make an important decision on the run.

Film and television are always running on the edge of disaster, and schedules rarely hold up long. Panicked phone calls at inconvenient times sometimes seem to be the rule rather than the exception. Think about the difficulties now, while you have time.

If you decide to go to the Go-See, or accept the call to set, can you actually make it? Shoot and casting locations are often hard to get to. Productions sometimes transport background performers to set, but don't count on it. You may need transportation late at night or early in the morning. Do you have a car? How well do you know your city by public transport? What would a cab cost from where you live?

Can you get there on time? How quickly can you be on your way if you receive a last minute call? How soon can you make arrangements for sitters, get hold of your boss to get the time off, borrow the car from your friend, rearrange your social life? Do you need to sort out wardrobe and supplies? You'll find some advice in the "Before the Shoot" and "Wardrobe" chapters for cutting down your ready time. Now think about the travel time to locations on the edge of town. Work the timing out door-to-door: waiting for the bus or getting the car started, allowing for weather conditions, mechanical breakdowns, off-peak schedules, parades, strikes, and plain bad luck. Be cautious. Allow time to find the place you're supposed to be. Your travel is not finished until you've reported to the extras holding area on set, and the casting person or AD.

Spend a little time on the "Scheduling Worksheet." Better now than under pressure after you get the call.

Purely from a financial standpoint, can you afford to be a performer? Of course you can, but the choices you are able to make will depend on your available money. Think realistically about how much you can spend on your career. You can draw up a formal budget, but most of us will make some rough notes on an envelope. What is your current financial status? Do you have money in the bank? What monthly income can you count on? What is it costing you to live now: rent or mortgage, food, utilities, credit payments, travel, entertainment?

To be more than a dabbler in the business, you are going to have to find spare cash for wardrobe, photographs, training, trade magazines and books, taxis, supplies and equipment, pager and answering machine and all sorts of unexpected things. What supplies have you got now? What will you need to buy? You don't need to spend a fortune, but no business succeeds without some money for training and publicity.

Get your bills and your bank book together, and work on the "Finances Worksheet."

The entertainment industry can be hard on relationships. It is difficult to explain what drives us, to anyone not in the business. Low income, poor working conditions, lack of security, long and unusual hours: it's hard enough to explain to ourselves why we do what we do! Would you travel out of town and miss your own wedding? (I postponed mine three times!) Would you accept a booking for that same morning when you have just come off an all-nighter?

Before the strains pull your relationships apart, how do the people you care about feel about your being in the business? Not only your spouse/mate, children, family and friends, but also your workmates, and colleagues in clubs, activities, and organisations. Will your boss allow you time off? Without sacking you? Break it down: in each case, what would the main problem be? I'm not just talking about the boss allowing you time off at short notice, or your significant other apologising for your absence at another family dinner; how do they really feel about it?

Life is more than working: at some point, you will have to choose whether to accept a booking or not, balancing the opportunity against the hassle. Look at the "Relationships Worksheet" and think about it now. Make your choices while you're not sweating.

Quick, without thinking about it, who do you know in the business? Don't worry about how well you know them, if you know a name, write it down. Even if you only have a vague idea that they are something in lighting, or work in a film office somewhere, write their names down. You are probably surprised to see a longer list than you expected.

Now, go to the "Contacts Worksheet" and sort your list out into hot prospects, the back list, and public names. You can work on the back list. Find out just what it is they do, promote them to hot prospects. The hot prospects are like a gambler's bankroll, but they just sit there like money under the mattress unless you use them.

But won't your prospects be embarrassed or annoyed at being used? That depends on how you handle it. I know a major film star who still calls the son of a minor co-worker, just to chat. If you are honest and sincere, simply opening yourself to their generosity, they will be flattered. Most people love to be assured they know more and have more power than you. Don't bore them with how good, and frustrated, and unfairly treated you are. Talk to them about their skills, compliment them, and ask their advice. Listen to what they say. Listen with your ears, not your mouth.

This book is about solutions. But this chapter is about problems. You can't use my solutions until you know they're right for you: thinking about the problems will help you come to your own conclusions for yourself. Your decisions will change, but making decisions is the only way to avoid being swept along by the tide, leaving everything to chance, relying on luck to get you out of the immediate disaster.

The Chinese sign for "crisis" combines the signs for "danger" and "opportunity." In this business, we live in crisis. Thinking things out ahead of time is the best way to turn danger into opportunity.

# TRAINING

You've heard of film stars who were discovered and achieved fame without taking any special training? Actually, they did get training, but they got it the hard way. They had to learn their skills on set. There are easier ways of growing as an actor.

Unfortunately, some people don't realise this. One minute they are the top in drama class at high school, where everyone looked on in awe at the greatest actor since Kermit The Frog, and the next they are in the business, totally lost, in a new country with different customs and a different language. There is no magic formula for success, but training helps the actor do the job better.

For every legitimate learning experience you see advertised or hear about from a friend, there are a dozen scams to take your money. Success or failure in this business sometimes seems a complete lottery, and wherever there are people with dreams, there are people selling magic potions to make the dreams come true. An advertisement in a newspaper, or even a flyer in the mall, isn't necessarily a bad symptom, but some guarantee work, or promise a major change in your abilities. Scams like these advertise training, but they're selling magic. Unfortunately, when the magic doesn't work, people blame themselves, not the scam artist.

Be wary of signing with an agency that insists you take their expensive course. The courses are often their main source of income. "It's a sensible investment to be properly qualified before we send you out on set." Sounds logical. Then they'll offer the more advanced course, "... for people serious about the business." If an agency seems to spend more time persuading you to take their classes than looking for work for you, be careful. You can spend two thousand dollars and never get on set.

Scams aside, people have unrealistic expectations of training. See a name that sounds familiar, pay money, and the world will open up. Shakespeare, New York, Los Angeles – surely the glamour will rub off on you? Things worth having aren't that simple.

Most Theatre Arts courses are an easy option to fill out course requirements. They can be exciting and satisfying, especially as a break from your main subjects, but professional preparation takes more than a few hours a week. You can't expect much from Playtime 101.

Even courses demanding a major commitment are rarely as good as their brochures want you to believe. The commonest complaint about drama graduates is, "They think they know everything." A college course can give you a distorted view of how much you know and what you'll be facing: even the star pupils of the best schools can't always make it professionally.

Classes are a fine way to expand and tone your skills and discover new ones. They give you a chance to learn more about yourself, your strengths and your weaknesses, but the classroom and the drama workshop are not the real world. Classes are no substitute for experience. You can't spend your life training. Get off the diving board: jump in or climb down, there's a queue on the ladder.

I'm not against acting training. Natural talent is not worth much unless you know how to use it effectively. Ignore those top actors modestly boasting it was just God's gift and a few lucky breaks: the comment simply makes for a more interesting interview than describing years of training and false starts. And notice you never hear from the naturally gifted performers who never get work.

When you're just beginning, professional training is useful to help you find out about yourself and get the detailed feedback that's so rare when you're working and mistakes are critical. If you're changing careers, you'll discover how much you have to offer in this new context. If you've got some experience, it can polish skills you've let grow rusty, and remind you that the best actors never stop learning, about the whole world as well as our little corner of it. The best training helps our discipline and concentration, and tautens muscles we've let go slack from specialising in the things we do well. If all it does is to knock us a bit off balance, that's good too: a contented actor rarely has the adrenaline to stand out.

Talent is necessary, training is useful. Some training. But again, beware the magic merchants: there is no simple formula for success, no single answer for everyone. If there were, people would be selling it for a million dollars a class.

Would you have surgery performed by a doctor who had just received his degree from a correspondence course? Would you have your dream house built by the neighbourhood high-school kid with an A+ in woodwork class? Then why would you pay good money to an acting instructor without checking for credentials? Although word-of-mouth from actors and crew is the best source of information about useful classes, try local theatre groups, public libraries, tradebooks, magazines, newspapers, drama bookstores and theatrical make-up suppliers, your agent (but see the warning above), your local university or college bookstore. Performer unions won't recommend a specific teacher, but they might suggest organisations where reputable classes are held.

No license is needed to teach performers: anyone can rent a room and advertise classes. To protect yourself, read the salespitch carefully, talk to the instructor, specifically about the classes, and generally to find out if you get along. If you don't like the instructor, you're unlikely to gain from the teaching. Do the organisers praise themselves and claim connections and experience you have no way of checking? Look for verifiable facts. Who do they mention as students? Do you recognise the companies or productions in their credits? What has the instructor done in the business *recently*? Beware of people whose credentials are impressive but ten years old; there's nothing worse than inside information that's out of date.

**26**

Talk to former students. Knowing how to do something and knowing how to teach it to others are very different. How have people like you rated the instructors as instructors? Actors, directors, casting people and DOPs (Directors of Photography) all know things from their personal experience that you might find useful, but teaching is an art in itself. Talk to people who have taken the same class, or a similar class by the same instructor. Teaching is a personal matter, and not everyone connects with the same way of teaching. Sometimes the best idea is to find someone who really liked the instructor, and see if what they are praising makes your skin crawl.

And ask yourself some questions, too. What do you want the class to do for you? Where do you want to be when it's over? What will the class lead to? Can you realistically commit the time and money you'll be putting out?

Look at the description of the teaching. Is it a general acting course, or does it focus on a specific area of study? Is it going to deal with twenty topics sparingly, or one topic in detail? Does it cover the areas where you need improvement or help?

Will they let you audit a class? Often, teachers will allow you to watch classes to see if they would suit you. It may cost you a little, but you won't have committed all the money or work if you find out it's not what you were looking for.

Are they set up to expand on current skills, or do they aim at the complete beginner? Even if you are new to the business, beware of organisers who only cater to beginners. Look for a professional class geared to different levels of competence. As you learn more, you'll want to move up into more advanced work with familiar instructors.

More advanced classes often ask for a photo and résumé from applicants. Don't worry if you've had little experience in their field, they often simply want to weed out total beginners. Some very popular teachers meet with applicants for a brief chat before signing them up, for the same reason.

Get a definite answer on how many people will be accepted. The best number depends on what is being taught: an improvisation class needs more people than an on-camera workshop. Some things can only be taught one on one, others are fine for as many as can hear the instructor. If the class is limited to ten people, you can expect more individual attention than if anyone with cash in hand is welcomed.

Long and short sessions both have their places: it depends what the content is. An evening can give you a start in a single area like income tax preparation, a lifetime is too short for comedy, or screen presence. Is the schedule fairly flexible or does it need a major commitment?

You can't always tell by what they're called, but there are general differences between workshops, seminars, and courses. All have their advantages and disadvantages, and each could be right for you in different circumstances.

Workshops usually cover a specific topic in depth and are relatively short and cheap. They deal with practical matters in a hands-on way and are set up for those seriously in the industry. They cater to a small group of people at about the same level, and are almost always given by people with current active experience. Teaching is mainly by example and by learning through controlled experiment. Workshops are unpredictable, because so much depends on your fellow-students. You're out of luck if you're in a group of zombies.

Seminars typically last one or two days and are closer to traditional school classes. A seminar leader is there to pass on specialist information and perhaps to start you working new things out for yourself. Good seminar leaders allow a lot of question and answer but individual attention will be rather limited. The main thing is to listen, take a lot of notes (especially of contact references for future use), actively process the information and ask questions when given the opportunity. You will waste your time and money if you sit passively and expect doors in your mind to be opened for you.

Courses combine workshop and seminar approaches, and run longer. Because you'll be committing more time and money, you'll need to do more research. What precisely does the course include? Will it be all you need, at least to make a start? How easy will it be to fill the gaps later on? What is the course load: can you keep going for the entire time? Even Madame Zelda's Modelling Academy and Intergalactic Talent Agency (Stay Home and Star!) might be right for you, if you know what you're getting into. Even the National Theatre School could be an expensive disaster if you don't.

Local colleges, universities and professional theatres often offer basic acting instruction, two or three evenings a week, with some weekend work. This sort of pre-beginners class is often quite hard work, though very enjoyable, but it will only give you an idea what serious training could do for you.

Accredited courses at universities and community colleges vary from English-Literature-with-a-dash-of-reading-aloud to theatre training of world standard. Notice I said "theatre" training. No drama school offers professional-level television or film training: that's a gap you'll have to fill for yourself. Maybe you'll be able to get some on-camera experience with the film school at the same college, or in the same city. If you're a mature student, you won't find it easy to get into an accredited drama course; you'll probably have to make up a patchwork quilt of shorter private courses in individual skills.

Courses differ in the length of time they run, up to four years, and the freedom you'll have during the course itself. Accredited college courses will take all the time you have. Will you have to work a second shift to pay for day-to-day living? Don't take on more than you can realistically manage. Even the most dedicated find it almost impossible to hold down any sort of job to pay the rent, once evening rehearsals and private study have been added to a long day at school. Drama is not a course for the faint-hearted. Private schools and college extension courses are typically more accommodating, but the training is seldom as good. There are tax advantages to full-time courses at established colleges, which smaller private schools may not offer. Ask before you enroll.

Cheap classes aren't always bad and expensive ones are often useless. You know how much you can afford, and how useful the class sounds. Certainly, $150-250 to work on something you know you should improve makes more sense than $2500 on general high-school dramatics. Find out, if you're paying for a series, whether you can get a partial refund if the class is not meeting your needs.

What additional material will you be required to purchase, above the cost of the instruction? Sometimes a cheap class is really a way of selling an expensive book. That may not be all bad if the book is useful and the class helps you to understand it.

The worst thing about any course, and most seminars and some workshops, is that graduates are given a false sense of security, a feeling that they know everything about the industry. After a while, and after more training by different instructors, most people realise the difficult grind and pressure of professional projects. Keep your ambition ahead of your current ability, but don't let your expectations grow faster than your proven talent. In your training, you may have been the big fish in the pond; once you hit the outside world, your little pool turns into a seemingly endless ocean filled with much larger and more experienced competition.

Whatever courses you take, your training is only the basis from which you start. In this business, people aren't interested in what you know or where you learned it – they want to see what you can do, now, for them.

# UNION AND NON-UNION WORK

When you are just getting started in your career, you may be asked to work on a non-union production. You will probably jump at the chance, hoping this will be your big break. You will be told, and it can certainly be true, that there are good chances of being upgraded with a few lines, and possibly even a chance to play a major character. It can be a valuable experience, but remember, most non-union work is looked down on by union people.

The non-union production is often made up of newcomers to the industry. With everybody operating at the same general level of qualification, you have a better chance to get that small role you're looking for. Don't expect star treatment or riches, but take the chance to learn how to function as a featured player. It may feel good to have lines and to be the centre of the scene for a few moments, but remember that most non-union productions are never finished, and very few are ever released commercially.

I'm not saying that working on a non-union or amateur shoot is bad, just that it is what it is. Being a hit in your high school play doesn't mean you are a successful theatre actor, and working in these small films doesn't prove your abilities. Take what you've learned to help you expand your talents where it really counts.

You will be excited about your non-union roles, naturally enough, but they don't count for much on a union set or casting session. I have talked to too many extras who think they are stars because they've done a few non-union roles. This attitude is totally unrealistic, and will do your career real harm. Don't try to blow up a university project into the next reincarnation of *Gone With the Wind*, when it was really just a little video only the producers' teacher and family will ever see.

At the start of your career any experience, good or bad, is the way to learn. Non-union jobs offer new opportunities for everyone, many of the crew doing the next job up the ladder from the one they normally do. Since the set is partly a training exercise, operations may not run quite as smoothly as a professional production. (Though things don't always run smoothly where everyone is theoretically qualified for their positions, either.) On union and non-union shoots, don't just bitch about the situation, take it as a challenge. Doing your job against the odds is an excellent skill to learn: producing good work under bad conditions is what defines a professional.

A set is an uncomfortable and dangerous place. Organised in a rush, adapted from something else with duct tape and baling wire, it's not a place to relax. Productions are always short of time, and there's always pressure to work longer, do more. Special effects that look dangerous on screen can actually be dangerous on set. No production ever has enough money for everything.

When you work on a union production, specific working conditions have been negotiated on your behalf. They may not always be obvious or even adhered to, but there are ways to have them enforced.

When you work on a non-union production, there are no such safeguards. If they're working on a shoestring budget, corners must be cut somewhere. Payroll is at a minimum, many people working on the set are volunteers, they use anything they can get for free, and they avoid spending money on anything they can do without.

Even on union sets, even for residual performers, space set aside for changing and storage of belongings can be dismal. On a non-union set, you can't insist on anything. You're like a bar band, making do with what you can find. Why would they rent an extra trailer during the bitter winter weather, when that money could be used to buy the last bit of film needed to complete the picture?

Safety precautions are of major importance to union productions. The government and the industry, including ACTRA, have worked out minimum safety standards to protect everyone working on the production. These precautions can drastically increase a productions' expenses, by as much as the entire budget of some non-union productions. Nobody wants to see anyone injured on set, but when a non-union production needs to stretch its dollar, safety precautions often suffer. Without the union's teeth, government regulations can be ignored indefinitely. We performers make this possible. We're eager to show our stuff, and we often go along with bad treatment to prove we are good team players. Injuries still happen on union productions, but on non-union or amateur shoots, you're doubly at risk.

On a union set, everyone has a job, everything is worked out ahead of time, and if you have a bright idea you'll be criticising someone else. The professional production cannot easily change scripts or shots. Any change means money: rescheduling shots, jeopardizing contracts, rethinking budgets. A union production is run by qualified and experienced people responsible for every aspect of the shoot, following very specific guidelines.

The non-union set is often less formal. Cast and crew all take their jobs seriously, but you won't find much star treatment. Since everyone takes on many responsibilities, input from all those involved in the production is more acceptable. If you have a good idea on set, it may be welcomed. It may even be followed. Performers are sometimes encouraged to work out their own variations. Even extras may have a chance to toss in their two-cents worth of ideas without too much fear of reprimand. Just don't get too pushy, demanding, or chronically annoying. You may be allowed to give yourself a line. Why not, if it works? The

**31**

production doesn't have to worry about upgrading your pay or credits. Even if you are getting a small honorarium, it will probably be a fixed sum, and, compared to the cost of the rest of the production, they're getting your performance for free. They're glad to exploit it if you're willing to give it away.

It's a cliché on union sets that the performers get meal-breaks, and are wrapped, when the money to pay technician overtime runs out. If everyone is working for nothing, or for a flat fee, there's no limit to how long the day can be.

I talked in "From the Top" about the poverty-level average income from the industry – and that's on union jobs. When working on a non-union or amateur production, the money will be even tighter. When I first started in films, I did four non-union shoots. Look at my fees: nothing from the first, travelling two hundred miles and working three days, one dollar from the second after twenty-five continuous hours, twenty-five dollars for a speaking role in the third, and then one hundred dollars for a main character in a music video – a big breakthrough into three figures! These figures aren't out of line for non-union work, where cast and crew routinely don't even get expenses for their work.

Residuals are fees paid to SOCs, Actors and principals when a commercial or television programme is aired. Extras don't get residuals, and if you are playing a speaking role in a non-union production, you probably won't get any either. A non-union production could conceivably go on to become a major success or cult classic. If by chance they do make back their money or even (gasp!) make a profit, what compensation will you get? Except for the extremely rare occurrence, the answer is simple: Zero. *Nada. Nothing. Zip. Zilch.* It was nice of you to donate your time, and we hope you had fun, but we don't owe you a thing.

Be very careful of anything you sign. It may look like a receipt, but you could be signing away all rights to your work. Without a contract, or with a waiver of rights, a producer can re-edit the show into a porno, or use parts of the movie in another film. What would happen if one day you did make it big, only to have that little show way-back-when crop up to exploit your success?

On union shoots, if you are stiffed for your fee, the unions and guilds will go after your money for you. In most cases, there is production money held in trust for just such occurrences, and you stand a fair chance of getting some of your money (especially if the production ever wants to work in your area again).

If a non-union production refuses to pay you what you're owed, you're on your own. Don't forget, not all non-union shoots are even registered under a company name. That makes tracing the person responsible for payroll very difficult. If you take them to court (at your own expense), and have an enforceable contract, you'd still better hope the production company hasn't been folded, or that there is still a credit balance on the producer's father's credit card. And of course there are the court costs. Realistically, without the power of the unions, once you have done your role, there's not much you can do to force the producer to do anything.

Obviously you can't make a living from non-union work. You may gain some experience or even minor recognition, but are your talents honestly worth that little? Don't fall for threats that you will be blackballed from the film industry if you "let them down."

Take any promised publicity with a pinch of salt; the likelihood is that the production will never be seen by anyone except the producer. "I am an artist, I'm not in it for the money" is fine, but it won't pay the rent at the end of the month.

Take the work if you choose to, but eventually you will have to draw the line at giving away your talents. It's tough enough to make it on a union actors' income. It's almost impossible to live on nothing.

# THE CASTING PROCESS

Why can't agents call us for work at decent hours? Why do so many of the calls have to be so late, or at the very last minute? Why does everything seem so disorganised?

The casting process appears to involve two parties, the agent and the Talent, but the bit you see is the last link in a long chain. The decision to contract you to appear on a particular set at a particular time depends on the results of hundreds of other decisions. Scheduling isn't like drawing up a school timetable. It's more like fortune-telling: making the best guess about the future.

Shows and series are organised like factories. Funding, Storyline, Directors, Crews, Location, Facilities, Accounting, Scheduling, Talent: every department waits for decisions from every other to be able to do their job. On set alone, the crew includes Lighting, Sound, Props, Wardrobe, Hair, Make-up, Electricians, Set Constructors, Continuity People, ADs, Transport, Craft Service, Locations. One wrong guess, one piece of information not passed on, and the schedule goes out the window.

The Talent department deals with principals and Extras. The principal casting director shortlists the performers who will carry the show, with the final selection usually made by the directors and production, but the responsibility of making the final selection of background performers falls on Extras Casting themselves. Principal Casting will usually be responsible for ten to thirty performers, but Extras Casting may be required to find tens, hundreds, or even thousands of extras each production day. The film *Gandhi* hired 300,000 extras. It's just part of the job for Extras Casting.

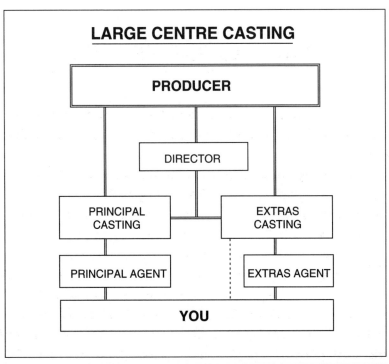

**LARGE CENTRE CASTING**

PRODUCER

DIRECTOR

PRINCIPAL CASTING

EXTRAS CASTING

PRINCIPAL AGENT

EXTRAS AGENT

YOU

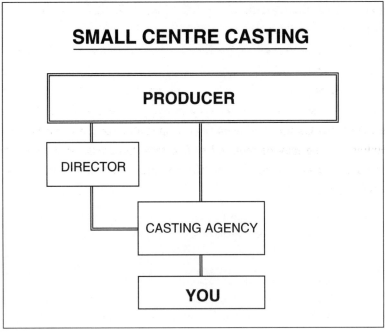

**SMALL CENTRE CASTING**

PRODUCER

DIRECTOR

CASTING AGENCY

YOU

## CASTING PROCESS – a quick overview

A)  PRODUCTION COMPANY AND EXTRAS CASTING

1)  PRODUCTION – hires casting director.
2)  CASTING DIRECTOR – meets with production to:
i) review script to determine:
- regular characters
- special characters
- general characters.

ii) decide if a Go-See is needed.
At the Go-See:
- Photos and stats are collected for the production file (bring your own photo and résumé for the casting director).
- Production may choose people to be assigned special characters.

3)  CASTING DIRECTOR – receives breakdown of characters needed for next day of shooting.


B)  TALENT AVAILABILITY CHECK

4)  CASTING DIRECTOR – contacts for availability
- EXTRAS AGENTS (providing the types/looks needed, how many people per category, wardrobe, etc.)
- FREELANCE EXTRAS (if time permits).

5)  EXTRAS AGENTS – contact their talent to see who's available for the shooting day (usually needing to call the extra back with a firm booking and the call time).

6)  EXTRAS AGENTS – call back the casting director with a list of their available suitable talent. The casting director will judge the selections made by the agents.

(Talent Availability will cycle through until appropriate extras are found for each character category needed for the shoot.)


C)  TALENT BOOKING CONFIRMATION

7)  CASTING DIRECTOR – receives the call sheet from the set and calls the extras agents and freelance talent with the call times for the next day, along with location and any additional information.

8) EXTRAS AGENTS – call their talent to confirm the booking, with time and location information.

D) PRODUCTION AND CASTING, LAST MINUTE UPDATES AND CHANGES
9) DAY OF THE SHOOT – the casting director calls the extras agents with any last minute updates:
• changes in call times or locations
• additional characters needed for that day
• replacements needed for no-shows or wrong looks.

(Availability checks, confirming bookings, last-minute changes – this goes on every shooting day until the end of the production.)

## CASTING PROCESS – the details

1) **The production hires an extras casting director.** In larger centres, the production will hire an extras casting director to be responsible for finding competent extras agents and performers. In smaller centres with no agents, all film and TV casting, residual and extra, is handled by a casting agency, which can deal directly with actors because of the smaller pool of talent in their area. Since the agent has been hired by the production, you won't normally be charged a fee or commission. The extras casting process will be the same, but the casting agency combines the work of the casting director and the extras agent.

Some casting directors work "in-house," from the production's main office. They may be hired by small non-union productions (who often save money by getting someone just starting out) or by companies based in small centres where they are the only game in town. Stations which produce many of their own shows, such as the CBC and larger and ongoing productions, have enough work and a big enough budget to attract an experienced extras casting director away from freelance earnings. In-house casting directors are in constant touch with the production and always seem to be rushed off their feet.

Most casting directors operate on a freelance basis. In larger centres, this means they could be handling five or more shows at once. If each show needed forty background performers each day, tracking down all the required talent would be next to impossible, so extras casting directors depend on the extras agencies in their area.

2) **The casting director meets with Production** to review the script, looking for general characters, special characters, and regular or continuity characters. General characters may be sorted out into street and club characters, for instance,

37

but are chosen for their overall appearance. Special characters may be Special Business Extras, but can also be single odd flavours in the mix: a robed African delegate at a conference, a hugely fat juror. Regular or continuity characters can be needed when a scene is shot over a number of days, or to be the locals in the coffee shop, say, in a series or in a feature when the locale is revisited in the story-line.

**A Go-See may be called**, especially if it's a new show or the producer is unsure of available talent. Often a production will rely on the casting director's knowledge of the business and the available extras. Where there is time, money, or special needs, the production will want to take a more active part.

3)      **The casting day begins.** The casting director receives a preliminary breakdown of characters needed for the next day of shooting. When the production has decided what scenes are to be shot the next day, the casting director is given the breakdown of the types of scenes, approximately how many extras will be needed and of what sorts, and special wardrobe requirements. This is not a final list. Before shooting starts everything may be changed by script rewrites, location problems, scheduling problems, weather problems ...

4)      **The casting director contacts extras agents.** Those who are in the casting director's good books get the job of filling a portion of the casting call. As much detail as possible on looks, wardrobe, etc., will be passed on.

This is where you can do most to get work: if they don't think of you, you won't get cast. Having good relations with extras agents will make your name the one they think of. Schmoozing and making nice have their place, but the best way to build a good relationship is to do a good job.

5)      **The extras agents contact their Talent**, the people on the agency roster who can handle the parts to be cast, to see if they are available for the shooting day. This first phone call is just to see if you would be available if cast – it's not a confirmed booking unless you're told it is or you're given your call time and location. Even if you're sure it's a confirmed booking, make double sure that it isn't just an availability check.

**The extras agents call** the casting director with a list of available talent. The agent is guaranteeing that everyone on the list will be available if booked. If you weren't by the phone, or if you haven't answered the message by the time the list needs to be in, you've missed the boat. The casting director has to trust the agents' judgement, but will look over the lists to weed out any known problems, misfits, or wrong looks.

**The casting director may call some freelance extras directly.** This will depend on time and the need for very specific character types. It's a professional compliment if the casting director calls you: twenty extras could have been hired in the same time using an agent. Do your bit, keep it professional and make it quick. Keep copies of the "Call Sheet Worksheet" by the phone. It will help you get the information you need.

Before you ring off, politely ask if this is a booking or availability check. Do not start casual conversations. The casting director is very busy. Say thank you for the call, and promise you'll be ready.

6)      **The extras casting director** is juggling chainsaws at this stage. The production's requirements are still changing, half a dozen agents are calling in with the progress they are making on their lists, there are too many lined up for the airport crowd and no Hare Krishnas available anywhere. The phone lines are buzzing.

7)      **The Production sends the casting director the call sheet.** This will be late in the day, when the next day is most predictable, because the crew has a guaranteed overnight break and BIG penalties for infringing it. At long last, the casting director can call the extras agents and freelance talent with the call times and final details.

8)      **The extras agents confirm the call** with the Talent who said they were available. Finally, this is a booking. You'll get the time and place, and assorted instructions. The call is almost certain to be very late at night, and even so the details are likely to be changed by tomorrow. Do what you can to get all the available details. Use the "Call Sheet Worksheet."

9)      **The day of the shoot.** The casting director is in early, because this is when anything can change. Another scene to shoot that day, a wrong weather forecast, or maybe someone forgot he'd just shaved off all his hair and shouldn't be playing a hippie now.

**The casting director calls extras agents** with new call times or locations, additional characters and urgent replacements for no-shows or people who just looked wrong. And the agents call their clients.

**Extras agents' emergency calls.** It's seven in the morning. You just got in after an all-nighter on another set, and you get a call to be on set in half an hour. If you get all the details, location, wardrobe, etc. and hoof it at top speed, you'll earn big Brownie points. When you get to set, don't make a big deal out of getting a last minute call. The Production may not even know there had been a problem. Just check in quickly, let them know who you're playing or replacing, and get into your wardrobe at double speed. Don't expect a hero's welcome: the casting director and extras agent know you've made them look good.

Extras casting is not an easy life. Each character placed may have required ten calls before a suitable performer answered the phone and was available. Even confirmation calls go wrong, with unanswered telephones and people suddenly remembering appointments elsewhere. The casting people will end their day hours after all the extras have been confirmed for tomorrow. A couple of hours sleep and they start again an hour before the first call time, checking with production, waiting for extras to arrive on set, hoping they are as advertised. Emergencies are dealt with and another shooting day starts. Meanwhile, back at the ranch, the casting director and extras agents have already started another casting day, looking at the preliminary breakdown for tomorrow.

## GO-SEE, LOOK-SEE, OR AUDITION?

It depends where you are, and extras agents often say Audition rather than Go-See (a.k.a. Look-See) because it sounds much more important, so they'll get a better turnout. There is a real difference, though.

A Go-See is a cattle call for background talent. It gives the production a chance to see what kind of "looks" are available to work as general extras. Normally, you won't be required to perform any special characters or pieces. If given a chance, however, use it to show off what you can do with even minimal direction. Be different, don't just copy the person beside you. Maybe that creative outfit you brought will help get you noticed.

In an audition, you are expected to actually perform. Trying for a residual role, you have been brought in to see if you are right for a specific character, and your talent will judged, not simply whether you look right. They will be looking for the person who can play the character, in the scene they have in mind, in the style of the show.

A Go-See should be treated as seriously as an actual audition, but the production is looking for different things. Be sure which you are being called in for; your preparation will be different.

If you ask other extras about attending Go-Sees, you will probably hear some complaining that it's a waste of time. Don't believe them. You won't be cast from every Go-See you attend, but you're still promoting yourself. Who knows what opportunities those other extras may have lost because they didn't want to waste an afternoon. For goodness' sake, Go – and Be Seen. Don't be too proud: use every chance you have to be better known. At the Go-See, the extras casting director, and sometimes the producer or director, will collect photos and stats for the production's files.

The producer and director may want some detailed control over the looks of the characters on their show. If they are at the Go-See, you will have a better chance of being one of the more prominent Background characters. You could get days of continuity or even be one of the regulars for the show. But only if you're there.

It may have been a while since the casting director saw you, and looks can change over a period of time. Have you lost some weight? Have you had your hair cut, or changed its style or colour? Have those blemishes cleared up? Do you have a few more wrinkles? The casting director wants a better idea of how you look right now. If you're on the list of the names they remember, you have a better chance of work. They may even realize that now you're perfect for one of their other shows. But only if you turn up.

A turnout of a few hundred extras may seem like an disorganised cattle call, but it tells the production the extras casting director is efficient and that means more work for the casting director. More work for the casting director means more work for you, if the casting director knows you are a casting call reliable.

# AGENTS

Do extras need an agent? YES. Definitely. Except sometimes.

You don't if you live in Chicken Feathers, Saskatchewan, where visiting films advertise for extras in the local newspaper. You may not if you have a major reputation and enough energy to do a terrific job and promote yourself at the same time. For the rest of us, agents are like necessary and powerful tools: you've got to choose a good one and know how to use it. The last chapter gave you the big picture of the agent's place in the scheme of things: now, here is the close-up.

In large centres, there are two sorts of agencies for performers: extras agents and talent or principal agents (sometimes called personal managers).

Talent agents deal mainly with residual work (principal, actor, SOC categories) and stage work. They receive a breakdown of the roles available in a production and submit suggestions to the Principal Casting Director, who chooses actors to come in and audition.

Most talent agents try to keep their list of clients down to 20-80 actors. They may submit two or three names per role and if they're lucky they can arrange an audition for about one person for every ten submissions. Talent agents make money by actively promoting the few people they do handle. As a matter of courtesy, talk to your talent agent, if you already have one, about getting an extras agent. Although some talent agents may handle extra work if it comes by, beware the extras agent who claims to be a talent agent as well. An agent handling hundreds of actors sounds like an ambitious extras agent.

An extras agent deals solely with background talent, mainly for film and TV, with some work in print shoots, small industrial productions, music videos, and special promotions. Because the casting personnel in the production office don't audition extras, they rely on the judgement of the agent to supply suitable people. The more clients the agency has, the better their chance of having the right people to fill the background. A film with twenty main actors may need 400 background performers to make it look real. The extras agent will keep a roster of 500-1500 clients in all categories, with all sorts of special skills: good guys, bad guys, young, old, male, female ...

How do you choose an agent? The problem may not be choosing, but making the best of what there is. Smaller centres may have only a casting agency, which does the job of an agent, but is paid by production companies. Some centres can support one local agent, who deals with all local casting, extras and main cast, in competition with agents in other cities. Larger centres do give you a choice, and I recommend you get as many good agents as possible working for you.

In Vancouver, Montreal, and Toronto, there are probably as many extra agencies as there are talent agencies. Some are efficient and ethical and the sort of people we would like as friends. Some aren't. Where there is a choice, I think I can help you sort out the duds. If you don't have a choice, I can help you make the best of the agent available. Don't be too worried by this chapter's warnings: you can honestly enjoy working with your agents. Read on, and use the Agent Checklists in the back of the book, and you'll make that more likely. A bit of common sense will help you to protect yourself against the thieves and con-men who collect where there are people with dreams and ambitions.

Who do you call? There's a section in the newspaper's classified ads: some look okay, most look a bit weird. Look up agents in the Yellow Pages phone book: nothing. Extras, Theatrical, Talent, Background: nothing. Loads of entries under Modelling, some called "... and Talent." Some also called "... and Charm School." Many modelling agencies also handle personal appearances by their models, at trade shows for example. Some actually have a real talent agency subsidiary for their clients, but this isn't what we want. In Toronto, agents are listed, all lumped together, in the Business and Industrial Yellow Pages. (Don't ask.) Your public library should have the current edition.

If you're a member of a performer union, call and ask if there is a general listing of agents in your city. In Canada, call your local ACTRA branch: there are ten, right across the country. The union's own agency lists are provided as submitted: ACTRA can't screen every new agency, nor endorse individual companies. They may have a pamphlet on Background Performers (and if you're interested, ask for the others on women's issues, children, etc.) and a listing of current productions: many ACTRA members are unaware that their union offers this valuable material. If you do drop by the office, check the bulletin boards for notices by agents, casting, photo services, and general news.

Non-members may find the unions reluctant to give them the same assistance: their offices are understaffed for the quantity of work they do for their members, and print material is expensive to hand out to everyone. Next time you're on set, ask a member if you can borrow any interesting material.

The very best thing is to ask around, if you have friends already in the business, and get the names of agents, good and bad. Ask a few people, and you'll realise a bad agent is sometimes just what you call one who hasn't got you work yet.

When people first look for an agent, they often either blindly sign on with their friends' agent or pick one at random from the classifieds. You've already shown more sense than some, by buying this book, but watch out for scam artists. An advertisement or a flyer in the mall may offer free auditions, tryouts, or "evaluation of potential" as a come-on. "Oh, Mr. and Mrs. Phule ... we've gone over your tapes and we're all just so excited! You have such natural talent and with a few inexpensive classes ... Once you are registered, we promise that we'll get you

**43**

work on set." Big Deal! A single crowd scene will meet their responsibility. Your $100 agency fee gets you one day on set, earning $40 (less their commission).

Respected agents don't hand out flyers in malls. If an advertisement promises your dream with no risk and no effort, they aren't talking to you, but to your wallet. It's nice to be flattered, but it can be expensive.

The extras agency is the way we plug into the casting process. We need its services, but that doesn't mean the agency is our boss. The agent and the background talent should be equal partners: the agent gets the client work and is paid a percentage of the client's fee. Each has duties and responsibilities, and each relies on the other. Remember, when you phone an agency, and when you go to the agency office, it's you who are auditioning them. Use the Agent Checklists to make sure you get all the information you need on the phone. Take them when you go to the interview. Go over your notes when the excitement has worn off; the cooler you are, the easier it'll be to make a good decision.

Extras agents take 10-15% of the money they get for their clients, but often also charge fees. There are registration fees, ranging from ten to a hundred dollars, and then sometimes administration fees as well, paid monthly, quarterly or annually, often in advance.

Be sure what the fee is for. If it's a registration fee, you may be asked to pay once up front, annually until you're established, or for each of the first three years, say. If you pay an annual fee, even though it adds up to more in the long run, you will save if the agency folds or if you decide that the agent (or the business) isn't for you. If it's a one-time fee, ask if you can pay in installments.

These fees aren't necessarily a scam. For every new client, the agent spends money on files and records, and often on updating the book of photos and stats of the clients for each extras casting director. Many beginners leave the business once they get bored. The agent's fee covers set-up costs, and is a sign of commitment from new clients. Beware of any fee that hurts. Ask yourself if the high fee covers necessary overhead and expenses, or if it is the agency's primary source of income. Can an agency that opened two months ago really justify charging a $100 fee? It's easy to open an agency, but it's very hard to run one successfully, and many agencies fold within weeks. (Don't waste your sympathy: the agency failed, but who's got your fee?)

I think agents shouldn't charge you fees on top of their commission if you are a full or apprentice performers union member. Your union status shows you're not in the industry on a whim.

Some agents want you to sign a contract with them, although it's not legally necessary. Remember that a contract is only written evidence of a deal two people have agreed on. If you are asked to sign anything, say you want to take it away with you to look it over carefully, so that you understand it before signing it. If the agent makes a fuss about this, and especially if you feel you're being forced to sign right now, you should ask yourself what they are so worried about. Be sure that the application or the information form isn't actually a contract, way down there in the fine print.

Don't accept a clause that says the agency will be your exclusive agent, which would mean you could not have another extras agent. (The "Agents, Take Two" chapter discusses exclusivity, and more, in detail.) Ask to have the clause struck out or write in "Non-Exclusive Representation" before you sign. Have them initial your change. If the agent insists on exclusivity, walk out.

How much of your money is the agent taking? Commission is normally ten or fifteen per cent, but is that from the gross or net amount? Most principal agents base their percentage on the gross (regardless of how much was deducted for permit fees or other union deductions). Some agents will have separate rates for cash calls, vouchers, or ACTRA members. Make sure you know which rates apply to you.

How will you pay? Agents often want you to have your cheques sent to them. That means they have your money until they tell you about it and you can get in to the office to collect it. Better to have your money sent to you, then send or take the agency its commission.

If there is anything in the contract you don't understand, have it explained before you sign. If there is something you're not happy about, ask if it can be struck out (often a clause is in because it's always been in, not for any very good reason).

If you are told, "Oh, don't worry, we never insist on that," have the clause struck out anyway: if it's never insisted on, it isn't needed in the contract.

Be sure you get an identical copy of anything you sign. Be sure the agent signs the contract. This is an agreement: you promise this, I promise that. There's no point in a deal unless both sides promise to follow it.

You must have a photograph: if you are just starting out, a good snapshot or Polaroid™ should do. If you stay in the business, you will eventually need a supply of black and white, eight-by-ten inch prints.

If the agent demands a proper B/W 8x10 inch photo taken by the agency photographer, walk away. Making money from the photographer's kickbacks is such an old trick it's embarrassing. On the other hand, if you are assured you don't need any kind of photograph, you should also walk away. How can an agent get you work without a reminder of what you look like? Sometimes the agent will take a quick shot of you for about $5 if you don't have a photo available.

If you are asked for 8x10s for their casting books, ask to see how the books are presented. A professional quality 8x10 is relatively expensive and you want to be sure the photos are organised neatly with stat sheets, not just tossed in loose.

When there is a more prominent or unusual character call on the break-down, your agent will need an 8x10 to send to the casting director. When you're ready to make a sizable investment in your career, get a professional photo taken.

**45**

Don't be caught by an agent or independent operator pushing demonstration videos. Demo tapes are expensive and even good ones are only useful for established performers. Be wary of extra agencies offering courses "... just to polish you." This is another old, old way of loosening you from your money. But if the cost isn't too high, then it may be worth it, especially if the agent has brought in an outside instructor.

Good agents have long office hours to serve their productions (and you). Production staff often won't know what characters they'll need for the next day until near the end of their current day of shooting. They rely on the agents who are available for late night calls. You'll miss a chance to work if your agent has already packed up for the day.

You should touch base with your agent regularly. However, some agencies prefer the "Don't call us, we'll call you" approach. It's really a question of style, but if you aren't allowed to call, you can't check how they're working for you, and it's easy for them to forget you altogether. If you don't contact them you'll lose a chance to be the actor they always think of when they're casting.

When you go for an interview, remember, you're interviewing the agent. You probably don't want a meat-market agent who is only interested in Pay Me, Thank You, Goodbye. Ask questions. More important than the answers, how does the agent listen?

When I ran an agency, I was swamped with new faces. Many of these people already had other agents, but I was always amazed how little they had been told about the business. I used to spend time explaining some of the do's and don'ts, and I would always make the same suggestion, "Check out other agents and sign up with anyone you feel comfortable with. If you want to sign up with us, fine, but don't jump into it." I wasn't being noble: I didn't want to work with people who hadn't thought seriously about this crazy industry.

Get a general feeling for the organisation. Are the phones busy? Listen closely. Are agency people chasing new clients, or are they talking to clients on the list already? Best of all, are productions calling in for extras? Be suspicious of a very ritzy office (whose pockets is the rent coming out of?), and avoid the obviously sleazy dump. Is there modern equipment like fax machines and computers? Is there enough staff, and are they knowledgeable and helpful with your questions? You may as well enjoy dealing with these people, you're going to be talking to them often in future, you hope.

Finally, let your gut tell you. If you are unhappy, even for no apparent reason, trust that feeling.

A good agent works very hard, and very long hours, finding you work on set. What should you be doing to be a good client for this good agent you've chosen?

•　　BE THERE　When you accept a booking, turn up! Don't cancel because you've been invited to the biggest party of the year. Being unreliable will cost you work. Don't decide a later offer from another agent sounds better. You've already committed yourself: backing out will leave a sour taste in both agents' mouths.

•　　BE HONEST　If you're called for a shoot and you've already appeared on the same episode, let the agency know. You may have to miss a day's pay but your agent will appreciate your professionalism. Chances are you can still be sent out once it's been cleared. If you keep quiet, and the casting director decides on set that you can't be used again, your agent will not be pleased.

•　　BE ON TIME　You'll usually sit around for hours in the holding area, but you can bet the one time you're late will be the time they need you right now. Or sooner. If you're not there, they won't know if they should wait or start looking for a replacement. Either way, your reputation stinks. Be there, be early!

•　　BE PROFESSIONAL　You're not just representing yourself, you're confirming that the agent made the right choice in selecting you. Good news gets back. Pay your commission on time. Agents will stop sending you out if they have to fight for their money. They've got plenty of clients who will pay them on time. When you get an upgrade on a job from the agency, give your agent a call and pass on the news. There may be a different commission rate for the higher category and this isn't the time to try sneaking the bigger cheque past them. Who got you the job which led to the opportunity in the first place?

•　　BE A GROWN-UP　Don't hound your agent, or whine. Checking in is fine but don't call twenty times a day. Time on the phone with you is time not talking to the casting director to get you work. Keep the conversation brief and to the point; show you realise how valuable business time is. Don't blame your agent for the fact you're not working. If you're right, complaining won't help.

•　　BE BRAVE　Let your agent know if there's been a problem on set. Most agents would rather know about an altercation than have the matter thrown up at them by the casting director. Forewarn them and they'll have time to prepare a response. They hate nasty surprises.

Being an agent is a terrible job; don't make it any harder. Treat your agents like people: a lot of them actually are people, and they all appreciate the courtesy. Work at being one of the agent's favourites; keep in touch, let the agent know how things are going, become a person in the agent's life, not just a name on a list. It isn't the best actor who gets the casting calls, it's the actor the agent thinks of when making up the list.

# STANDING UP FOR YOURSELF

A production never has enough time or enough money. Someone has to take up the slack. Don't get paranoid, they are not out to get us especially, but extras are often an easy solution. It's up to us to decide how much to put up with: we can't expect the best of accommodation, but we must refuse to be put in danger. Hysteria and name-calling will get you known as a trouble-maker, but we are professionals and entitled to defend our dignity. Being afraid to say anything makes a bad situation worse. We can look after ourselves, and use our power to help each other, just as Neighbourhood Watch and Vertical Watch protect our homes.

Abuse is any sort of bad situation people are forced into unfairly. Being abused isn't simply being uncomfortable, it has to do with the reasons for the discomfort. If you are freezing, but the production is scurrying around trying to round up heaters on an unexpectedly cold night, that's part of the job. If you're freezing and everyone else is in heated wagons, you're being abused. In our business, like every other, not many people want to cause harm, but ignorance, laziness and selfishness cause harm nonetheless. Abuse of all sorts, sexual, racial, and purely personal, exists in the entertainment business as much as anywhere else. Scripts deal with crises in people's lives and productions themselves seem to exist in a state of (more or less) controlled crisis: both facts blow on the fires of people's prejudices.

Everybody is unique and comes packaged with a personal set of ideals, morals, ethics, motivations, and personality. For all sorts of reasons, we often have to cut other people some slack. At some point, we decide enough's enough. On set or at a go-see is not a great time for a long speech of outrage, but there are other ways around most abusive situations.

Scripted abuse is entirely more complicated than the real life abuse we deal with at work just as anyone may have to. If a character says, "Come here, jewboy!" does that abuse the performers? Playing abusive characters, and playing characters who submit to abuse, isn't easy when it goes against your own feelings, but it can be justifiable in the context of the production. It depends on the script. You may not see the script, you may have no real idea of the story, you may have to judge by the bits of the scene you are involved in.

A scene's reality can become abusive to the performers. If the scene is a coach-load of travellers freezing after an accident on the highway, it will probably be shot on a cold location. You can legitimately complain about the freezing holding area, but how long should you be forced to shoot a scene when they need to see your breath on the air?

As usual, it's your decision. At what point do you draw the line, and what do you do then? It's your choice, and it's a hard one.

Casting stereotypes are a way of life, but the behaviour of people of many ethnic and racial backgrounds is stereotyped by the industry: the bug-eyed Negro slave and the Chinese laundryman aren't entirely in the past. Racial stereotypes are an abuse built in to the casting system, and you may find yourself called to portray some characters which you view as demeaning. If a stereotyped character upsets you and you are called by your agent or the casting director to play what you consider a demeaning role, let them know you appreciate the call and calmly explain that you wouldn't feel comfortable playing the part. This doesn't demonstrate weakness on your part. Rather, it shows maturity. The performer unions have committees who will be glad to hear of productions containing grossly demeaning characters. Scripted characters are not meant as an assault on ourselves, and we are not being judged as though we actually are the characters we portray, but there are times when your gut reaction is too strong to ignore. Awkwardness reads on camera, and the production would much rather not use you if you're uncomfortable with your character.

Women, visible minorities, and those who are physically outside the norm find it difficult to be cast where the character could be, but doesn't have to be, visibly different. There is an assumption in casting that generic characters are "normal" white men. In some ways, this is worse than clichés about racial character. Why shouldn't the receptionist be in a wheelchair? Why has it taken so long to see any black nurses or East Indian doctors? Does the doctor have to be a man and the nurse a woman? Can the lawyer only be Jamaican if it's an immigration case?

Women performers are shortchanged – literally, because they average two-thirds the earnings of men, and also in the parts they play. Over half the population is women, but less than a third of lead roles in Telefilm projects are played by women. The better, ground-breaking shows will continue to improve the situation: many are now using role reversals, or at least acknowledging the fact that women can believably portray characters which once may have been considered to be for males only. We are seeing female judges outside family court, women lawyers and mayors, tough bosses of trucking outfits, without comment, without a big thing being made of it.

Always take any opportunity to play a non-standard character. Take the roles as house-husband or male secretary, the woman SWAT officer or Her Excellency, Madame Ambassador. Society is changing and the screen world is catching up. Slowly. Push your agent. Watch for opportunities to help make those changes. There are agencies specialising in colourblind casting, and with rosters of actors who are wheelchair-borne or otherwise physically different. No matter what prejudice is the barrier to your casting, find out the opportunities in your area, get active on union committees if you're a member, and open up your casting chances.

Racial harassment is probably less common here than in the world in general, but it is still very real. We are artists and craftspeople; this is not a perfect world, but we should be doing our best. People of every colour and ethnic background work on sets, as technicians and in production, as well as talent. If you simply can't work in that situation, then please go elsewhere: we have enough tension while shooting without dealing with your stupid jokes and the tension they cause between you and the crew, cast, and other extras. If your lighthearted humour makes somebody else uncomfortable, you are in the wrong. If you can't deal with your feelings against another group, get another job. However unbiased we think we are, tiredness and tension sometimes make us think things we're ashamed of later. Deal with that as best you can; don't let the feelings out.

The script can make things worse, as we play characters less civilised than we would like to be. If the production is set in the past, the problems can be worse still. I remember one shoot about the integration of blacks in Boston schools. There was group of young performers playing the black students, some of whom complained loudly that the Afro wigs they were wearing looked ridiculous and that there was no reason why their own hairstyles shouldn't be acceptable. Another regular complaint was, "I wouldn't have put up with that [stuff], so it doesn't make any sense to pretend I would." No-one felt easy about the language used by white characters in the script. Needless to say, tempers and feelings were very strained on set, and the situation was only made worse by comments from various other extras. At best it would have been a very difficult topic to cover, but the reaction of the African Americans, and the racist comments from white extras, meant that tempers were unnecessarily strained. Remember, attitudes change; in a historical piece, the characters and their actions will be based on attitudes at that time. Ordinary conversation from the fifties could sound violently racist nowadays. If you are in such a set-up, deal with it, don't make the situation worse. If you know you aren't going to be able to work with the set-up, don't accept the job.

Sex sells in our society. Unfortunately, women are usually the ones used to do the selling. You see it in print, in commercials, and in the movies and television. Scantily clad females wandering around nonchalantly, often in outfits that have very little to do with the characters. The days of the old "Jiggle Shows" are not completely gone: audiences have just decided that there should be scripts to go with the jiggle. And it is audiences. Producers can (and I think should) lead their audience forward, but they often have advertiser's dollars dragging them back.

Maybe you find it easy to play the obvious sexy scenery parts, but you feel awkward playing hookers or toy-boys. We can't all do everything. If you're too embarrassed to portray a stereotypical hooker, simply tell your agent and leave those characters for someone else to play. If you're relaxed enough to play the part for the day, have fun with the character. Play make-believe and dress-up. Maybe learn something about yourself.

Productions abuse women – and men – by their casting assumptions, but that man dressed in drag for the set, or that woman dressed as a hooker, is an actor, doing a job, like you. You wouldn't run screaming from an actor playing Frankenstein's monster; why assume the sexy creature next to you is available for your steamy glances?

Sexual harassment exists on set, mainly against women. It's actually not so bad for extras, who are typically in and out in a day, but bigotry follows no rules. Harassment in a working relationship festers, and can swell into a real problem for everyone. When you're on a set with sexy characters, treat those around you as the actors they are. If you don't do anything about offensive remarks you hear, you are weakening the abused and strengthening the attacker. Decide whose side you're on – you can't be neutral.

On set or off, there are opportunities for harassment whenever someone has power over someone else. Casting decisions are made from the gut more often than not, so that personal and business decisions overlap. Without necessarily going as far as the casting couch, when a favour is granted, a favour is often expected in return. And favours are often sexual. Isn't that illegal? Certainly it is, but the situation isn't often clear-cut. "Come over to my place for the night and I'll make you a big star" is clearly sexual harassment. The fact that the casting director always finds work for friendly young men, or the agent calls on the people who sit in the office and flirt, could just be coincidence. One thing you can be sure of: if you think there's a string attached to the offer of special treatment, there probably is. In most cases, you'll dance on the string and not get the special treatment.

> "If your common sense tells you that you're being harassed, you probably are. Your response should be immediate, direct and firm. Indicate verbally, as well as by your actions, that you are not interested in such comments or behaviour.... The intensity of your reaction should depend on the circumstances.... Talk to your fellow-workers.... Call an ACTRA representative to report the incident and get further advice.... You may wish to inform the producers...."
> *(From the National ACTRA Women's Committee)*

Homophobia exists, even though the world of the arts traditionally accepts homosexuality. Heterophobia, too, of course: straight bashing is no joke, even if gay bashing is more common. The industry has a tradition of ignoring the way you look and your sexual preferences, as long as you do your job well. Not everyone you see wearing leather and studs will be gay, not everyone in a wool vest and suit trousers will be straight. And it doesn't matter. You aren't being asked to accept or approve of their preferences. You are being asked to ignore the differences and allow that they are professionals as well. If they weren't competent at their job, they wouldn't have been hired. Concentrate on your job, and let them do theirs.

The employment of minor children is allowed only in special circumstances in North America. The entertainment industry in the States is one of the very few places children are allowed to work. In Canada, it has theoretically been illegal for children to work on set, but now the Ontario government has developed a Code to guard against abuse of minors, and it is expected that similar measures will be adopted countrywide. Although performer guilds and unions take great care to set specific guidelines for children's work, the new child performer codes will govern not only union sets but also non-union sets, where there have been no rules at all until now.

We all want the best for our children, but sometimes pride can cloud our judgement where they're concerned. Who wouldn't be proud to see little Johnny or Susie on the big screen? They're so cute and talented; we beam at the thought of sharing them with the world. It's dangerously easy for parents to neglect their children's rights on set for fear of upsetting the production. We don't want our child to let us down and it's tempting to give in to the rigorous demands of film-making. "I know he's a little tired, but don't worry, he really can handle it." Your children are obviously having a great time, so wouldn't it be okay to let them stay just a little longer than the regulations say?

Please say no. Children haven't the judgement or the experience to know what's best for their own health and safety. They depend on their parents to make the decisions (though they may not always agree with the parent). Even if your child seems fine on set, please help ensure that productions follow the regulations. Get a copy of your responsibilities in following these regulations from your local union office, and be sure you know precisely what your child will be doing. Try to be near set at all times; if there's a chaperone in charge, arrange to meet the person so you'll know who is looking after your child. Allowing a company to bend the regulations sends a message to all productions that it's okay to bend the rules for any child on set. We all remember the horror stories, the tragedy with the helicopter on the *Twilight Zone* set, but all sets are potentially dangerous, all the time, not just late at night in special stunt situations. Children try to please the parent figure, and they believe what they're told. Their voices are small: it's up to us to make sure they're heard and their special needs respected.

And that's all of us: when children are on set, we should all watch over them. See the "Union Matters" chapter for more details of the rules for children.

Stand up for your rights. Everyone, not just extras, gets treated badly from time to time. Every time you think you've learned your lesson, there's a new way of slipping it to you. It's very difficult, in the on-set pandemonium, to know when, and if, you should stand up for your rights. It's easy to say that any abuse should be corrected, but this isn't always possible at the time. Often a really unbearable situation turns out to be more justified when you think about it the next morning without the previous night's tiredness and frustration. All you can do is try to work out whether the situation warrants a serious complaint, whether the complaint has to be now or can wait, and whether there is a way round the problem. One thing is sure: if you think it's a bad situation and you don't do anything about it at all, you'll feel worse than if you had done something and it didn't help.

It's not unusual for personalities to clash at work, especially at the end of a seventeen-hour day. Personally, I can't bear extras who do as little as possible, and I guess many extras feel I take my work too seriously. I have my priorities and they have theirs. As long as we're doing our job on set, who cares? You're not there to win a popularity contest. You won't get much sympathy for crying, "Miss, Tommy doesn't like me!" Take it as your responsibility to ensure the differences in attitude cause no problems for the production.

Most of the unpleasantness on set is just bitching. It isn't worth making a court case over, but it can wreck a day, and sometimes blow up into something worse. Bitching about waiting or rushing, heat or cold, doesn't help but it's human nature. If the bitching is justified, do something about the problem. Bitching about people is corrosive: don't just mumble agreement to dodge the situation. A disgruntled extra putting down the crew or production needs reminding that everybody can have an off day, and that the crew may be a little frazzled at the moment. No need to make a holier-than-thou sermon of it, just point out that everyone's in the same boat.

Prejudiced remarks, about someone's sex or race, shouldn't be part of our life. If you're the target, don't play the game. Move, after making it clear why. If someone else is a silent victim, quietly check with them. Perhaps they're too embarrassed to speak up, or prefer not to draw attention to themselves. At least show them your support. You might be able to defuse the situation by talking discreetly to the offender. If you make it sound as though you know it was spoken unintentionally (which it often is), the problem may be remedied without anyone else noticing.

Contractual rights are another problem area. You and the producer have signed a contract (that's what your voucher represents) and theoretically you should both stick to the contract absolutely. Of course, there has to be certain amount of trust, of give-and-take, or we'll achieve nothing.

A five- or ten-minute mistake in your signing-out time at the end of a day shouldn't be a major concern (maybe at some point in the day you wasted that much time by wandering out of earshot or not following your instructions).

If you don't agree with your hours on the voucher as you sign out, and you can't resolve the situation quickly and amicably, tick the Don't Agree box. If the person signing you out is upset about that, calmly say they may well be right, but you just need to check it out. Say you've both worked too long today to worry about it. "Let the union figure it all out for us" is a easy way for everybody to save face. As soon as the union office is open, call them and ask to speak to the Steward for that production: fill them in on the details so they can follow it up.

Don't wait a month down the road – by then it's too late for them to do much. If you were a cash extra, contact the union so they can help ensure this isn't becoming a production habit, but you'll probably have to wave the money goodbye.

Does the production seem to be ignoring the extras? There's no water left or you're sitting unshaded in the hot sun? The crew has been working together for some time, but the extras are usually a new group each day. It's easier to "forget" people if you don't know them personally. The easy solution is to quietly tell the person in charge of the extras about the problem. You can check in again to remind them in about twenty minutes. If there's still no response, and the problem is becoming severe, you may need to take stronger measures: if it's a union production, call the union office and ask to speak with a representative to see if they will deal with the situation. An empty doughnut tray is not a severe problem: dehydration is.

If you have a problem with the special shooting conditions for a scene (heights, animals, live firearms, etc.), speak to the people responsible for the extras. Simply let them know about your concern. They'll do their best to have you work away from the source of intimidation, or possibly hold you for a different scene. They will help you if they possibly can, even if you should have known about the problem from your call details. They would rather work around you than cause an accident.

Most people are reasonable most of the time, and there are times when it's reasonable to let an infringement go by. Ask yourself: has the overall treatment of the extras been good? Is the matter fairly trivial, annoying but just a matter of inconvenience or slight discomfort? Are you just nitpicking?

Situations alter cases. Suppose I have not had the substantial snack that allows the production to work me six hours before lunch without a late meal penalty. Strictly according to the book, I should get the extra fee.
- If I reminded the ADs, then I've tried to be helpful and will claim the penalty.
- If I hadn't been aware of the time myself, I'll usually claim the penalty.
- If the lack of Substantial was one of many problems on the set, if the treatment of the extras was very poor, I would fight for the penalty.

When the problem has been taken care of, it's always nice to give a little thank you. It lets people know that you understand how busy they are, and it tells them you appreciate their attention to the extras. Besides, they get so few thanks on the set, you'll make their day.

What if it's serious? Generally it isn't, and so far we've come down on the side of avoiding problems getting worse, and suggested quiet ways of dealing with things. There are times, generally after the velvet glove is worn out, when you have to use the steel fist. Ask yourself these questions:

- Is anyone's health or safety at serious risk?
- Is someone being sexually harassed, or threatened with physical harm or loss of work?
- Is it a serious breach of contract or ethics?
- Is the abuse intentional?
- Are the production personnel aware of the problem, and simply ignoring a situation they should be dealing with?

In these situations, and the list could be much longer, you have to do something. You do. Not "someone." You. Every once in a while, you'll come across a situation which is very serious, or even dangerous. Someone joking around with prop firearms is serious, someone drunk or drugged in a position of responsibility can lead to a dangerous accident. Neither of these is likely, but don't ignore the evidence of your eyes: tell an AD. Don't worry about being a snitch if you're saving someone's life.

If the production is putting you into danger, they are breaking the law. If it's a union shoot, they are also breaking union rules. Trying to stand up for yourself (or others) may cost you a little work, but would you rather be dead? Don't buy their threats: do you want to work for people who hold grudges or label you a troublemaker for saving your own skin? You may not think you have much power, but the performers unions have Liaison Officers on set (OSLOs in Canada), and Stewards, and the local office has someone who can help, or at least an answering machine that's checked frequently.

If you are working on a non-union shoot, you are protected by the law and by the fact that most abuse, even serious abuse, comes from laziness and contempt. If you show you are serious, you won't be forced. Without the union behind you, you may lose your fee, but that may be a better choice than frostbite or another five hours in thick smoke.

Unfortunately, if you stand up and complain, on a non-union shoot, or if the situation is too urgent to go through channels, be prepared to stand alone. A reputable advertising agency, signatory to an ACTRA Agreement, recently had a scene on a bouncing aircraft wing, with two wind machines blowing, up to thirty feet over a concrete floor. One performer out of the fifteen was brave enough to refuse to do it. The others trusted to luck and two inches of foam on the ground. They weren't warned of the risk they would face and they weren't paid a risk fee.

In that case, the union was called, but after the event so they couldn't do anything about it. If you're a member or a permittee, give the union a chance. It's there to sort out problems, by explaining where you have misunderstood the rules, or at the other extreme by threatening the producer with closing the set. In a general grievance, the union will guard your anonymity. Your name won't be mentioned and in most cases you can accomplish a lot by having them onside. Most performer problems on set come from honest mistakes or the production taking shortcuts to save time or money. No-one wants to mess with the union for the sake

55

of a stunt that may be cut anyway, or for the convenience of the Locations Manager.

If your problem, however small, seems to have been only one of many abuses the production is trying to get away with, talk to the union representative, so that the union is playing with a full deck in future disputes.

Extras are at the bottom of the totem pole, but there's no reason why we always have to suffer. We may be treated like mindless sheep, but we don't have to treat each other the same way. Look out for your workmates, look out for yourself.

Let the union do its job. Don't let the production, or anyone around you, mistake your silence for consent. Bitching in undertones doesn't help the situation. Speak up, or you'll face worse situations in the future. No, you won't be blacklisted: that's a meaningless threat, or an excuse for the lazy-minded.

# BEFORE THE SHOOT

## CHECKING IN

Now that you have an agent, naturally you must be prepared for calls to set. Many new extras sit by the phone, waiting for it to ring. The agency said they would call you shortly after you signed up, but so far you've had no reply. Could the phone be out of order? Nope, there's the dial tone. So what could be keeping them?

The easiest way to find out is by calling them. You should be in the habit  of checking in with your agent(s) regularly, every two or three days when you're first starting. You're the new face in the books. You want to make sure that you aren't forgotten in the rush of calling the regulars. You want to be a regular.

Is it better to call late afternoon or early morning? Ask. Agents have dif-  ferent work styles: fit yourself in to each agent's preferences. After a while, your agent will become accustomed to hearing from you and will keep you in mind.

Keep the calls brief. Simply let the agent know that you're available and ready at a moment's notice. Keep track of when you phoned in, what your reception was like, and any new information you may have heard. If your agent says there may be a large casting call coming in, ask if you should call back later in the day. You may be suitable as one of the characters.

## GETTING YOUR CALL

At last your agent phones you. Make sure you always have pen and paper nearby. Use a copy of the Call Sheet in the back section of this book. Don't try memorizing all the information: write it down! This is probably only an availability check, but get what information you can. Keep that Call Sheet handy; with luck, the next call will confirm the booking.

After fifty calls, your agent can lose track of what information has already been passed along. Use the Call Sheet Worksheet to be sure you have all the necessary information before hanging up:

- Call date (what day you are shooting).
- Call time (what time you must be on set).
- Production (name of the show).
- Location (address of the shoot).
- Nearest Intersection (gives you a basic idea of where you'll be travelling to).
- Character (what sort of part you are playing).
- Wardrobe (any special clothes or props; how many changes you'll need).
- Contact (who to check in with when you get to set).
- Cash or voucher (how you will be paid).
- Any other special information you should know.

**57**

You may want to copy all the information on an index card that you can take with you to set. If it's an unfamiliar location, pull out your map to get a general idea how far it is, accessibility by public transit, alternate routes in case of traffic problems, availability of parking, and so on. Put the index card in the pockets of the clothes you'll be wearing to set.

## MAKE THE COMMITMENT

Once you've accepted a booking, you're committed. Don't cancel because you receive a big invitation or because you're too tired. Once you've accepted a booking, be careful about accepting a booking for another show. Your booked call may be for six hours, but you are obliged to stay, being paid extra of course, until they're done with you. If you have the chance to do more than one shoot in a day, have your agent check with the casting director about your need to leave by a specific time. If you're told that you might not be finished on time, then you must turn down the shoot you haven't actually accepted.

If a real emergency does come up (sorry, your goldfish dying doesn't count), use your best efforts to make good on your commitment. I once went to the funeral of a very dear friend, and then grabbed a cab to travel two cities away to speak at a seminar. It may sound callous, but even the death of a friend or loved one isn't an excuse for not letting people know you're unavailable. If you simply can't make it, contact your agent as soon as possible. Calmly let them know your situation and have them inform the casting director right away.

Unfortunately, standing by the commitment isn't always a two-way street. Changes can happen on a shoot, the weather may be bad, the production office may be behind in their shooting schedule and need to reschedule. There can be a last-minute cancellation of your booking. If there is still time, you can try getting on another shoot. Whatever happens, take it all in your stride. There is little anyone can do; these things happen. Legally, if it was a firm booking, and not just an availability check, they're obliged to pay. You want to take Megga Films to small claims court for your $100? Industry practice is that performers have to put up with this sort of unavoidable last-minute change. Ranting and raving won't help matters.

 If you were booked on a set and arrive to find yourself cancelled, you will usually be paid. If there's a problem, let your agent work it out with the casting director. The set isn't the right place to raise a fuss. If your agent closes shop early every day, there may have been no way for the casting director to pass on the news about the cancellation. The same holds true if you simply couldn't be reached, perhaps because you don't have a pager. That's not the production's fault. I've heard of extras who purposely unhook their phones so nobody could reach them to cancel a booking. This not only makes you look unprofessional and unreliable, but it wastes everybody's time. In such a case, you have nobody to blame but yourself if you don't get paid (although most casting personnel are usually reasonable).

When you accept a booking, you must always do your best to fulfill your responsibilities. At least let someone know if you cannot be there. It's not always easy, or fair – but whoever said this career was going to be simple?

## WARDROBE

Once you have received your call, get your required wardrobe ready right away. Make sure your wardrobe is clean. Did you forget that you wore those jeans to roll around in the mud for that last shoot? Make any necessary repairs (loose buttons, etc.).

Even if you're called in to play a cop and the production will be supplying the uniforms, bring along a suit. They may decide to make you a detective instead. Bring some ragged clothes as well (they may need a tramp). Bring along anything that will change your appearance enough for you to be used again. People thought I was crazy, but I used to carry around ten times as many outfits as were required between shoots. Sure it was heavy (at one point, more than 100 pounds, travelling by bus), but I was always prepared. I may have been playing a street bum, but I often brought a suit and dress shoes along anyhow. More than once the casting director pulled me aside and sent me straight to another shoot, this time playing a business executive. They may have had enough outfits on their truck to clothe me for the scene, but the casting director knew I had my outfits with me.

Okay, so that's getting carried away a little and most of the stuff was never used, but the aggravation of toting it all around town paid off. The wardrobe department was always delighted with the variety, and they've paid me back many times by helping me when I've needed special costumes for other shoots or for auditions.

Keep a variety of clothing prepared for all your special characters ahead of time. That way you'll simply have to grab the proper outfits. This will also save you a lot of panic time if you're called at the last moment.

Buy some sort of travelling bag for your wardrobe, nothing too elaborate or expensive, since there's always a chance of it getting ruined or stolen on a set. Bargain stores often sell zippered bags for about a dollar. If they get too tattered, you simply replace them. If a buck is still beyond your budget, then just use a garbage bag over the hangers. It may not look pretty, but it'll get you by for the day.

Don't wear your wardrobe. Wearing comfortable street clothes to the set will not only save wear and tear on the wardrobe to be used, but also give you a fresh, comfortable change after a sixteen hour day. Bring a light windbreaker just in case the production goes overtime and you don't get wrapped till the brisk early morning.

Avoid those dangerous colours and patterns: bright reds and oranges,  white, black, heavy pinstriping, anything with an logo.

You may be spending a lot of time standing around, so make sure your shoes are comfortable. Above all, make sure they're soft-soled. Hard-soled shoes make a lot of noise as you walk across a set, which is hell on the stars' quiet dialogue. Even stick-on soles will help.

## OTHER STUFF

It seems a fussy thing, but with warm days and hot lights on the set, it's very hard to keep cool. Trickling sweat can play havoc with heavy make-up, not to mention personal comfort. Do yourself a big favour and think about a fan. A folded paper fan can be stored in a pocket. Handheld electric fans provide greater relief between takes, but cost more, are a little harder to hide, and require charged batteries throughout the day. They're both well worth the investment.

It may not look like rain, but a folding umbrella may save you from sunstroke. Make sure you have your name on it and don't expect to carry it into the scene.

## ALWAYS ON STANDBY

The biggest frustration about doing Extra work is that you can never be sure when you're going be called for work. Or if you'll ever be called again.

You should always be prepared for any last minute calls to set. It may be 2 a.m., but if you're lucky enough to be called to set immediately, don't gripe about the hour. Just grab your stuff and go. They could as easily have asked someone else, and if you get known as always available, you'll get more work. Keeping that assortment of wardrobe handy means you can now enjoy an extra few minutes in the shower as you try to wash the sleep from your eyes.

A good agent should be available twenty-four hours a day; so you should be no less accessible yourself. Make sure your agent is aware that you understand the need for late calls, and that you welcome them. They hate having to wake people up, so of course they would much prefer dealing first with the people who don't mind.

If you work at another job, or simply want to go out for a while, a pager will help ensure that you don't miss any film work opportunities. Also, your employer would probably prefer that you receive calls on your pager, rather than through the company's business lines. If you're easy to contact, your agent will likely phone you before another extra.

You may have just finished a sixteen hour shoot, but if you can handle a back-to-back (work all day or night on one shoot, and still go on to another), then you may almost work enough to make a living. You can usually grab a quick power nap on your way to the next location, or in the holding area. Do your utmost to accept all extra work with a smile (now's the time to use your acting skills). The second pay cheque of the day will help make up for the days or weeks that you won't be working.

## ¦ READY

*y* to forget something when you're rushed or half asleep. Make sure that you're organised ahead of time. If you get an urgent call to set immediately, or if you feel like most people before dawn, you simply haven't got the luxury of wasting a half hour get your things together. You've got to be out the door and on your way within five minutes. Besides a ready set of wardrobe, you may also want to put together a small tote bag armed with a few supplies to be used strictly for on the set. Suggested contents:

| | |
|---|---|
| $5-$10 for cab, meals, etc. | Mini Sewing Repair Kit |
| Small change for bus, phones, etc. | Mini Appointment Book |
| Aspirins | Pack of Wet Towelettes |
| Camping Mirror | Paper and Pen |
| Cigarettes and Lighter | Photos and Résumés |
| Comb or Brush | Shoe Polish |
| Contact Phonebook | Snack (pop, chocolate, gum) |
| Contact Lenses Kit | Soap and Small Towel |
| Crossword Book | Spare Batteries for Pager ✓ |
| Deodorant | Toothbrush and Toothpaste |
| Emergency Money | For men: Shaving Cream and Razor |
| Folding Umbrella | For women: Make-up, Tampons, etc. |
| Map | *straws* |
| | *temporary tattoos* |

These items (plus any others which you may wish to include) will remain in the carrying bag for use on set *only*. They form your emergency travel kit for when you simply don't have enough time to get ready. As soon as you get home, replenish or refresh the items as necessary. That way you'll always be ready at a moment's notice.

## FINAL CHECK

Before you turn off those lights to catch a few ZZZs, take off your jewellery and run through a quick check to make sure you haven't forgotten anything. The "Call Sheet Worksheet" may remind you of something important.

Well, you're reasonably prepared now, so you had better hit the sack and get rested up. You've got a big day ahead of you, when you go on set.

# PICTURE'S UP

# AN EXTRA LIFE TO LIVE

2

Bob is reading "the book," lying on his back on a loveseat. Jane sits in a firm chair beside him.

JANE
(In a terrible Sigmund Freud accent)
Zo, Mr. Voolff, vhy do you sink a goot hextra you vood make? Are you too fat, or too skinny ...

BOB
No, but these Worksheets are great. This Casting sheet's full of good stuff, Gran.

JANE
There are two words I won't hear in this house, and one of them is Gran. I know what I am, I don't have to write it down in a Worksheet.
(She is waving the Casting Worksheet from the book)

BOB
Do you think I'm a "Group Leader" or a "Giggle-o?"

JANE
(Snappishly)
I think you're goofy.

BOB
Aw, come on! (Looking at book) No, hold on, here it is. Goofy hey? (He marks it on the list, then realises.) Aw, really?

JANE
When you're grown up, you'll know what you are.

                    BOB
No, that's the point, it's not what you
are, it's what you look like. You look
like a lawyer, you don't look anything
like a ... well, ... a Gran.

                    JANE
I've told you, two words I ...  (Realising
what he said) I look like a lawyer?  You
really mean that? Really? No shit?
(Realising what she said) Oh dear.

                    BOB
Sorry, the G-word ...

                    JANE
And the S-word.

                    BOB
No shit.

                    JANE
No shit.

# ON YOUR MARKS

Congratulations! You've had your first booking from your agent and you'll finally get to be on film. With your excitement and anticipation, and a little dose of fear and apprehension, you spend a sleepless night waiting for the big day. Will you do okay? Will the production like you? What if you do something really wrong and never get called in again?

It takes a while to build a reputation, either good or bad. Unless you do something really spectacularly stupid (and I have seen cases that still boggle my mind), you simply aren't important enough to be picked out and blacklisted forever. We spend time and effort reminding casting people why they should want to use us again: believe me, they don't have the energy to remember every dumb thing everyone does.

If you spend your time thinking either how great you are or how terrified you are, you will certainly make a fool of yourself. If you focus outward, keeping your antennae alert, like a new bug on a windowsill, you'll stay ahead of trouble. Focussing outward, concentrating on what other people are doing, working on what you have to do, is the best way to forget your fear.

"Going to set" is one of those odd expressions. It means going to the two- or three-block area where the filming is being done, and when you're there it means going to the fringes of the circle of technicians and cameras around the main action, and when you're there, "Going *on* set" means going to the area that is going to appear on camera.

I'm going to be talking about a well-run union set, because that covers most of the work out there, and the rules and structure of the organisation are specific. Remember, though, that on a non-union set, or the odd badly-run union set, there are no rules and no guarantee what will happen. You won't go far wrong taking this advice anyway, but sometimes the situation may not be at all what I am going to describe. Do you want to hear the story about the non-union production where everyone turned up on the first day to find no set, no crew, no producer? I didn't think so.

Relax, you'll survive. You've been in new situations before: the same rules will help you, the way they did at kindergarten, the way they did at the junior prom.

**Look.** Watch everything and everyone working around you. It may look like chaos, or idleness, but see how every trade has its own responsibilities and skills. Each works around the needs of the others; not always cheerfully, but with respect. Once you realise how hard they are working, and how and why they do what they do, it will be easy to respect them. If you respect other peoples' work, you'll get consideration in return.

You're not an outsider on someone else's territory here. Although everyone seems to know everyone else, long-lasting teams are only possible in successful series. These are just people who are used to slotting in to a new team without fuss: and you're part of the same team. If all you do is treat people like people, you will get noticed and make friends. There's a depressing thought.

**Listen.** Listen to what people are saying, even if they're not talking to you or the other extras. You aren't gathering dirt for the tabloids, it's not nosiness, you won't blackmail your way into a part. It's simple: if you pay attention, you may hear what the director wants to accomplish, what the DOP's lighting problem is in the scene, or what's required to fill the picture. The better you understand how the scene is working, the better you'll be able to deliver the performance needed. If you know why the AD in charge of the extras is telling you to move quickly through the scene, you'll be the townsperson who is excited to be getting nearer to the band, in a bunch of extras who are simply marching along. That may be your best chance for an upgrade. Directors and crews enjoy working with people who make their life easier by working the scene properly.

**Learn.** Years ago, performers were laughed at by people with regular jobs. If you had a regular job, you started as a learner and spent a while going around with your mouth open, being stupid. Eventually you knew enough to be able to stickhandle your way through most situations. If you stuck around long enough, you got your own locker and a parking place, and you got promoted to being an expert.

Performers never stayed long enough to get the locker, were always looking for work, and laboured day and night to make minimum wage. Performers were secretly paranoid about not being successful, never stopped talking about their job, and were always taking classes.

Nowadays, things are changing so fast in almost every industry that it's the learners who are winning out over the experts. Actors and directors are teaching seminars for executives who need to be able to function on their abilities, rather than relying on their familiarity with the routine. There is nothing sadder than seeing someone who built up the Widgets department from nothing, when no-one uses Widgets any more.

Actors and directors train in a different college of The School of Hard Knocks. In this business it has never been possible to learn everything: there are simply too many variables. Different crews, directors, different scripts, even a different set can mean all previous bets are off. Even on a long-running series, only the core cast and department heads are around long enough to get bored. If you're hoping you will eventually be able to ease off and coast, think again. Why do you think it takes so long for the scene to be lit, or for the star and the director and Wardrobe to decide on a colour for a tie? Because no-one knows the answers.

Decisions on set, for everyone, are more like painting a picture than building a wall. There is no right way, there isn't an instruction book, you have to work it out for yourself.

As you go through the day, remember the bug on the windowsill. Keep your antennae moving, be ready to jump, physically and mentally, don't slump and think that's the best way to avoid attention. Never be satisfied with what you can already do. You can never know too much. When you stop learning, you may as well leave the business.

**Help each other.** That's allowed. Help out another performer who looks lost – you may be paired up together later, and have to rely on each other knowing the way around. Ask questions of anyone who looks accessible. (Remember, though, you are low on the totem pole, so be *very* sure before you risk disturbing anyone, crew or talent.)

Here's the address, where's the set? Check your call details: are you really where you should be? Look for the rented trucks, look for the orange cones in the road, cruise the outside of the area and look for the signs. Panic.

Don't expect to find a parking place anywhere around: the production will have locked off the curbs for blocks and grumbling residents and commuters will have overspilled into the next postal code. When you do find a spot, check what risk you're running of being towed. A fat fine is one thing, having to schlep down to the pound late at night after a day on set is no fun at all. I haven't driven to set in seven years, I find the problems worse than the advantages. I travel in on public transit, and when I'm wrapped, like Blanche Dubois I rely on the kindness of strangers. Drive around some more. Panic.

All the casting directors, agents, and extras that I've spoken with agree on one matter: *Be on set ten or fifteen minutes early.* I say take that advice and throw it out the window! Be there at least *thirty minutes*, and *preferably an hour* before your call time! Why so early? Simple: it's better to be an hour early than five minutes late. You could get lost or have trouble finding the set. You may be stuck in a traffic jam, or oversleep. Even if you're only minutes late getting to set, you risk being bumped and replaced by the time you arrive. You'll lose the fee and, worse, the casting director may tell your agent to use someone more reliable in future. I once arrived fourteen hours early; I just wasn't sure if there would be any transit service on the day of the shoot. That may have been extreme, but I sure wasn't late.

If the worst happens, and you are late, don't make a big production number out of it. Check in immediately with the casting director or AD in charge of the extras and hope they can still use you. Apologise discreetly, but don't go into a detailed explanation unless you're asked. You won't be: they've heard every excuse in the book. Check in with the Wardrobe people and change into your outfit straight away. Then on to the Hair and Make-up people if necessary. Once again, apologise discreetly to any crew members you may have held up. Time is of the essence, so work extra hard to help them get you ready.

Arriving late is a pain for everyone. Arriving ahead of schedule gives you a better chance of upgrades or featured shots. A production will often want to have some characters made up and wardrobed as early as possible, and there you are, in a small group, ready to be noticed. If you're ready when they come running into the room because they suddenly need someone to play the riot ringleader, you'll be the one who gets the upgrade.

It makes the AD's life a lot simpler on a big shoot if they don't have to race around in a frenzy to sign in everyone at the last minute. These are the people who will be your contact on the actual set; it only makes sense to keep them happy. When the ADs have to decide who to wrap and who to keep at the end of a long day, they often like to keep those who put in the extra effort. I've got more than my share of overtime (as much as an additional eight hours at time and a half) simply because I'd been around since the dawn's early light. Find out the names of your ADs for the shoot: since crews move around to different productions, there is a very good chance you'll be working with them again. Give them a chance to treat you like a real person, earn their respect, and you'll be one of the in-crowd.

Speaking of that, you're not in until you're signed in. As soon as you've parked, and walked around the buildings again, and finally found the set, check your call worksheet details or index card again, or your diary if you forgot the card, for the name of the extras' contact person. In this business, getting people's names wrong is an insult. Look for an AD (one of the crew members with a walkie-talkie), ask where the contact person or the extras' holding area is.

The contact person, who will sign you in, will be the casting director, a PA or the third AD; check your call details yet again. The Vouchers may not be ready yet, but there will probably be a list. Check in to be sure the person responsible for the extras knows you're there. If they make a mistake and lose you in the rush as call time approaches, it's your fault. Get your name on paper.

If no one is available to sign you in, wait in the holding area for them to arrive. If no holding area has yet been established, wait off to the side, out of the way. Keep your eyes peeled: it's your job to sign in, it's nobody's job to find you. For some reason, people tend to wait in doorways: this gives you a view of two areas, but it also puts you in the way of two sets of busy people.

If the holding area is just being set up, offer to help. If you behave as if they're doing you a favour – say it'll kill time for you – you'll be less likely to get up anybody's nose. If the crew doesn't mind, make "Extras Holding" signs, set up chairs, any grunt work. You'll be more comfortable with your surroundings and feel more like part of the production. Don't look for any special favours in return. That's very uncool. And a waste of time.

If you were smart and arrived early, there'll still be a good spot to set your bags down and relax. Try to find a hook to hang your suit bag, or a piece of floor to put it out of harm's way and out of the traffic. Even if you're expecting to wear your grubbies, you don't want them buried under latecomers' bags or trampled underfoot. And you'll have something smarter in your bag as an option, anyway, won't you? You haven't brought anything irreplaceable to set, but keep an eye on your stuff. Things are stolen, sometimes by outsiders benefitting from the confusion and crowds of unfamiliar faces. Regrettably, not always by outsiders.

Since you've already checked in and know the procedure for this set, you can help any later souls. Be very cautious. Don't play the seasoned pro too much, or you will annoy the ignorant, who will feel you're lording it over them, and the expert, who will be outraged that you can't see their expertise. You will make the director shriek with laughter if you mistake her for a newby and point out the sign-in sheet.

It's always nice to get a call to a set where there are very few extras. You're treated with a little more respect and dignity (since there are fewer people who require pampering). With larger groups it's always chaotic. On the other hand, shoots that require hundreds of extras for that big crowd scene give you a better chance to find out about other agents and what's happening in the industry. It may not be very organised and the lineups are longer, but at least you're working.

Once you get more familiar with the scene, this will feel like a peaceful time, before everyone arrives, and I've often used it to listen as the crew sets up their equipment. You can pick up a lot of information about the types of scenes they have scheduled for the day: listen for hints on what the director or production might want. If you're informed, and present what they're looking for, you'll have a better chance of an upgrade.

The morning munchies that craft service brings in for the extras are always grumbled about. Nobody is allowed to admit they are welcomed and appreciated, any more than a teenager is allowed to admit liking broccoli. (In the privacy of this book, though, thanks everyone.) The doughnuts aren't (usually) stale, and the coffee... well at least it's strong enough to wake the soundest sleeper. Rev up your courage and grab a cup. It's all free, and you'll need a pick-me-up for what an extra must do best. Don't be tempted to scarf down the buffet laid out on the craft services table or in the craft van. This is not for extras unless specifically invited, which can happen on a small or non-union set. Generally, craft services is for the main cast and technicians, and you'll get frozen out right quick if you try to push in there.

Waiting-R-Us. About 90% of your day on set will be spent in the holding area. Extras are always complaining that they're tired of just sitting around without being used for all the shots, but then they complain about spending endless hours stuck on the set itself. There's no satisfying some people, and it's all part of the job. Some directors schedule especially long days, and of course they can afford the luxury of extras standing by for the crowd scene if they ever get round to it. I remember one feature film starting on Monday, when we waited fourteen hours and never saw the set. On Tuesday, we were called to set after twelve hours. After six minutes, they changed the scene they'd planned and sent us back to the holding area to be wrapped. Wednesday we were used for two hours at the end of a sixteen hour day. We didn't complain. The overtime was great and we were used for another six weeks of continuity (where they use the same people to portray characters throughout the project).

So, how do you kill time when you're stuck in the Extras Holding room? There's no giant screen TV, all the good stuff is happening on set at the other end of the building, you're trapped, and you're bored out of your skull.

Scan the room and listen for the people who are discussing work, current and rumoured shoots, working conditions on local sets, character and show style information, etc. This is useful stuff, the small change in the networking system. Chat with the jocks – "What about them Reds?" – or the housewives, of both sexes – "Oh, it's more chartreuse, surely?" – but don't lose the chance to plug into the bush telegraph. This is where being a nomad means you can add together different people's feelings and rumours and see a little way into the future. You can't count on everything you hear, but wisps of information build up into a solid picture, often before there has been a formal announcement of new work or a new agency. Comical stories about the sets, new shows, good and bad experiences, skills: you've already got a wealth of information to exchange. Don't barge into these conversations with your ideas, there's often a guru in the group who won't welcome a rival, but take part and feel your way. Share what you have and be grateful for whatever you get in return.

Are the make-up, hair, and wardrobe people trading production information? This is valuable stuff. The crew know the inside information about all the upcoming shoots – they often sign up for positions a month or more in advance – and willingly share the details with other crew members. Some crew members feel inhibited or touchy when those outside their group get a little nosy. If you come to know and work well with these people on other shoots, they'll often be glad to let you sit in on the exchanges. Just don't force the invitation.

Those crew members who deal with the Talent can be approached. If they're alone and not working against time, one great way to start is by asking for a moment of their time for advice on how you can make their job easier. Most will be more than happy to give you a little advice. As they see that you are serious in your interest in their work, without ulterior motives, they'll quickly relax. Find out their personal preferences about working with extras. Knowing their quirks, habits, or pet peeves can help relieve tense situations when dealing with them in the future. Some crew members appear very stern or severe, handling pressure with gloomy intensity, while nothing ever seems to faze others, who seem inex-

**71**

haustibly bubbly. Knowing and understanding their moods under these situations will help develop a good working relationship, and signal you when to shrug off unintentional offenses. You'll be working with these people a lot in the future: learn what makes them tick.

If the casting person or AD in charge of the extras isn't busy, you can use the chance to talk briefly to an insider about what's happening in the industry, and get another viewpoint. Just as with the crew members, if they seem preoccupied, let them get back to their work or thoughts. Don't overstay your welcome. They may enjoy a little chat, but they really aren't looking for you to spend the entire day with them.

Have you met someone really new to the industry? However new you are, you're likely to be of some use to them: you're reading this book, aren't you? Many newcomers feel very self-conscious, as though they're the unwanted outsider in a crowd of seasoned pros. Others will jump right in, figuring you'll never spot them as first timers, and expect you to praise their "obvious" talent. Be the one to start the conversation: help the shy ones to feel relaxed, take what the arrogant ones say with a grain of salt. A group comfortable with each other in the holding area makes for a solid team on set.

Sometimes you'll spot extras who seem to be off in their own world. When you're on set, you'll see me wandering around the room or back and forth in the hallway, with a face to scare children as I pace relentlessly. Like many others, I use these moments to build nervous energy, focus and concentration. Don't feel put off, these are just techniques to prepare the characters. I'm not really that nasty. Now, shut up and get away from me!.... Just kidding.

If you just need to relax a bit, pull out a crossword or a good trade book–like the one you're reading now! I still carry *The Actor's Survival Kit* around with me on sets for constant review. I read each trade book again every couple of months, just to remind me of subtle points I lose track of. I even plan on carrying my own book: amazingly enough, I often forget I'm the one who wrote it, and discover wonderful ideas when I read the manuscript. Learning a craft all the time, it's very easy to forget what you've already learned. Even good habits can get neglected – review yourself often to keep your career in peak shape.

The holding area may be a quiet room, or a space on a busy sidewalk: this is your home away from home. If you think back to when you were a teenager, the same rules apply here as they did at home, at college, or even now, maybe, if you share an apartment. In the holding area, of course, you may have two hundred roommates.

Keep it clean. Someone else may have made the mess, but be civilised, clean it up yourself.

Keep the noise down. The set may be nearby, and microphones are sensitive enough to pick up even minute noise. If the shooting is taking place elsewhere in the same building, be careful about stomping around, as many of the older constructions may transmit the banging throughout the building. Whole mornings of shooting have been wasted trying to work round an elevator running at the other end of an empty college building. Even before shooting starts, no-one wants to set up a romantic scene next door to a bus terminal waiting room.

Do you smoke? Smoking is a problem. Even ignoring local by-laws, there are a lot of non-smokers out there, and some have severe allergies. I like to smoke at work, so, when I first arrive at the holding area, I ask the AD where smoking is allowed. At least try to find an area away from the crowd, where smoking will be tolerated, and use the butt-buckets, not the ground. If you're allowed out, stay within earshot, smoke and get back. These days, they're doing you a favour.

Where are you going? Don't leave the holding area. You're signed in now, and are on call until the production wraps you. They have a holding area so the ADs will know where to find you. Time can't be wasted asking around and searching for someone who wandered off.

If you need to make an urgent phone call, and you're very grand, you can use your cell phone. Otherwise, you're unlikely to find a pay phone, so it's up to you if you want to risk annoying the casting director or third AD. They hate to set a precedent, but if it is truly an emergency ...

You may be bored and feel like walking around a bit, or going to the local store for a snack to kill some time. Before leaving the area, check with the casting director or the AD in charge of the extras. If an AD isn't around, don't assume it will be all right. This includes times when you just want to go outside for a smoke, or if you must leave the immediate area to use the washroom. Oh, all right, if you're taken short, leave word with a friend, rush off and rush back.

When you're told that you have time to step out for a few minutes, make it fast. Don't wander away shopping for twenty minutes (I've seen it happen). As soon as you sneak off, the production will be going crazy trying to get you on the set. Of course, as soon as you get on set it's hurry up and wait time again.

This is your home, at least for the next few hours, and you're trapped. Make the most of it: if you didn't get much sleep last night, flake out on the nice soft floor for a few minutes. Bring a long book, crossword puzzles, some cards (four-handed Euchre is popular), or whatever will keep you entertained for long periods. Why not read those trade magazines you just bought? Knitting is good, working on your car and practising your trumpet are not.

Talk nicely to your friends. Here's your chance to find out how busy the other extras have been, and to ask about their agencies. You may discover a new agency worth looking into. Pay close attention when the conversation turns to the new shoots coming into town. You may hear who's casting the projects, and what characters will be needed. If you have any information, share it: what goes around, comes around. Without taking down the conversation in shorthand, note the main facts in your diary, for transfer into your files when you get home.

If you're new to the industry, talk to the veterans. People love to give advice and suggestions. Just don't believe everything you hear, even if everyone agrees. Everyone thought the earth was flat at one time. Watch for confirmation and use your common sense.

If you're working on a commercial, you'll have a regular contract, giving your work category. Otherwise, the casting director will sign you in and take your SIN (Social Security number in the States) and your address. If you're not a union member, you will find out if you are going to get a voucher or not. The voucher is your contract and will be signed by a representative of the production, with your hours worked, at the end of the day. Don't lose it.

In Canada, the CBC has a voucher format in tasteful pink, but most extra work is on ACTRA Independent Production (IPA) sets, and there are three sorts of extra vouchers. There's details in "Union Matters," but for now there are:

**blue**   ACTRA vouchers used for ACTRA members,

**green**   Apprentice vouchers, for people who have committed to the union, but who haven't yet done enough work to qualify for full membership, and

**yellow**   Permittee vouchers, which entitle non-members to ACTRA rates when ACTRA quotas aren't filled.

If you're not a performer union member, you'll be told if you're on cash or voucher: union members are always on voucher. Vouchers pay more per hour than cash calls. The casting director, and sometimes selected agents, will decide who gets the available vouchers and who gets cash at the end of the day. Naturally, the non-union extras who are best liked and most trusted tend to get the Permittee vouchers.

Wardrobe personnel eventually come in to check on the clothes that the extras have brought. Lay yours out as best you can, and listen as Wardrobe makes choices before you, so that you can organize your stuff with the likeliest most available. Are they choosing slacks and straw hats for the beachwear scene? Put your scuba gear and the bikini off to one side. Still visible, but second choices. They will eventually get to you and make their selections, with possibly another selection for a second outfit. Don't complain that your number one choice isn't used; Wardrobe is putting together a look for the crowd around the central idea, not all following it exactly. You may have the ideal outfit, but someone earlier in the process may have filled that slot. Don't make a big thing of how much you have brought. Read the signs before you launch into your thinking about the variations on the wardrobe requirements. Even if they seem interested, be brief and businesslike: you're a salesperson with a busy customer.

If the production is providing costumes, perhaps for a historical piece, or uniforms or work clothes, you should still have brought some of your own choices, but be very cautious about pushing them. Your police blues may be smarter, your nurse's uniform may be authentic, but Wardrobe is pulling together the whole group. From their point of view, your real Ghanaian headdress could just be an embarrassment in a group of near-misses they whipped up from stock.

If you put together the right choices when you headed for the set, you'll have the bonus that the costume Wardrobe chooses for you will actually fit you properly. If you decide to leave all the work of outfitting you to the wardrobe department, or if there are very special requirements they are supplying, don't complain if the outfits are a little uncomfortable. Showing up really early for your call gives you a better chance to get clothes from the wardrobe department that actually fit. Each piece they stock is chosen to be wearable by a dozen other extras over the next weeks, but they don't carry stock to fit every combination. For example, the production may have six pairs of shoes, sizes 7,8, and 9: when everyone who shows up wears size 8 and has nothing suitable of their own, then some will have to make do with shoes too small or too big. The lucky ones get to stuff paper in their big shoes. The last in line, with only small shoes left, will have sore feet at the end of the day. If you are an odd size, you will do well to pay particular attention to our "Wardrobe" chapter. Wardrobe Works Wonders, as the sign says, but they simply can't buy new clothes for each person. Don't expect everything to be tailor fitted. Save your grumbling for when you get home.

Once you know what clothes to wear, change quickly. There should be an assigned changing area, and usually there is (perhaps just a washroom), but make do with what you have. There is little room in this business for shyness or embarrassment. Don't worry, the wardrobe people have seen it all before.

If they've provided the costume and it's really uncomfortable, let them know and they will decide if there is any way to change it. Since the wardrobe personnel are very busy, they simply haven't got the time to make permanent adjustments. Their job is to do camouflaging quickly. You will sometimes have to settle for the minor alterations being held together with tape, pins, or staples for the day of shooting. If the pants are too big, wear a belt. If a jacket is too tight, decide not to wave your arms. Face it, you only need to wear the clothes for a day or two, so you'll have to make do. If the fit is really bad and you offer back-up clothes of your own, they may agree to use them instead of squeezing you into their stock. But only if your things are essentially identical to their choice, and only if there's time to discuss it.

Be especially careful of any uniforms or pieces of wardrobe that the production has supplied. Don't leave bits and pieces of the outfit lying around. If you're told to remove a hat or other item for the scene, give it to an AD or wardrobe person while you're shooting, or ask where you should put it. Treat everything with care; it may be fake and not as tough as it looks. Some of the stuff will look pretty scruffy close up, but it has probably done a good job in more films than you've had hot dinners, and the production will pay dearly if they can't return it undamaged to the rental place.

Once the wardrobe department has approved your appearance, do not make any alterations. If you've brought your emergency sewing repair kit, perhaps they wouldn't mind if you resewed their work a bit more securely. Ask them first – if they need to pull the alterations out quickly at the end of the day, they will be counting on ripping out safety pins and duct tape, and they will not be well pleased to have to pick apart your fine sewing.

The wardrobe department may well ask you to remove your watch and jewellery. It may clash with the style or period of the film, or glitter too much in the lights. It's best to leave it at home. Too many people have access to a working set for your jewellery to be safe anywhere except on your person, and if you're in a beach scene, or playing a ballet dancer, you won't have too many pockets for your watch or your diamonds.

Hair and Make-up is the scene of more tears and tantrums than anywhere, even now that improved lighting has made the styling very natural and painless. Fortunately, hair and make-up people obviously take Niceness pills, and try to have you leave their table feeling better than when you came in. Time is always tight for the crew, so they need to prepare you and all the other extras as quickly as possible. Help them as much as you can, and get a smile in reward.

In most cases, the best thing you can do for them is wash. It's not a pleasant thing to talk about, but Hair and Make-up bitch more about B.O. and dandruff than anything else. Use an antiperspirant: a deodorant will have no effect on the smell of nervous perspiration.

The hair and make-up people are responsible for your appearance, but there are times when they will not have time to do more than check you. Background performers often don't need more than a quick check from the experts, a brush of the hair and a dab of powder to take the shine off. Outdoor scenes may not even need that. A combination of special needs and performer mistakes, however, can turn your straightforward Hair and Make-up time into Horror and Misery.

Unless you are told otherwise by your agent, omit your morning make-up. Your regular application and the make-up required for use on the set can be very different. In your usual day, you don't worry about the effect of film lights and film stock, color and contrast flares, nor about presenting the image of somebody living a different life from yours. Don't insist your make-up will be okay. The make-up people have their reasons for doing things their way. In most cases, they would like you with a clean bare face, a blank sheet for them to work on, so make it easier for them do their job.

However, it has been known for some agents to forget to ask whether their performers should show up with make-up done, so always bring your own make-up, and a small mirror, to be on the safe side. The rule of thumb is: if you are unfamiliar with the show and haven't been asked to apply your own make-up, then play it safe and don't. But bring it and have it available just in case.

If you are booked as a regular on a show, ask Make-up if they would like you to apply a base before heading to set the next time. Sci-Fi and horror productions, particularly, often have very heavy make-up schedules and it may save the Make-up department time if you already have a foundation applied. If you are working regularly on a show, you can be more trusted and be able to be more help. It doesn't hurt to ask.

When you're in the make-up chair, be ready to move your head, close your eyes, look up, look down, rah rah rah, whatever they need. Don't fidget. It is very frustrating for Make-up to have you squirming and looking around the room while they are working on your face. Work with the make-up person: trying to read what the make-up artist will do next, while looking in the mirror at your face being transformed, in an unfamiliar place, with people bopping in and out saying very important but totally mysterious things to each other, is a good exercise for keeping your focus and concentration when you're on set.

Those sandwiches may be absolutely delicious or that doughnut may really hit the spot, but wait until you're out of the make-up chair to do your eating. If you're chewing food, or even gum, it's like asking the make-up people to do their job on a moving target. Besides, how would you like to be working inches from somebody's face while they're dribbling gobs of food from their mouth? It's not a pleasant working position. You are being paid to do a job and so are they. Let them do theirs quickly and you'll be able to get back to your snacks soon enough. It's simple courtesy.

After Make-up, if you've had lipstick applied, use a straw if you want to  drink anything, hot or cold. It means your make-up will stay fresh and require fewer touchups later. Bring your own straw in case the make-up or craft service  people don't have any. The make-up people will appreciate your attention to minor details.

Tattoos are a source of fascination on set and quite often the director will want to feature more visibly those who have them. Just as often, real tattoos make real problems when the scene makes them inappropriate. If you have a tattoo, Make-up won't be able to cover it, and Wardrobe may have to spend time hiding it. A discreet rosebud won't likely be a problem but bikers' knuckle messages will cut down on your range of casting. The solution is quite simple. When you think the scene might use them, bring a variety of temporary tattoos from a bargain store for the make-up people to choose from. You can stick them where they'll be most use, even on your face and hands, where they would have cost you work had they been real.

When you're wrapped, you'll often find there is a long line-up to take make-up off. You can dodge this by going home with your make-up on, which can be very embarrassing and next to impossible if you're in a horror monster scene. (Although it has sometimes got me a seat on a crowded bus.) Better to bring along some moist towelettes, cleanser and even a small container of water. It's a very inexpensive investment, and very welcome at the end of a long sweaty day.

There are some shoots where a five-o'clock shadow may be acceptable or favoured. If it seems likely, but you didn't get a clear indication from your agent, and you aren't sure if you should shave beforehand, bring your bristly face and a mirror and battery shaver (electricity isn't always easily accessible). A shaver is also handy if your beard grows quickly and you need to get rid of that shadow midway through a particularly long filming day. Shaving cream and a blade razor will do, but you'd better be prepared for a dry shave since hot water may not be available. Remember the importance of continuity between days of shooting: if you had the stubble on one day, you'll probably need it again for the next.

Be prepared for a quick haircut if the production requires a specific hair style, maybe because it's a period piece or you're portraying a cop. Sometimes a production may be able to hide your long hair under a cap, but if they can't or won't, they'll give you a trim. If this isn't acceptable, let your agent know ahead of time. You may have to give up the job to keep your locks. Think ahead, be reasonable: if you're in a regular street crowd, and they want to clip you down to the bone, you can legitimately refuse, if you're playing a cop and you're a bit shaggy, you must expect them to trim you. Take a deep breath and smile: your hair will grow back. Remember, the difference between a good haircut and a bad haircut is ten days. If you're surprised and outraged by a hairstyle demand on set, you can of course refuse the haircut, and storm out of the trailer. If you do, be prepared to storm right on home and have a very irritable agent calling about the complaints that have come in from the production. Much better to pay attention when you get the call, and know what you're going to set to play.

The purpose of the Hairdresser's work is to make you blend in to the scene. That means you can't change things to suit your ideas of attractiveness, or your comfort. Once they have set your hair, do not change it! You make the changes, but the crew gets the blame for not having done their job properly. Boy, will your scalp sting when they take out your improvements! If you're in a real frazzle about the look, ask the hair people about possible changes while you're in the chair. Don't hold your breath waiting for them to agree.

Let the stylists do their job. The hair and make-up crew are trained and experienced in hair for camera. They know what kind of look is needed for the shoot, and they know what will make you look good on camera. I've seen a Hair Artist spend more than half an hour setting one extra's hair in a very elaborate style needed for the scene. Ten minutes after they had finished, she had undone all their work because "I don't look good with my hair done up. I like it hanging and long!" She caused all kinds of delays on the set and was never called again for that production. Doubtless her agent got an earful about her!

Wardrobe and Hair and Make-up have taken less than an hour, now what do we do? Wait. The networking and preparation we talked about, certainly, and the crosswords and cards, but the most important thing is to wait. Be ready to move at a moment's notice, but for now, just relax and wait.

# ON SET

If you're not in the first scene of the day, you may be waiting for it to be finished. But it's only three lines in the script:

```
173          TODD GETS OUT OF CAR,
        THE KIPPER KILLER HITS HIM,
                  HE FALLS.
```

How long can that take? Most of the tape and film run through the cameras is never seen by the audience: in a good day's work on a television show, the production hopes to tape two or three minutes of programme time. On episodic television, they schedule a new episode, twenty-two minutes of acting, each week. At a killing pace, as much as two episodes. It can take seventeen hours to shoot one thirty-second commercial.

Finally, it's time to go on set: here comes the AD: it's time to strut your stuff. And it's time right now; don't dawdle about as though you were getting ready for a casual stroll. When you're called, you follow.

Keep the noise down. The sound of fifty extras chattering as they approach the set can be very distracting for the crew and director. Stay in a tight group, try to keep out of the way. There are a hundred people running around trying to do their jobs. Orders are flying, equipment is crashing, the director is arguing about the set-up for the next scene. Don't add to the racket, and when you hear "Quiet," it means "Shut up! Completely! NOW!" Take it as a direct order to you. "Yes, you." Forget about the noise the crew may still be causing. Don't give them a fall-guy when they're looking for someone to blame. "Shhh ..."

You may be in a high traffic area, but try not to get in the way. The art is to stay where you were put and observe what you can without wandering about. Keep your eyes open, remember the antennae on the bug: as the crew rushes by with more equipment, manage to take a half step back out of the way in time.

This is a huge operation. The people you can see now are only a fraction of those working on the set. There are more people in trucks and cars and taxis, more in the production office, and many more who will be brought in to do specific jobs as the project goes on.

You may not plan on working as a crew member, but learn as much as you can about what they do. These are serious professionals like you and the more you can learn about how they do their job, the easier it will be for you to do yours. Why is this specific equipment being used now? Why is backlighting so important? How does the smoke machine change the look of a shot? Watch how the boom man mikes the room, and how the lighting department flags the spots and sets up the key lights. See the gaffers waft in more smoke and stand actors on apples.

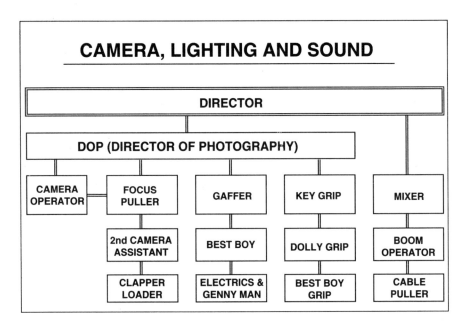

# CAMERA, LIGHTING AND SOUND

| DIRECTOR |
|---|

| DOP (DIRECTOR OF PHOTOGRAPHY) |
|---|

| CAMERA OPERATOR | FOCUS PULLER | GAFFER | KEY GRIP | MIXER |
|---|---|---|---|---|
| | 2nd CAMERA ASSISTANT | BEST BOY | DOLLY GRIP | BOOM OPERATOR |
| | CLAPPER LOADER | ELECTRICS & GENNY MAN | BEST BOY GRIP | CABLE PULLER |

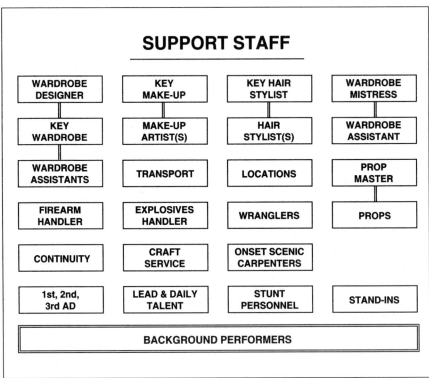

# SUPPORT STAFF

| WARDROBE DESIGNER | KEY MAKE-UP | KEY HAIR STYLIST | WARDROBE MISTRESS |
|---|---|---|---|
| KEY WARDROBE | MAKE-UP ARTIST(S) | HAIR STYLIST(S) | WARDROBE ASSISTANT |
| WARDROBE ASSISTANTS | TRANSPORT | LOCATIONS | PROP MASTER |
| FIREARM HANDLER | EXPLOSIVES HANDLER | WRANGLERS | PROPS |
| CONTINUITY | CRAFT SERVICE | ONSET SCENIC CARPENTERS | |
| 1st, 2nd, 3rd AD | LEAD & DAILY TALENT | STUNT PERSONNEL | STAND-INS |

| BACKGROUND PERFORMERS |
|---|

Did all that sound like gobbledegook? Sorry to show off. It's just trade jargon; you'll pick it up soon enough.

Now's the time to inspect the set itself. Imagine possible ways to fill the scene with the extras. Are there usable props? How will the cables stretched across the floor make walking troublesome in different areas? Eventually, all these things will run through your head automatically, but for now work at getting a head start on the problems and opportunities that will come up during the shooting.

Lifting an anonymous plate in a background cafeteria crowd may not make you an Olivier, but then Olivier probably wasn't much turned on by doing his late career TV commercials. This is your job: take it seriously or you may not have it long. Take the job seriously by accepting the characters you play as being normal. Accept the situations as documentaries from someone's life. Take the job seriously but laugh at yourself! It's natural for your alien creature to run around in silver underwear, but you can have fun with it. If you feel ill at ease, others working with you will feel uneasy too. That nervousness reads on film. If you can laugh at yourself and enjoy the amusement of those around you, everybody will have a better time. I purposely ask for the wackiest characters: it's the really weird ones that have all the fun!

Time passes. You were dragged here at half a run, and now they're not ready for you. You signed in at seven, and here we are at eleven and they're still not ready for you.

Let's look at the schedule for the morning, assuming this is the standard location shooting day for a feature film or movie of the week:

**The Location Manager** was here yesterday, making sure everything was the same as when he signed the rental agreement, and getting the keys. The production crew chose out of his folder of available places, and visited the likeliest to plan how to use them, and what equipment would be needed.

**The crew** got here an hour before any performers, putting up the set and bringing in the equipment from the trucks, following the DOP's list of instructions.

**The DOP and director** arrive, to see the set in three dimensions for the first time.

As they fit their planned scenes into the real set, the set decorators turn it into real life and the gaffers get a basic set of lighting instruments out of the storage area, onto set, up on stands or attached to the overhead grid, powered up and focussed.

**Blocking** moves the main cast around the acting area, just to get a rough idea of the problems. This is where the DOP uses that doohickey hanging round his neck: it's a camera lens, to give a better idea of what the camera will see when the time comes. The talent leaves, and the work continues. The extras who are working as stand-ins move and stand in crucial spots to represent their principals.

**81**

Lights are moved, fixed, changed. Sound sits off in the dark and worries. As the set and set dressing is completed, the colours for the lights are fine-tuned.

**Camera rehearsal** brings the Talent back, and here you are, ready to be worked into the scene they've been working on continuously for hours. Sound is relieved to find there is enough room for his boom man in the corner after all. The scene will be played exactly as planned, the camera will carry out its moves, and everyone will find out how it looks on the monitor.

Now things are roughed out, background action is planned. When you're given specific directions by the director or one of the ADs, follow them to the letter. This isn't the time for you to start getting creative or to interpret the scene your way. You may be asked to do some pretty silly things, but do them anyway, if they're safe (and legal). The production won't be glad to hear that you have a better way of doing something. They're paying the bills.

Listen for your instructions, don't waste time by having to have information repeated. For now, this is only rehearsal, but behave as if the camera were rolling. The director will be watching for the effect of the extras, so give him the effect.

When you've been given your starting position by the director or the AD, look around for reference points. You may spot a blotch on the floor, see that you're starting directly beside the corner of a table, or near a fire hydrant. It sounds obvious, but don't judge your position by other people, who may be moved away without your realising.

In rehearsal, just as in shooting, the scene starts when the director decides. The first AD makes the necessary calls:

**Camera Action** when the camera is moving as the scene opens.

**Background Action** is your cue, generally just before

**Action**, when the scene as a whole starts.

You may be given a cue other than Background Action: you may start on Action or on a word of dialogue or piece of activity. If you are to do a crossover (i.e. walk through the scene as a passerby), you may be lined up off-camera for the third AD to tap you on the shoulder when you are to pass through.

Whether you're relegated to the distant background, or brought in to work in the main scene, always give them your energy and focus. If you're brought in for the principal performers to have someone to talk to, help the actors by giving them something to work with. It may be a stern look, a brilliantly happy smile, or even just a crossover at the right time. Whatever the scene calls for, give them something (something silent) to react to. Don't worry about the camera seeing your face, play the scene for the production and actors. This isn't the time to hog the spotlight.

The director will always use an extra who can help make a scene work rather than one who is concentrating on being featured. Rather than weaseling into a prominent position so that you're highlighted, or into the shadows so you are hidden, give them what's needed to help the shot work. It's only human to want a little more attention, something more important to do, a little more money. Serve the scene; the production is the most important thing and your chance will come.

Do what you're told, but be aware of how your position will affect the main performers. Unless you're told otherwise, don't block them from the cameras' view, and beware of blocking their light. The key lights will have been placed to highlight the principal performer on his or her marks. If you see that you're casting shadows across the performer's face, even if it's because they're out of position, it's up to you to shift your position slightly.

As an extra, you get no scripted dialogue, but obviously people in real life can be seen and heard talking, so what do you do? There's an old habit on the set to simply repeat "Rutabaga, Rutabaga, Rutabaga" over and over. Amazingly, it actually works for some people, but why not have a real (mimed) conversation in character? Feeding your belief in the character with appropriate dialogue will make your job easier. Remember to keep half an eye on your instructions and the necessities of the scene.

It's usually easier to have a crowd miming its chat, record the principals' dialogue, and add crowd noise in post-production. Don't try to make up for the lack of speech by flailing your arms about in grand gestures. Use your hands as your character would, don't conduct an orchestra. And remember that only half the people in a chatting crowd will be talking – half will be listening.

How can you carry on a conversation when you don't know what the other person is saying? How do you respond in turn? You will have been given an outline of the situation, so you know the sort of chat that will be going on. Just play out the scene with a real conversation in your mind. React to the other person as though they had actually responded to your words. I remember a mimed chat in a bar, when after we were cut my partner asked me to finish my exciting action tale. In fact I was telling him all about my life as a pickle, but his interest (and my enthusiasm) had made the scene flow better for both of us.

On stage, you exaggerate your actions so that the people in the back can see what you're doing. In film and TV, the director and editor decide what is going to be seen. You don't have to do anything to get attention, the camera will come to you if your actions are important to the story. If you exaggerate just to get attention, the director will shoot around you or cut the scenes you wrecked. Don't freeze up like a store dummy, just let your body believe in the situation.

There are times when the director calls for big emotions, wild panic or a riot. This isn't always easy, but look on it as free therapy. Your shyness makes you catatonic, you move like a zombie, but the scene must be played. Jump in. Feel the adrenaline! Play the scene for all you're worth. It's just the same if you're told to yell or scream at another character. "Argg," "Boo," "Hiss" just don't cut it.

You'll always find a dozen extras doing the standard groans and yells. Be different and creative. Get mad! Have a ball! (Keep it clean.)

These weird shots can be the most fun if you throw yourself at them. I was in a scene where we were to break out of some cages and dive into pink slime spread on a cold floor. It was an alien drug that we just couldn't resist — yuck! I went at it so enthusiastically that the director upgraded me to Special Skills Extra. That earned me an extra $200 for the day, and the same director happened to be casting at my first principal audition. He remembered me very well and I got the principal role. No matter if you're "only an extra," if they can use what you're doing, they'll love you.

Don't get so carried away that you forget what the AD told you to do, and when. This is not for real, it's only for pretends. Be careful you don't really hurt anyone. Oh, yes, that happens. I've seen an actor coldcock an RCMP trainee in a training film.

A prop can be your best help from the production. It could be a tray, a glass, a sub-atomic particle disrupting Mark-IV laser, or a sheet of paper. Whatever you are given, use it. What can you do with a piece of paper? Read it, examine it, make notes, search for a pertinent paragraph, file it, make a paper airplane or a pirate hat, crumple it, tear it, eat it. Think what your character would do in that situation. A nurse, a business executive, a crazed psychopathic killer on a weekend pass – the prop gives you a tool to show your character. If you can find a way to use it quietly. Two practical points: props are often fake and they can be very fragile. Props are often noisy – clinking glasses, ruffling papers, clanking chains – remember the sound man and try to keep it quiet.

Two more points, about firearms: the law of the land, union regulations, and plain common sense say that any gun you are given as a prop will be a fake. Don't assume that it is. Always assume that any gun could be loaded with live ammunition. Don't play cops and robbers between scenes, and never aim a gun directly at others or yourself. A bullet is more likely to kill you, but blank ammunition can easily blind or cause truly horrible scarring.

If live ammo is being fired, whether you are firing it or not, ask for earplugs. They're invisible even in close-up, and they can stop permanent hearing loss. I once played a character with a tiny gun only three inches long. I smiled as I turned down the earplugs, but I fired the weapon once and almost had a heart attack. My ears were still ringing a good ten minutes later. Ask for earplugs. Use them.

Pay attention to any tiny moves you are given. They're the important ones! The director may have you shift over just an inch to one side. Watch their hands: camera left means your right, and vice versa, but they don't always remember the difference.

Know your beginning and ending points. During the sequence, keep track of what you do and when you do it. Using your peripheral vision, link where you are and what you are doing to what is going on around you. You're reading a newspaper, and as soon as the lady in the yellow dress walks past, you put away your paper and leave in the other direction. Don't watch for her, use your peripheral vision, be aware that the yellow blur going by is your cue for the action. When the camera moves to another angle, you will have to repeat the gestures as accurately as possible each time. This is expected of you, it is a skill you must practice. It's much harder when they do a pick-up shot (starting to shoot in the middle of a scene) hours (even days) after you did the original scene. The longer the gap, the harder it is to remember everyone's actions. If you can remember yours, you will be noticed.

When you're working in a large scene, forget about the camera entirely. Instead, let yourself get caught up in all the action around you. If you're supposed to be cheering for the home team at a hockey game, cheer, even if you don't like the sport. Don't just mimic your neighbour. Feel the excitement for yourself. Get the rest of the crowd involved. Lead the wave. Yell at the players. Taunt the cops. Don't worry about upgrades, don't try to draw attention to yourself, just get right into the whole atmosphere and have fun with it. When was the last time someone paid you to go to a big blow-out party?

However, your enthusiasm may catch someone's attention. Before I became an ACTRA member, I accepted a cash call for a weekend shoot. There were two days of riot scenes with about 350 extras. On the second day, the director pulled me out of the crowd and gave me a couple of lines to say. Instant upgrade to Actor category, an ACTRA credit, and a cheque for $600.24 (after deductions) for one days' work! You're never out of a good director's sight on set, and motivated performers really catch the eye.

Pay close attention to where you're stepping (funny, you never see any of these cables on the screen, but now it looks like a regular snake pit). Move around quietly. Even if you are a 400-pound lumberjack, they'd prefer to put your footsteps in later as Foley sound. You can wreck the scene's main dialogue with as little as the noise of a shifting chair, or even a pitcher of beer being put down.

If you need to see where the camera is, catch it out of the corner of your eye. Don't look directly at the camera unless specifically told to. Your character doesn't know there's a film being shot. If you're told to react to the camera as though it were one of the actors, look at one side of the lens. The director will usually tell you which side to use. If you're not given a spot to focus on (the eye line) pick a point on the camera mounting: this will be the actor's eyes for you. Don't look directly into the camera lens unless you're told otherwise at the time.

When the action is set in a crowded area like an airport, stadium, or street, the extras are used to suggest a continuous flow of traffic in the background. There may only be twenty or thirty extras to represent hundreds or thousands of people, so they need choreographing. Crowds are naturally patchy, but the bare patches need to be under control. It's very easy to end up with an empty space behind the actors when the camera reaches them for their scene, so they look as if they're completely alone. It's the AD's job (and yours) to fill these gaps. You're no good to anyone if you can't be seen. It's obviously useless to walk behind a wall where you won't be seen at all, but if you're in a crowd and you can't see the camera, you might as well be behind that wall. Help them by moving over until you can just see the camera lens. Time your move, within your instructions, to fill the gaps or dead spots where there is no action taking place behind the main actors. Vary your speed a little in comparison to the other extras: not everybody walks at the same speed in real life.

Believe it or not, walking down a street can feel very awkward when you're doing it for a camera. We have a tendency to concentrate too hard when we feel people are watching us. If you have a reason for walking, though, you'll quickly stop worrying how normal you look. Pretend you're late for work. Maybe you're enjoying a relaxing stroll after a fantastic date. Vary your pace slightly so you're either passing others or they have to brush you aside as they scurry along. If you're paired with someone, talk to them. Walk hand-in-hand if it feels right for your characters. Check out that store; there's a big sale. And if you trip or stumble, don't worry. It happens all the time when you're out walking. Don't panic, just pick yourself up and carry on. No-one will even notice, unless you make one of those stupid "I Goofed" faces.

When you've crossed through the scene and are off camera (out of the camera's sight), stand out of the way and keep quiet. The scene could still be shooting. You don't want to be stumbling about, knocking over the lights. Keep your eyes open: another AD may want you to cross back (especially if there are very few extras available for the shot). They may want you to change your appearance slightly. Remove your jacket, wear a hat, or just move at a different pace. No funny walks, please.

At the end of a sequence, you'll hear "Cut!" If you're still on camera, freeze where you are. Take note of where you've ended up. The director is now doing one of two things: looking at the end picture, or fine-tuning the middle. You may be told to end up more to the left or given an entirely new track to follow during the sequence. Then you'll be sent back to firsts (returned to your starting point) for the next try. Don't dawdle! They need to shoot the scene as soon as possible. Rush right back to your opening spot and let them see that you're on the ball. The ADs will be noting who they must babysit, and who can be counted on to do the job they were hired for. Leave the production with a good impression. Let them see that you understand how valuable their time is.

Most of the changes between one rehearsal and the next will have nothing to do with the extras, or even the main cast. This is a technical medium, and you will traipse back and forth until the technicians are happy. Use the repetition to be able to put your instructions on automatic and enjoy the character.

It sounds like a lot to do (and that's only the start), but as your professional habits develop you will be able to perform without consciously concentrating on the details.

Joy, oh joy, oh bliss. An upgrade! They've just given you a specific line to say, out loud or in mime, and now you'll be famous the world over. Well, maybe it's not much of a line, but at least it's a start. And your basic fee went up from less than a hundred bucks to over four hundred. Plus residuals. Congratulations!

So now what? They don't expect you to get it right on the first take, do they? What if you blow it? Suddenly you start feeling the pressures of really having to deliver. The best advice I can offer comes from *The Hitchhiker's Guide to the Galaxy* – "Don't Panic!" You've likely received the upgrade because the director saw you were coming up with good stuff as an extra. You can obviously be trusted with more. You already know about hitting your marks and analysing the scene, so just go out there and do the same, plus your little line. You still aren't the lead, your scene won't make or break the film. Relax, have fun, and enjoy the upgrade.

There, that wasn't so bad, was it? What next? Don't worry about it, one of the ADs will take you to the side and fill out your contract. That's right, you will now have an official contract, suitable for framing and showing off to all your friends. You'll be walked through each step of the form, and if you have any questions, just ask. With a union contract, make sure they've written your name and address and SIN right and you should be fine. It'll be a while before you can negotiate anything over the minimum fee. If it's a non-union production, well then there may not even be a contract to fill out, you'll just have to hope that anything you've signed so far doesn't give away all your future rights.

If it was a union production, contact the union; let them know you were upgraded, and ask what is needed for membership. Don't rush in (see the "Union Matters" chapter), but deciding not to become a member right away may affect your qualifying for membership later. Find out exactly what's involved, and take a day or two to work through your options.

Before you leave for the day, you may want to ask who you should contact later about getting a dub. The ADs know you're excited about your big moment, and will do their best to help you. And don't forget to let your agent know.

Enough of all this warning and advice stuff, let's Roll Cameras! Let's Bring on the Empty Horses!

I'm sorry, more advice stuff. Once the camera is rolling, things start getting really technical and really complicated. The rest of the section is useful stuff, it will solve problems for you, but you don't have to know everything all at once. Build on what you already know, bit by bit, and the new information will blend in so it feels like your own ideas. Don't worry, before long it feels natural. For now, fake it until you make it.

When things are as good as they are reasonably going to get, the director decides to lay one down. Actually, taping or filming shouldn't make any difference, in fact that's the whole point: the final rehearsal was approved because that was what was wanted. In fact, the performance is always a little different from the rehearsal, because everyone's heart is going a little faster. More calls from the first AD:

| | |
|---|---|
| **QUIET ON SET** | Everyone, producers, the suits, stars, everyone. |
| **LOCK IT UP** | Crew stops other work, sometimes, in the studio, literally close the doors. |
| **WE'RE ROLLING** | Not a rehearsal, the camera is running, the red warning lights outside are on. |

| | |
|---|---|
| **ROLL SOUND** | and the sound man calls |
| **Speed** | when his tape is running |

The Camera Operator says:

| | |
|---|---|
| **Mark it** or **Slate** | and the clapper loader identifies the shot |
| and **Frame** | to show he has the opening picture set up. |

The First, or the director, continues:

| | |
|---|---|
| **Camera Action** | if the camera is moving as the scene opens. |
| **Background Action** | is your cue, generally just before |
| **Action** | when the scene as a whole starts. |

You will probably do more repeats of each scene on camera than you did in rehearsal. These will all be for technical reasons, unless a performer does something really stupid. Which happens.

This first scene of the day will probably be the master shot. You see it all the time: the characters run up the escalator (recorded yesterday, possibly in another building) and the scene changes to a wide shot of the office, with you and me and a dozen others bustling about in suits. Remember, each time you run the scene you're making another piece of material the editor is going to sew together in post-production to make a seamless whole. After the wide shot for a scene has been made, the balance of the shooting must match it. Don't change your actions because you've just thought of something wonderful you could do. It's too late. The cover shot lays the base for all that follows. Your skill after that is to do everything so that it looks the same, keeping it alive and natural take after take.

After take, after take.

 Just as in rehearsal, when you hear "Cut," stop still and hold your position. You will be told if you're to return to Firsts (start again from your opening position).

**88**

Finally, you hear "checking the gate," which means the take looked good, and they are checking to see if a whisker of film has fallen into the focal plane of the camera. This is the cameraman's equivalent of your taking a snapshot of your thumb covering the lens. If the gate is clean, then they have their shot and are ready to go on. Good news ... you've done your job well.

If you're told to "hold your position," the production wants to see where everyone is. The next scene may pick up from this point and your end position may very well become your new starting position when they shoot from another angle.

The other reason for holding your position is getting room tone. Every space sounds different when it goes quiet. Tiny background noises appear, and the hard or soft nature of the space changes the quality of the sound. The mixer, or sound man, will want thirty seconds of silence so that the editor has enough to slip in as pauses, and to build his effects on. It is very difficult to stand silent for thirty seconds, but in this situation if you don't shut up it is very easy to be ritually slaughtered by a crew wanting to move on.

At the start and end of a take, and after wardrobe and hair, throughout the day it seems, the crew is taking Polaroid™ instant pictures. No, they don't think you're adorable. They're keeping track of the continuity for each shot. The production wants to make it seem that everything was filmed in order in a single take. In fact, scenes are usually shot in pieces, out of sequence, over a number of days (or even months). When continuity breaks down, the different shots don't match. The actor enters in a brown suit, with a full glass in one hand. They shift to a closer shot, and he's in shirtsleeves, his glass is empty, and a half finished cigarette has appeared in his mouth. As he exits in the wider shot again, he's back in his suit. Months later, the editor and the director are putting the scene back together, and look at those shots in tears.

If you've been on set and rolled up your sleeves during a break, make sure you roll them back down afterwards. There is a worried continuity person with a clipboard and a giant binder (the show bible), and every department looks after its own area, but how would you like to make sure that every little item was in its proper place at every given second? That shirt was buttoned up, she had the glass in that hand, he lit the cigarette on this word in that line. It's a nightmare unless everyone does their bit.

As soon as the scene is over, return your props, or keep them with you at all times. Don't leave them lying around, figuring they'll eventually find their way to the proper place. If something breaks, let the prop people know right away. The propmaster shouldn't be upset as long as it wasn't through your negligence. Props do break and they can be fixed, given time.

They called "Cut," they checked the gate, the First called, "Moving on!" You were sent back to holding, and now you're back on the same set about to do the same scene again. Is this déjà vu? Did they see the moment when your concentration slipped? Don't worry about your mind – and don't flatter yourself that they noticed your slip.

If you watch TV and the movies closely, you know that the camera flips back and forth among the actors. The ordinary audience member doesn't notice this intercutting. If the show is well edited, the camera is doing what your eyes would do if you were there following the conversation and looking at whatever was most interesting. On the screen it looks as if the show had been shot using a number of cameras, but that is rarely so. A live to tape interview may use two or three cameras, but in scripted productions expense means they only use one, unless the scene cannot possibly be repeated ("Okay, Harry, drive the blazing limousines through the glasshouse!").

Each scene is repeated with different lenses and from different angles (otherwise you would see another camera in the background of the shots). You may have shot the master in the actual office, but now you're in a mock-up of part of it. The set is changed, now we are only seeing a part of it and the lighting is changed. Your moves and actions will look the same on camera, but they will almost certainly have to change as well.

It's often no more difficult than recreating all your actions as precisely as possible, just as you did in rehearsal and in the retakes of the last shot. Your biggest difficulty will be in reorienting yourself, now that the set is all turned around. You may also need to cross through some occupied areas (where did those cables suddenly come from?) and squeeze awkwardly past the camera (without hitting it) as though it weren't there.

Sometimes it's more complicated. Your last scene was the master of the office. The principals came in the main door and looked off camera left to see the boss. Your action was to walk from the camera left door to the desk with the flowers, and sit down to type. This new shot shows the principals' POV: your real life action will be the same of course, but you're in a different set and the camera is pointing in a different direction. This time you will start camera right, cross very slowly in front of the camera, and squidge yourself against the wall out of sight until the dialogue is finished. You've been asked to cheat the shot. Sometimes your move, or actions, or just the angle of your body, may not look right to the camera's eye in its new location. When this happens you'll be told how to fake it so that it looks real.

As you get more experience, you'll begin to see the problems as you return to set, and be looking at your own solutions. As usual on union sets, this means that you'll be in a better position to understand your instructions, not that you'll be able to come up with suggestions.

Extras may not be cleared back to the holding area between shots: they may park us in a convenient spot to be on hand when they need us. So what do you do while everyone else is busy and you're stuck on the sidelines?

First, don't make the noise worse. Four departments, each filled with tension and attitude, can set up a roar like a beer tent. The director will be contemplating the next shot or discussing how the scene should be set up. That's not easy above all the noise and chatter around them. Shhhhh...

Don't sit on any chair unless you are pointed at it by the third AD or extras casting director. Chairs on most sets are like gold: searched for and guarded against claim-jumpers. Never ever sit on a canvas-backed folding chair with the star's name on.

Watch the crew in action and see what they are trying to do. Check on the new obstacles you'll have to manoeuvre around. Note how the camera will be seeing the action from its new location. Pay attention to what's happening around you, look for your edge.

Leave the crew craft table alone. They're not being mean when they grumble about extras hogging their food: besides the fact that many of the crew unions deduct a portion of the crew's contracted fees to pay for part of the service, the crew have to grab a quick morsel on the run when they get a chance. It is very annoying when they have to fight through a crowd of extras and then be called away before they grab a munchie. They're on the go all day: be courteous and leave their table alone. If you're really thirsty and have been stuck on set a long time, ask the AD if there's a table for the extras nearby.

Most actors are pleasant enough. If they start a conversation, they've given you a present, be careful of it. If they ask for your opinion, then offer it briefly. If you aren't asked, then keep your ideas to yourself. From stars to day players, they're probably working at keeping track of their lines for the next scene, getting into character, watching the camera angles. Like you in the last paragraph, they're looking for their edge.

Normally, you work five hours on set before a meal break, but sometimes they work you for another hour. When they do, they have to bring in substantial snacks (sandwiches, etc.) to keep you going. This is one of the minimum work conditions the unions have negotiated. Unfortunately, substantials turn extras into vultures, swooping on the craft service and grabbing every morsel possible. Relax, stay cool. This is simply a snack to tide you over until lunch, not a full meal. Save room for later – only one serving per customer – because right now you've only got a few minutes and it's back to work.

Lunchtime! I know it's 2 a.m., but it's still called lunch in this business. Most films will provide some sort of meal, but they aren't required by ACTRA to do so if there are restaurants available in the area. If it's a non-union shoot, assume you won't be fed unless you're told otherwise.

On your own is always a possibility, even in a purpose-built studio. Studio buildings are sometimes equipped with a lunchroom run like a franchise. If you are downtown in daylight, you could very well be on your own for lunch. If you insist on eating, then bring a few bucks with you, just in case the meal isn't provided by the production. Or brown-bag it.

**91**

If you decide to head away from the set for a while, be sure to leave your props with the proper personnel. Don't leave the location wearing wardrobe provided by the production. If you're unable to change, wear a jacket over the costume, no matter how hot or ridiculous you feel. This often happens with street scenes and cop uniforms. There are heavy penalties for pretending to be a policeman, intentionally or not, and judges don't have much sense of humour. Your life could be at risk, too. That's true in spades if your uniform has a gun.

"Lunch provided" may be anything from an appetizing hot buffet to a depressing lunchbag of a sandwich and small salad. There's nothing much you can do by complaining, unless the food is literally rotten. It's free, so enjoy what you have. Maybe you should have brown-bagged a cookie anyway.

Eating with the crew can be a great treat, and happens particularly when there aren't many people around on set. The new IPA contract gives union members the same food as crew. Welcome to some of the best catering in the city!

Wait for the crew to serve themselves first. They've been working non-stop and must return to the set first to set up the next shot. The same rule applies to allowing the Actors to eat first. You're a guest, be nice.

Fifteen minutes before the lunchbreak is over, get ready to go back on set. You can still relax and let your meal settle, but if you're in extras holding, the production will know that you're available at a moment's notice.

Gather up your props and adjust your wardrobe. Were your sleeves rolled down? Did you have on a tie? Were you wearing a shawl? If you need a quick washroom break or want to brush your teeth, do it now. Don't wait until the queue forms when the production wants you to go back on set.

The rest of the filming day is more of the same. Even on union vouchers, you can be held for as many hours as they have money to pay you overtime for. Well, actually, to pay the technicians overtime for. Mostly, you can expect the standard six-hour call, with overtime fairly frequently. By the end of the day, everyone is tired, including you, and it's hard to stay on top of things.

When the director says "That's a wrap," you'll witness the most extraordinary transformation of humans anywhere. People who appeared near catatonic for the last three hours suddenly burst to life, the weariest of slugs move at lightning pace as they storm to the long signout line leading to the exit.

While everyone is racing to get in line, why not relax and get changed at your own pace? Unless you have two shoots back-to-back, you don't have to get frustrated in the queue; you can change, wash off your set make-up, ensure the proper crew members get back their props and wardrobe, grab a last pop, and join a now much smaller line to sign out. The casting director or AD will still be there – and you're probably still on the clock. Let's bring some order to the sign-out chaos:

**Before you change**, take your props back to the prop department. The crew are anxious to head home too, so don't be discourteous. They've tried to help you during the day; show them your appreciation and return your stuff. They aren't in the mood for a treasure hunt.

**When you've changed**, make sure all the wardrobe belonging to the production is returned. Some shows won't even let you sign out until you've been initialed by the wardrobe department. If you see some outfits tossed in the corner, take them back to the department with yours. Your returns may be organised and hung up, theirs may be in a pile, but you've made the wardrobe department's job a little easier.

Lineup is still long? Well, grab a cloth and water (or those wonderful moist towelettes you brought) to remove the worst of the make-up.

Hmmm... the line is still pretty long. Look at the mess the extras have left the holding area in. Make a start on the half-empty pop cans and disposable coffee cups. You're not being paid to be a maid, but it only takes a minute. Besides, the line should be reasonably short by the time you're done.

Now you're signing out in a relatively composed manner. If it is Casting signing your voucher, thank them for the call and let them know you're available for other shoots. After the chaos of the other extras hurrying to get paid and leave, Casting or the AD has a moment to breathe and there's time to check if you might be needed again for the current shoot. Leave them with a good impression. First in, last out: that's the sign of an extra who really enjoys the job.

On the way out, if the hair, make-up and wardrobe people are still around, stop by and give them your quick thanks for their support today. As you're leaving the set, just a nod and a smile as you pass can leave the crew and director with a good feeling about working with you. Before you grab the bus or get in your car, give your agent a quick call – if it's still early enough in the day – to let them know you're wrapped and available once again. If you've brought enough wardrobe and are willing to work a back-to-back, you may be off to another set right away. Fill them in on any big problems you may have had on set: it's better they hear about it from you, rather than being caught off-guard by a complaint later.

If it's homeward bound, as the adrenaline rush slows, exhaustion will soon take over. You've had a busy day, you've had a long day, you've had a good day: you've done well.

**Home at last**, no messages on your answering machine, your feet can barely drag you to your bed. If you're not working often, you can collapse now. When you're busy, though, you won't have time to do a pile of clean-up in the morning. Today's crumpled costume pieces, and the notes you made during the day, will be lost or useless if you don't make a start tonight. Take a couple of minutes to unwind your sweaty dress shirt and refill your aspirin bottle. Pull your scraps of notes out of your set bag and make sense of them. It really does pay off.

**Sleep. Sleep.** Last-minute calls can come in at any hour, and that means work, so don't turn off your pager! You don't have to choose to be on call twenty-four hours a day, but it will cost you money if you're not. Agents and casting people will soon learn you're ready for work calls at odd hours, and they'll call you rather than have to apologise to someone else.

**Pillow, pillow, pillow.** Get a good nights' rest. You deserve it (and who knows when you'll get your next chance for sleep). Nighty-night.

# CAMERA LENSES

Even if your scene makes it through the editing room without being cut, you may not be able to recognise yourself in the finished product. The camera may be aimed directly at you, but if it's focused on a tight shot of the main actors, you'll be an unrecognisable blur moving behind them.

Get to know the different types of lenses. If you're close to the director and cameraman when they're preparing a scene, listen for the type of shot and the lenses they will be using. Find out how tight or wide the shot will be (wide cover shot, close-up, extreme close-up, etc.). Listen for any special effects the production will be creating (slow motion, dreamscape, enhanced speed, etc.). With this knowledge in hand, you'll be thinking about what the scene will need before the third AD comes over with your instructions. You'll understand why you're being asked to play the scene a certain way, adjust your pace or alter your actions artificially. When they reshoot a scene, you still need to repeat your actions as accurately as possible, no matter which type of lens they use, but now you have an idea how they are using the extras to create atmosphere in the shot. Watch a few shows to see the difference in effect when the background and performers are blurred behind the actors, and when they are seen well. Knowing what the camera will actually see means you are collaborating, not just doing what you are told.

"We need a long lens," "let's go short," "use a 50," "let's go a wide 20." If you're interested in learning more about lenses and shots, hang out with the camera assistant or check out your local library, specialty bookstore, or college. I won't pretend to be master of all the combinations, but let's see what the little Bluffers' Guide to Technology has:

**DOF – Depth of Field** If you look at an oil painting of the prairies, you'll see the fence in the foreground, the elevator in the middleground, and the thunderheads in the distant sky. You'll see the details: the twist of wool on the fence, the Wheat Pool logo on the elevator, the birds in the clouds. This picture has a large DOF, everything is in focus, from your arm's length to the horizon.

In reality, we don't see that way. What we are interested in seems to be in focus, and the rest of the world blurs out. The director wants to use that effect, by showing a crowd in wideshot (all in focus, to show it's at an airport), tighten in on a medium shot of the star (in focus) looking across a crowd (fairly blurred); we hear her name called, she turns, we zoom in to a medium close shot of the child and the kidnapper (in tight focus) and the legs of the crowd moving past (completely blurred out).

95

Lenses with large DOF can hold a clear image anywhere from infinity. With a small DOF the picture will be in focus within a five-range only.

**SHORT LENS**  A short lens has a wide angle of view and deep focus, and will pick up more of the background and the area surrounding the main actors. The audience is meant to be interested in everything in the picture, because it's all in focus.

**LONG LENS**  A long lens has a small DOF and a narrow angle of view, and is used for selective focus (narrow shot). With a long lens, although the camera is far away, we still have a close shot (head and shoulders) of the actor. The area closest to the camera will be muddy and out of focus, the middle ground where the scene is played will be in focus, and the space behind the main actors will again appear muddy. In this shot, the director will be using the extras to shadow the scene (provide blurred movement or atmosphere in the background).

**20's, 50's, 100's**  The higher the lens number, the longer the lens and the narrower the shot. The lower the number, the shorter the lens, and the wider the shot. Your actions are likely to be seen in more detail when they're using a smaller numbered lens, and more shadowed or muddied when they call for a higher lens number.

Here's a very simplified chart to give you an idea about how closely the size of the lens will mimic our own eyes.

| LENS SIZE / FILM | 20 | 50 | 100 |
|---|---|---|---|
| 16mm | Proper Human Perspective (25 size) | Narrower view, selective focus | Very tight view, very selective focus |
| 35mm | Wider View, not as selective focus | Proper Human Perspective | Tighter view, selective focus |

If you're lost, don't feel bad, most principal actors (and some directors I've worked with) don't understand all these lenses either.

# PROFESSIONALISM

**pro•fes•sion•al** adj., n. __adj.
1 of or having to do with a profession; appropriate to a profession: professional skill, a professional manner.
2 engaged in a profession.
3 **MAKING A BUSINESS OR TRADE OF SOMETHING THAT OTHERS DO FOR PLEASURE.**

*(Gage Canadian Dictionary)*


Extra work is a professional business.

You're not doing extra work as a career, just for fun? That's not an option, if "for fun" means carelessly and selfishly. The people working around you take their careers seriously. The production hasn't brought you in for your amusement; they have a serious job to do, and they want people who contribute to the final product. They are paying your fees: you were hired to be a professional, and that's your job, even if you aren't the star of the show.

This doesn't mean that you can't have fun at your job. You're an insider in a mysterious and exotic industry, and as an insider you'll learn that productions aren't one big success or one big disaster, they're made up of hundreds of tiny jewels and tiny flaws. Don't be a flaw.

If you're in the job for the long haul, don't let others con you into believing that an extra isn't important. Extras often see themselves as second class citizens: it's very common for Background Performers to be treated as second class citizens, but don't justify the treatment by behaving that way. If you are somebody dependable and professional, you will be noticed, you will get the interesting jobs and you will get more of them.

Being a professional is more than simply showing up on time and earning your pay for the day. Half-hearted attitudes and low energy deserve little respect, and get it. Respect is a two-way street, so value your own contribution to the show, and respect and understand the importance of the work done around you. Your efforts may not be praised, but your value is massive and the production knows it. We don't get much feedback in this industry but, believe me, directors do prefer to give upgrades and lines to professionals. And who knows, someday you may be the star.

Professionalism is a pattern of habits we don't think about any more. Train yourself, invest some time. Attitude and habit can really help you through those frustrating days.

How well are you prepared for extra work? I don't mean contacting agents or having photos printed: do you have what it takes to succeed in this industry? It's tempting to say either, "I'm terrific. If people don't like me, that's their problem," or "I'm useless. I'm not surprised people don't like me." These are actually the same cop-out: blaming everyone else for what only you can change. If you look at yourself without guilt or pride, just to see what is there, you will see the strengths you can build on and the weaknesses you can use. Our frailties make us human and give us our uniqueness and strength. Know yourself, and turn your problems into profit.

Go the extra mile. On the days when you really don't want to do any more than you really have to, force yourself. Work on your good habits. Why bring ten spare outfits when they only asked for one? To establish a good habit. Why show up an hour early? It becomes habit. Why give 110% if you're only being paid minimum wage? Because professional habits are the same if you're a cash extra or a principal performer. Develop bad habits now and they will return to haunt you.

Take responsibility; don't duck it with, "I wasn't told I needed that / that's the crew's job / it's too much trouble / it's only extra work / it's not my problem."

Take pride in your craft. Don't blow it by arriving unprepared, chattering between takes, idling back to set or back to your first position. One extra thinking about his uncomfortable shoes can ruin the big panic scene. If you do your job professionally, attention to even tiny things will become second nature, and once it has become a habit you won't have to spend energy on it.

Keep your concentration focussed. If you're meant to just sit in a chair throughout the shot, listen to the atmosphere of the scene. Work out what the main performers are trying to present, and how they use their movement and voice to accomplish it. Maybe the principals are rehearsing without the extras; don't slack off, don't take a break to talk to your neighbor on set, watch the blocking. The director is looking at the major focus of the shot; soon the extras will be brought in to fill any dead spots. Watch for those dead spots, think about how the actors will cross through the scene. When you're called, you'll already know how you can help the shot.

There's nothing more dangerous than badmouthing the script, unless it's badmouthing the series. Every set has influential people wandering around. The writer, all shades of producer, clients, editors: all with some responsibility at some stage and all with six-figure incomes riding on the project. They may not order you off the set immediately, but don't be surprised if you're in the first group that it's unnecessary to keep.

Don't Drink and Drive. And don't bring it to set. Okay, everybody has a drink or two now and then, but even a quick beer at lunch is a no-no when you're on set. Save it for after the shoot: you need all your focus and concentration for the job at hand.

Drugs don't work: you may feel better, but people around you certainly feel worse. Drug-taking in the industry is common, but illegal drugs can destroy your career before it starts. Be warned by one who has seen the wreckage; everyone thinks they can handle it fine, including some of the major celebrities you hear horror stories about in the tabloids. I've seen talent destroyed overnight.

Be generous with what you know. Help out when you can: you won't look any better if people around you are failing. James Krenov, a master carpenter, says in *The Impractical Cabinetmaker*, "I've picked up a bit of know-how, yes. It is not my private knowledge, but rather it is my way of using what little I have learned that happens to be right for people like myself." Don't push your thoughts where they aren't wanted, but give them away to good homes.

# POST-PRODUCTION

# AN EXTRA LIFE TO LIVE

3

In the living room of Bob's house, Jane is looking at a brochure from an acting studio.

> BOB
>
> No way, I just got out of all that! I'm not going back to school. Don't you start in on me. (He glares off, at the kitchen.) I get enough of that from Her!

> JANE
> (Automatically)
>
> "She's" your mother. Anyway, these aren't classes, they're training. You train for your Haiku, don't you?

> BOB
> (Automatically)
>
> Aikido. But that's great  and I'm good at it. She, okay Mum, says it's a waste of time. But it's my time, right?

> JANE
>
> I don't think it's a waste of time, I think it's a Special Skill. Why don't you learn how to use it to make money? Look. (She hands over the pamphlet)

> BOB
>
> Combat Mime? That's weird. Hey, this fellow wrote a book! Hey! I read it! That's amazing!

> JANE
> (Dryly, under her breath)
>
> You read a book? That *is* amazing! (To him) Well, are you going to try it?

                    BOB
I'm gonna talk to him. It was a great
book. And it's in the evenings, so She
can't complain. So what's up for you? They
got a "Poetry in Shakespeare" thing.


                    JANE
I'm going to the On-camera Intensive --
three weekends and I keep my videotape.
And then I'm taking Aikido from you at the
Y on Tuesdays. You're going to turn me
into SuperGran.
                    BOB
She'll be really ticked about that! Hey, I
didn't tell you they gave me a class to
teach!


                    JANE
I do my research. (Simply) You didn't tell
Her either.


                    BOB
                (Embarrassed)
No, well, I'm gonna tell her. Soon.

                    JANE
            (Heading for the kitchen)
Come on, you go high with your Aikido
class and I'll go low with Heck's Granny.


FADE TO COMMERCIALS over the kitchen door, behind
which we hear muffled wails and much clattering
of pots.


                    END

# WARDROBE

A major selling point when you're an extra is your wardrobe – the selection of clothes you bring to set, ready for the wardrobe coordinator to use when putting the scene together. Most of the time you will be told what sort of things to bring and how much, but look on that as your very minimum. Even though the wardrobe department will usually have some outfits on hand, you should still be prepared. There may be 30 or even 400 extras on set. The production simply won't have enough to dress everybody well. They can usually find bits and pieces to make do, but, as a professional, you should bring some supplies of your own, whether you were asked to or not. Unless you've been assigned a specific outfit from a previous day or through a wardrobe fitting, bring a variety with you.

Even if you're told that you'll be given a uniform once you get to set, always try to bring additional outfits. You may be scheduled to play a cop, but someone may not show, or they may decide they need a detective instead. And people don't always fit the uniforms stocked.

The wardrobe department may be on their own to outfit everyone on period or futuristic shoots. Having your own clothing for at least some period work will increase your chances of being used on set. Also, your own clothes will be comfortable. People depending entirely on the wardrobe department will have to make do with whatever happens to be available for that day. It may fit, or it may not.

There's no prize for having just the right thing at home; however there is credit, and praise, and more work in future, for the extra who has the outfit that's just right. It's worth carrying the extra garment bags to get a reputation for always having something just off the wall to spice up the mix.

Don't rely on what you have in your closets already – productions are set in different years, different countries, and different neighbourhoods. If you only have college grunge or suburban respectable, you won't suit most groups you're going to be part of.

Many beginners make the mistake of buying a whole new wardrobe when they first start. I've even met parents who have spent thousands on clothes for their children, believing it would guarantee them a career.

Bell-bottom jeans, multi-coloured shirts, and a jet pack ... not quite your usual fashion? Well, get used to it, because films can use some very peculiar combinations. It would look bizarre on the street, but on set it all fits.

Don't worry that you are making a fool of yourself. Acting is a serious job: these offbeat outfits are your work-clothes. Enjoy these odd ensembles. If you seem to be comfortable with the situation, chances are you'll be featured or used more. The production hasn't got time to worry about background performers who are too embarrassed to do their job. They want professionals who can perform.

Start your wardrobe search deep in your own closets: is there something that makes you look like a fashion faux pas? Keep it. Keep the out-of-fashion clothes, keep the shirt you must have bought when your mind was possessed by aliens. Spread your wardrobe net wide. Rummage and garage sales, flea markets,  thrift stores; they are all sources of hard-to-find items. Even garbage day can be a bonanza at spring cleaning time. I'm not saying you should start picking through garbage cans. However, if you see a box of old clothes on the curbside, take a casual glance.

Years ago, I saved a winter vinyl coat from the garbage and put a little work into it. Some terrible stitching, a bit of model paint, some small chains from the hardware store, and a lot of pins to hold it together – Voilà, a Punk/Biker jacket! Completely generic and without profanity. The coat has brought in work on over 200 sets.

A good wardrobe collection doesn't have to cost a lot. Some thrift stores sell by the pound and have special sales where the clothes sell for as low as 25 cents. I once bought 4 jackets, 16 suits, 8 pairs of dress pants, 10 shirts, 4 hats, 4 ties, and a belt, at a total cost of $25. Even better, I sold one of the suits to a film and got $25 back, so the entire collection didn't cost me anything. Put the word out among your friends. If you can't use their old clothes, perhaps another extra or even a wardrobe department could find a good use for them.

You won't use these outfits on every call, but they may get you noticed. You're a professional: be prepared. When you arrive on set, it'll show that you went the extra mile just for that specific production. Okay, so you really just stumbled across the clothes by accident, but the production doesn't know that.

The Wardrobe crew are always fascinated by weird pieces, and unusual outfits create opportunities to be seen. This is the make-believe world of film. Often the unusual is usual.

Some rules:

• Never wear your own jewellery to set, unless you are prepared to take it off and carry it around with you. Remember, if the production provides your costume, you may not have a safe pocket. If you wear a Medic Alert medallion, be sure it can be tucked out of sight.

• Never wear anything with a trademark or commercial slogan: companies spend big money to have their names featured on screen, and your Coke™ T-shirt won't be welcomed on a shoot backed by Pepsi™.

• Beware of tight checks or pinstripes – the outfit will look as though it's moving all over the place, even though you're standing still. The camera sometimes has trouble focusing properly on the detail.

- Colours pose problems: bright reds, yellows and whites flare or flame up on the television screen. On the other hand, very dark or black outfits will be lost in the shadows. Medium blue is very dangerous – a specific shade (called chromakey blue), can play havoc on any show using special effects. Some of these effects use what's called a blue screen which makes everything chromakey blue invisible to the camera. Wardrobe will play safe and not choose midblues for these shows.

Should you omit these colours from your wardrobe? No, simply find colours that are slightly off. Instead of buying a pure white shirt, get one that's slight off-white or eggshell. For reds and yellows, you can get some that are moderately duller or darker. This will help cut down the flaring effect. As for black outfits, they are used more often than most people in the industry think. Many shows look to creating a dark or moody effect. If the show is lit for this type of setting, you will probably be asked to wear your darker clothes. Just don't load an entire collection with black clothes. Plain pastel or earthtone prints work very well for most sets. They are easy to mix and match, accessorize, and rarely bother the camera. They should form the majority of your collection.

Make life easy for yourself – organize your wardrobe in colours and styles.

Group your outfits into styles: casual, business, period, funky, evening best, shredded worst. As you work on different shows, you'll quickly learn which type of characters you're most likely to play. Set aside at least one complete outfit reserved strictly for your usual characters. For example, I always have one main outfit ready for a Street-Tough or a Criminal:

Pair of torn jeans (light blue)
Tattered T-shirt (light grey)
Vest (black)
Biker/Punk jacket (the one I made myself)
Spiked wristband (in pocket of jacket)
Spiked glove (in pocket of jacket)
Biker rings (in pocket of jacket)
Two bandannas (1 red patterned, 1 black with skulls)
Wide black belt
Pair black half-boots (soft soled)

It's not quite what I would normally wear down the street, but that exact and complete outfit has been used on more than a hundred shoots.

Keep a small stock of some bright colours, solids or patterns. Even an outfit that looks outrageous for normal wear may be perfect on set. If a show wants a cheerier, brighter look, or if they need some noticeable colour to break up an otherwise dark shot, the wardrobe department will likely adore it.

**106**

Always buy at least one good white shirt. It shouldn't necessarily be pure white, but only slightly off-white. This shirt will support any dressier or business type characters.

Finally, the black outfits. T-Shirts, dresses, dress pants, leathers: they all have their place on certain shows. You can add further depth by adding a few very dark browns or greys. These will often be used for sombre shoots.

If you want to increase your work as business or executive type characters, bring suits that include dark navy, medium brown, medium grey, and at least one lighter shade of blue, grey, or tan.

As you build a useful collection of outfits, keep them organised by colours and types. There's no point in having all that good stuff if you can't find it when you need it. Don't categorize just your clothes. Do the same for accessories, costume jewellery, and props. Pick up some small containers, film cans, yoghurt tubs, and label them.

Panic can really set in when you get a last minute call to set. You scramble through closets and drawers trying to remember where you put that special shirt. The matching pants? Five frantic minutes later, you find them. Whew! Well maybe you can air them out on the way. Wait! You forgot those tattered running shoes you used last time. Panic-Panic-Panic!!!

You simply won't be guaranteed enough time to get organised if you're needed right to set. A little preparation can do wonders for your nerves.

Pay close attention to what type of clothes you are actually asked to bring to set. If you aren't told to bring any changes, bring extras anyway for variety. Even if Wardrobe is supposed to be outfitting you, circumstances change. The more outfits you carry with you, the better your chances for meeting those changes head on. I've had a casting director send me to another shoot at the end of one days' filming simply because I had more changes with me. So far my record is three shoots in one day. I wouldn't have received this extra Extra work without my extra wardrobe.

Try to carry along at least one completely different style with you, rather than just more of the same. At the start of the new season for a recent series, I was told to bring Upscale and Funky clothes only ... "NO GRUBBIES!" Well, I had seven outfits which the wardrobe department loved. And then I brought out one more selection, my grubbies, the Street Tough outfit listed earlier. I've worn that outfit almost every episode of the series this season and have become a regular in the bar scenes.

You've spent good money on wardrobe for the set, now go one step further by protecting it. You may have to shoot in some very severe conditions. There won't always be clean storage areas. Cover your clothes with a cheap zippered garment bag; a garbage bag will do in a pinch. You may want to invest in a sturdy tote bag, something flexible enough to hold all your supplies without becoming unwieldy.

It pays to take care of your set wardrobe, even the grungies. As soon as you get home, sort out what needs attention, and hang up the rest. As soon as you can, mend the casualties. Put aside any clothes that need to be washed. And wash them. It's a terrible feeling to realize, when you're packing for a last minute call, that the outfit you need is still covered with mud from the last shoot.

Wardrobe people work on many productions through the years, so it's very likely you'll see them again on another shoot. They do appreciate your efforts to make their job easier. I've been fortunate enough to develop a comfortable rapport with many of the wardrobe people on various sets. You don't have to go as far as I used to – I sometimes brought as many as thirty changes to a day of shooting – but I've been repaid tenfold.

Early in my career, I had won principal casting in a big TV series. On the day of the wardrobe fitting, I packed my bags with a large selection of personal wardrobe. It was a long bus ride, but I had a role, the day was sunny, and I was in a great mood. By the end of the journey, the weather had unexpectedly turned very bitter. I got off the bus in a snowstorm – and here I was in a light jean jacket. The wardrobe people remembered me from my extra work and were impressed that I had once again gone to so much trouble with my wardrobe, although unfortunately not much of it was right for this specific shoot.

As I was about to leave, they asked why I wasn't wearing something warmer for the weather outside. I explained that my winter coat was basically worn out. They said they had just bought a new winter coat for my character and they would see if I could buy the coat at a discount from them after the show.

The following week, I arrived on set early (habit again), so I went to my trailer to relax. My wardrobe was hanging there, and when I tried on the long winter coat, I noticed a tag attached. Just a name tag, I thought, until I turned it around and read:

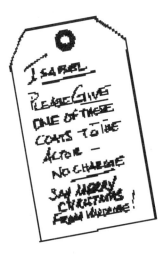

I still wear the coat every winter and think of their generosity. I kept the tag as a reminder of how wonderful the crews can be.

The Wardrobe crew is your best friend on set. They can be your best ally. The easier you make their job, and the better you make them look, the more they'll push for you to be upgraded or featured. They receive little appreciation on set, but make sure you thank them for doing their job. And thank them again when they do more.

To my friends in wardrobe,
who have done more
(and broken rules on my behalf):
Thank you all again.

# AGENTS, TAKE Two

Exclusivity and commission, agency logos on your photos, and checking in with your agent. All problem areas, no easy solutions.

## EXCLUSIVITY

In the United States, you can have as many agents as will take you on, until one signs you on exclusively and gives you extra services and some of the Personal Manager treatment. The rules of the game are understood and it has worked for years.

In Canada, principal agents decided in the early days to insist on exclusivity. One of the principal agent's main jobs is to get you higher fees and better conditions, and without exclusivity, productions would only work through those agents prepared to accept low fees. Exclusivity doesn't lose you anything, because all principal agents receive the same casting calls from casting directors through a casting breakdown service. They all try to cast for the same roles so you don't actually lose opportunities by only having one agent.

The situation is different for extra work, although many extras agents also insist that you accept no work from any other extras agent. I don't think this makes sense, for agent or client: exclusivity costs you money, because one agent will supply performers to just a few of the day's shoots, rather than for every production, and it doesn't help the agent, because it makes it harder for them to sign on the number of performers needed for a good extras roster.

Agreeing to exclusivity to an extras agent may cost you more freedom than you realize. Most will still allow you to accept background work from a direct call by casting – as long as they still get their full commission. Others will ban you from accepting any outside offers at all, even if you're willing to pay them commission.

Exclusivity means you can't use any other agent: check that you aren't banned from searching for a principal agent as well. Some say you can still work through any other agent you want, but since you're "exclusive" and they're "really being nice by bending the rules," you must notify them of any calls and pay them the full commission. If you did accept work through another agent, they would get their 10-15%, and your "exclusive" agent would also get a 10-15% cut. Kiss your paycheque goodbye.

Exclusivity does make life simpler when the agent is dealing with extras who are not very well organised: they never find you have been double-booked, and they never have to fight over who gets the commission. The key to getting non-exclusive representation is to convince the agent you're organised and ethical.

It surprises most beginners to find that most of the best extras agents are  actually receptive when you request non-exclusivity. They know that if they're keeping you busy, you'll always be in touch with them first, so they don't fear competition from fly-by-night agencies. They know you are only covering all your bases, and they also know that they are good enough to earn the majority of commissions you will pay, by keeping you working. Non-exclusivity by itself may be a good reason to sign up with these people and give them your professional commitment and approach to the industry. They deserve it – they're worth their weight in gold.

Let me explain why you should try to persuade your agents not to insist on exclusivity in your case. Assume you are signed exclusively to Agency A:

• Not every agency gets all the casting calls, and today your agent has two ballroom dancing crowds. You don't dance, so you don't work. Agency B had an office and a football crowd. Pity, you weren't signed with them.

• Your agency had a falling-out with one of the four main extras casting directors in town, and won't be receiving many more calls from them in the future. You've just lost 25% of the available casting. That casting director liked your work, but will never see you again. A couple more agency fights with casting personnel and you're dead in the water.

• Today, your agency is so swamped with casting calls, they have to let one slide. Agency B is searching for extras for that very same call, and they would have time to call you, if you were on their roster.

• Your agency is best friends with two or three of the extras casting directors for your area. Agency B does a major part of their business with a different casting director. If you were with both agents, you'd cover the bases.

Having a second agent, or more, can make the difference between working and starving. You can, and should, persuade your agents not to insist on exclusivity, but how do you argue your case? You don't, you negotiate. Go through this list until you can put it in your own words, and say you will follow these rules in exchange for non-exclusivity:

• If the first agent calls with an availability check and the second with a booking for the same shoot, you will accept the booking only after checking the first agent hasn't upgraded you from available to a booking. (If the first agent still has you listed on standby, let them know you'll be accepting the booking from the other agent, but that you appreciate their efforts.) The agency which booked you gets the commission. You don't pay commission to the other agent, since they didn't get you that job. Next time, maybe they will be the one to book you.

• If you have accepted a booking, then you will stay booked! You won't cancel because another agent offers a better deal. If the second call is for a major opportunity (such as a residual role), then you'll check with the first agent to see if there's any chance of finding a replacement for you. If they say no, then you'll just have to accept it and fulfill your original commitment. If you let the first agent down, then both agents will have a bad taste in their mouths about you.

• If you have already appeared in the episode                    nt to book
you on, especially if it was through another agent,               now. Most
of the time, the casting will still approve you to work again on the show. If they
don't, there's always the next shoot, and you've saved them from needing a last
minute replacement for you.

• If the first agent calls with an availability check and the second with a
booking for the same shoot, you will accept the booking only after checking the
first agent hasn't upgraded you from available to a booking. (If the first agent still
has you listed on standby, let them know you'll be accepting the booking from the
other agent, but that you appreciate their efforts.)

Under these rules, the extras agent will be giving up exclusivity but gain-
ing someone who will be working for them. You'll have to show your agents you
won't make their life more difficult: be on your best behaviour, keep your commission up to date, and let them see how organised you are.

You'll want to set up some sort of filing system to check the amount of
work each agency finds for you over the year and see who is doing the best job.

If you do have an exclusive agreement with your extras agent and you
receive a direct call for work from casting, take down the call information and tell
the casting person you will call them right back, that you just need to confirm that
 you aren't already booked on another show. Call your agent to check you're clear
to take the job offer, and to reassure them they'll still get their cut from your pay.
They're not likely to refuse your request unless they've booked you elsewhere. If
they do object you'll have to turn down the spot, and you've learned a valuable
lesson about what you can expect for the future. Call the casting director back and
let them know whether you're available or not as soon as possible: calling them
hours later may cause them real problems. That's a poor payback for making the
extra effort to offer you the spot directly.

## COMMISSION

A large chunk of an agent's income is the ten to fifteen per cent you pay from
each fee you get. They want that money flowing in smoothly and reliably, as the
work goes out to their clients. Why should your agent have to wait and chase you
for your commission? On the other hand, you did the work, so why should you
have to wait for your pay?

The simplest solution is for the agent simply not to offer any more calls
to people who don't pay their commission quickly. This works for cash extras,
who get paid at the end of the day, as well as voucher people, who will get their
fee later. There are agents who work this way; it saves them paperwork and hassle,
it weeds out troublemakers very early on, and it doesn't seem to lose them money
in the end.

Some extras agents insist that vouchers be filled in with the agent's mailing address. Then the agent receives your fee, and you have to pick up your

cheques from the office, writing a commission cheque when you do so. This delays your fee and the agent's commission. If you're busy working, you will get your mail and you can write a commission cheque, but you may not be able to get to your agent's office.

Some agents even cash the cheques themselves. They say this is the only way they can be certain of receiving their commissions promptly. Unfortunately, the extra is left chasing the agent, keeping track of what work has been done and which cheques have arrived, and making trips to the agency to pick up the fees that have come in. Without any fraudulent intent, if the agent puts your cheque into the agency account, there are always more important things to do than pay money to someone else. This is all perfectly legal and businesslike. If you put the agency address on your voucher, the production will send your cheque to your agent. If you let your agent cash your cheque or pay it into an agency account, and don't write a letter of protest, you have given up Power of Attorney over your cheques. You would need to write to the agent and the agency's bank to withdraw the Power of Attorney.

I think you should be trusted to receive your own fees and pay your commission like a grown-up. Agents have plenty of power over extras. If commission isn't paid in full and promptly, the agent simply cuts the extra off from more work.

---

**AGENT:** Extras-R-Us Talent                     **DATE:** Nov. 05, 1995

**ATTN:** Ms. A. Gent

**FROM:** John Smith
789 Any Street
Somewhereville, Ont.
A1B 2C3
Pager: (416) 555-1234

**RE:** Commissions

| PROJECT | FILM DATE | CALL TYPE | DATE PAID | AMT REC | COMM RATE | COMM DUE | TAX | TOTAL DUE |
|---|---|---|---|---|---|---|---|---|
| "The Film Star" | 10/23/95 | Voucher | 11/05/95 | $100.00 | 15 % | $15.00 | $1.05 | $16.05 |
| "I'm Rich" | 11/04/96 | Cash | 11/04/96 | $ 42.00 | 10 % | $ 4.20 | $ .29 | $ 4.49 |

ENCLOSED: 2 cheques in the amounts of $16.05 and $4.49 (Total $20.54).
Please hold my receipts in my file and I will try to pick them up in a few weeks.

THANK YOU AGAIN FOR THE CALL,

*John Smith*

---

**113**

When I ran the agency, I told my extras to mail in their commission when they had a chance. I received most of the cheques within a couple of days. Out of more than two thousand casting calls, I only had to remind two people who were late paying their commissions. I received both cheques in full in three days.

Whether you're paying in person or by mail, provide your agent with a proper breakdown for each payment. If you've been sent out for eight shoots in a week (it's very possible), a breakdown will help keep everyone's records straight.

You can use a form like the sample on the last page. The lay-out is unimportant. Type and photocopy it, or run copies on your computer, so that you and your agent each get a copy for your records.

Always get a receipt for commission paid. Your agent should give you one in exchange for your cheque, or get your copy of this form signed, if you're in the office, especially if you're paying cash. If you're mailing commission in, your agent may hold the receipt for you, or you can get up to date when you do manage to get in. Be sure your receipt shows each shoot you've paid your commission for: that can save a lot of arguments. An agent may send you a breakdown of your commissions at the end of the year for tax purposes. If your chequing account returns cancelled cheques, that can be a back-up. It's a good idea to write separate cheques for each shoot: you may have to pay an additional bank charge for each cheque issued, but it saves a lot of confusion when you can look at your records and see which shoots you have actually paid commission for.

## AGENT LOGO

Some agents insist you include their logo, the agency name and contact information, on the front of your photo. It might seem logical to include their advertising – that way casting will see who to contact whenever they look at your picture – but it does involve some risks.

Your principal, or talent, agency's name can have a big impact on your casting. Since they'll be your sole long-term principal representative and you won't likely be freelancing for these roles, including the agency contact numbers may be beneficial.

An extras agency name, however, won't help you. If you have more than one agent, you'll need a different photo for each, since agents won't submit your photo with another company's name on it. This means higher photo costs, with no benefit to you.

Are you sure your agent has been around long enough to warrant the cost of a special print run? There are a lot of operations out there that move from one cheap office to another. When they move, you'll need a whole new printing to update their address and number. And how will you know which version the casting director is using?

Casting directors argue with agents, that seems part of life. If so, when they see the hated agent's name at the bottom of your photo, will they associate the bad vibes with you?

Which agent will be listed on the photos you give personally to Casting?
Listing any agent on your photo will severely limit future freelancing calls. Is this
name going to be part of the agent's exclusivity deal? Are you prepared to forfeit
that area of self-representation?

If you've decided to advertise your agent, how will you display the
agency name and contact information? Don't expect too much help from the agent
you are advertising. Larger and more established agencies supply photographers
and repro houses with the required art work, (occasionally larger than the performer's name). Sometimes the agent will just provide you with stick-on white
paper labels – not enough for all your photos, so you'll have to use the label on
your master shots. Before you stick anything on your precious master, think how
the label will reproduce. If you have white borders, and the label is small, it's
easy: the white background of the label will be virtually unnoticeable against the
white border. However, if you had borderless prints made, especially with a dark
background, the label itself will draw attention. Ask the agent if they can give you
a clear label with white printing.

A simpler solution would be to provide the stock of photos, and give
them permission to apply their own labels or ink stamp (much more cost effective
for their purpose) as needed. That way you only have to have your name put on all
your photos. You save by ordering a larger number of a single reproduction, and
your agent(s) get their advertising.

## CHECKING IN WITH YOUR AGENT

You don't have to call your agents. Your commission pays for them to call you
when there is work available. Very true. It is possible to sell any product by sitting
back and waiting for chances to come along. This is the easy way, but you can do
better with a more active strategy.

Keep your agents up to date with your availability, find out about any new
projects coming up, keep your name firmly in their mind. Not only will your
name be in the front rank for regular casting, your regular call may come when the
agent is trying to solve a tricky piece of casting. With a large roster, it is very easy
to forget even your best performers.

Don't be a pest. There's no need to phone every single day. Certainly
never call twice a day, unless your agent suggests it: perhaps you may be needed
for a shoot coming in later. Keep the conversation short. Just let them know that
you're available and ready at a moment's notice. Keep it cheerful, keep it short.

Generally, when I ran the agency, my phones were ringing off the walls,
and I used the quiet times to organize the paperwork that came across my desk. I
still encouraged people to check in regularly, as long as the conversation was kept
on a business level. Once I had made a note that they were available, I wanted to
be back to work. Unfortunately, some of my clients assumed that, because I had
picked up the phone, I was free to chatter. I once had a call from that sort of per-

son, put the phone in the desk drawer and found half an hour later the extra was still talking. I had moved over to another line on another phone, so I still got my calls out – and that extra was not cast that day.

Dropping by in person can be a very good idea, as long as you don't make it a daily habit. Check that the agent doesn't mind – paying your commissions is always a good excuse, since everybody is always happy to see money. Going in is a very good idea if you look drastically different (new hairstyle or color, grown a beard, etc.), to let your agent see your new character possibilities.

Whenever possible, make an appointment, but don't expect more than five or ten minutes of their time. Don't try to book a meeting more than a day in advance; call just before you set out. Circumstances may have changed, and a phone call may save you a wasted trip. It may not: a casting call can come in at the last minute, so your agent may be free when you call and overworked ten minutes later. If this has happened, say you'll catch them again, and let them get back to work. They'll appreciate your understanding.

If you drop by without calling first, there is a good chance that your agent will be too busy to see you. Leave a message with the receptionist to let your agent know that you were there. If you see your agent free for a second, just pass by, say hello, and leave.

Check in with your agents often, either by phone or in person. Don't hound them twenty-four hours a day, but be around as often as possible, and as much as is acceptable to your agent. Become part of the landscape. Do it right, and your name will be at the top of their lists for casting calls. Agents should encourage you to check in and let them know your availability. If they don't want to hear from you, then chances are that you will rarely hear from them.

# RÉSUMÉS

When you're looking for a regular job, you use a résumé to present a prospective employer with a condensed chronological history of your work experience and skills.

In the film industry, for extra work, we present our skills and ability to portray various character types. Rather than giving a list of the productions we have worked on, we want to make it easy for Casting to see physical details and skills which they may find useful. To do so, you should understand how the casting director will use this information.

### PRINCIPAL RÉSUMÉ VS. EXTRA RÉSUMÉ
When principal casting directors look for Talent to audition for a particular role, they want your résumé to show specific acting experience. They want to know that you have worked before, and what sorts of work you have done. Your sizes and minor skills are of lesser importance. Instead, they must feel secure that you have enough acting skills and experience to portray a full role.

In contrast, an Extra casting director will search for those who fit the production's requirements for the "look" or "feel" of a character. Extras are meant to provide an atmosphere for the scene rather than to carry the scene itself. Their physical appearance is more important than their actual acting talent. For this reason, the Extra résumé will concentrate on your physical appearance and various real-life skills. Acting ability and professionalism will get you hired more often, but if they want bikers, they want BIKERS.

### I DON'T REALLY NEED A RÉSUMÉ FOR EXTRA WORK
I hear a lot of extras say that a photo is all you need. While it's true that your "look" will determine what characters you'll be called to play, you will miss out on a lot of work without a proper résumé. Quite often the Casting is asked to supply people for given sizes of wardrobe, or with specific skills (athletes, dancers, etc.). You may be perfect for these spots but you'll miss the chance if the casting people aren't aware of your qualifications. You may feel they know you well enough to remember what you look like, but they deal with too many people to remember if you'll fit that 46" jacket. Their choices will have to be based on the exact information they get from a quick scan through the résumés in their files.

### BUT I HAVEN'T DONE ANYTHING YET
That's the beauty of doing extra work. Most of the time, your lack of experience won't be used against you. A properly presented résumé will gain more work for

**117**

you than a poor résumé with extensive film experience. You don't need to have done any film work: you simply need to provide casting directors with the information that is most important to them, and in a manner that's easy for them to use.

## WHAT SHOULD I INCLUDE?

I've seen some incredible résumés where people went on for many pages, listing every single set they've ever been on.

*Film – "AREN'T I GREAT" – I was in two scenes. One as a passer-by crossing the street by the stars. The other was in the bar scene when Johnny Wonderful walked by and I opened a newspaper right by him.*

The casting department simply hasn't got time to rummage through a ten page history of your work. Having done extra work on a specific show will not necessarily mean they will want you for their new project. Listing every show you've ever done does nothing to help them select you for the next production. If they have specific qualifiers for a character, and your résumé is too unorganised to determine your suitability quickly, you'll be passed over for the next person.

## TECHNICAL GUIDELINES

These are solid suggestions, based on having looked at thousands of Extra résumés. Make different choices when you're sure of yourself, these aren't Golden Rules. Except the first one:

### *YOUR RÉSUMÉ SHOULD BE SINGLE SIDED, ONE PAGE ONLY!*

Not half a page, not a page-and-a-bit. It will be one full 8½x11 inch page! Now comes one of two problems: what if you have absolutely no experience and end up with an almost blank sheet, or what if you have too much experience to fit on only one side? That's where knowing what to include, what to exclude, and how it should be displayed will come to your rescue.

Some suggestions about the details, especially useful if someone else is doing your layout:

**PAPER:** 8½x11 inch or A4. (If people use an 8x10 résumé in your area, to fit the back of the standard photo, lay out on a full page and photocopy down to 91%)
Plain white or very light plain pastel (do not use highlighted borders or images) Medium grade stock, 20lb or heavier

**BORDER:** ¾-1 inch all around

**FONT:**   Use a plain typestyle which is easy to read, such as Helvetica or Courier. Avoid script or fancy fonts like Gothic or Futuristic.

Your name and union status may be in a different font from the balance of the résumé, but not so different that it's the font that gets the attention.

**SIZE:**   If you can do your résumé on a computer, I suggest putting your name in bold 24 point, subheadings in bold 12 point, and the text in 10 or 12 point. The date of résumé revision at the bottom looks good in 4 to 6 point.

A typewriter will do a perfectly good job, if you make sure the typeface is clean and not too small. In this case, put your name at the top in rub-down lettering at least a quarter inch high.

We want to present a very clean, precise, uncluttered layout. The casting department should be able to locate any specific information quickly and easily. The résumé is not your life history. It gives chosen information in brief, bulleted notes. If the casting director is forced to read your entire résumé just to see if you fit an outfit, you'll likely be skipped over. Time is too valuable to read through your autobiography when the production is waiting for a casting call to be filled.

The layout I'm going to suggest is probably a good one to follow, at least to start with. Look at the example at the end of the chapter. Your first résumé will be fairly bare; as you gain experience, and credits, rework it. Here are the areas to include:

THE HEADING
- Name
- Union Affiliations or "Actor"
CONTACTS
- Direct Contact
- Your Agents and Alternate Contacts
GENERAL STATS
- Height and Weight
- Hair and Eye Colour
- Wardrobe Measurements
BASIC LISTING
- Physical Features
- Wardrobe and Accessories
- Driving
- Film Experience (Optional)

**119**

SPECIAL SKILLS
- Sports (**Adv**anced and **A**verage)
- Advanced Skills (Dance, Music, etc.)
- Other Professional Level Skills

OTHER SKILLS
- Miscellaneous Skills

WORK RESTRICTIONS
- Limitations on your availability

SPECIALTY CHARACTERS/COMMENTS
- Main typecasting areas
- Additional comments or notations

DATE STAMP
- Date of Revision

## THE HEADING

Your name is your trademark, so it should be highly visible. It's the headline. It must stand out at the top of your résumé in large, bold, uppercase letters. Palatino or Helvetica are good fonts. If you don't have access to a computer which can produce large lettering, leave enough space for using rub-on lettersets. Your name **must** stand out above all else.

Directly below your name will be your union status. If you are not a member of a performers' union yet, just put ACTOR (whether you're male or female). Don't make the common mistake of putting RÉSUMÉ! It's obvious that's what it is.

Normally you would simply centre the name at the top of the page, but if you have access to a computer and digitized miniature photo (or at least one that will reproduce clearly by photocopier), you could include it at the top left of your résumé. Adding the photo is not necessary, but can help tie a face immediately to the information. A good photocopy shop should be able to advise you whether your photograph will reproduce well. If the photocopy will appear blotchy, just leave the photo out and center the name instead. A clean, clear heading is better than a bad attempt at appearing clever.

| PHOTO | **JOHN SMITH** ACTOR |

_____I draw a separating line between sections._____

## CONTACTS

I'm not talking about lenses for your eyes, nor about all the famous people you know in the industry. I'm talking about how the casting directors and productions can reach you for work. Sure, they may have used you on set before, but don't expect them to keep your phone number on their Rolodex. Extras come and go too quickly to record each person's number individually.

Five lines of type should be enough. Start with your direct contact phone numbers: your home number (res) and pager (pag). Directly below the phone numbers, I usually include a message "Calls accepted at all hours." If this is there, the casting director needn't feel guilty about contacting you when the call times arrive at 2 a.m. I'm prepared to work at a moment's notice: if you don't want phone calls after a certain hour, say so here.

Some people include their address in the CONTACT area. I would suggest not doing so – no-one's going to write to you about work. And I may be paranoid, but there are too many crazy people out there. You may get the odd emergency replacement call if you give your nearest main intersection.

While we're talking about crazies, many people have a pager to avoid listing their home phone number.

Under the label ALTERNATE CONTACT, list your agent(s) or anyone else who can be absolutely relied on to track you down and relay a message if a call comes in. Listing your agent(s) will also make it easier for casting directors to call you to set if they haven't enough time to make individual calls. They don't necessarily all deal with the same agencies, but if they are planning to call an agent with a list of people needed and they know which agents represent you, you may be included as a specific request.

Breaking the section into two columns, DIRECT CONTACT on the left, ALTERNATE CONTACT on the right, with proper headings, will help if you need more space. Otherwise, just center the information.

Each of the next three sections is divided into two columns, to make a mass of information clearer. The headings will be in the left third of the page. The point-form data will be in the right two-thirds. Go to the RÉSUMÉ WORKSHEETS in the back and start collecting the information for these sections. Remember, don't cheat. Not even a little bit.

## GENERAL STATS

Now comes some of the most important information the extras casting director will need: your physical stats and measurements. Unlike the principal actors, who will be custom fitted for their costumes, extras are often hired according to who fits what is available. There might be a separate wardrobe fitting, but this is usually only to determine what minor adjustments can be made. More often, Casting will simply be asked to bring in people who can fit the ready-made outfits.

Notice that the résumé doesn't mention your age or age range. Your real age is no use to casting people, provided you're not a child, and, unless you have enough experience to accurately determine your true camera age range, leave it off the résumé for now. Age range is a product of your face and manner, and gives Casting a general idea of how old you look for potential characters. It's worth using the Casting Worksheet to learn about your range. If a casting call came in for people who are 40-ish, and you were 42 but looked more like mid-30s, you might not be quite right for this particular shot. However, if the call was for people 30-ish, you might get it despite your real age. Don't narrow your chances by putting the wrong camera age range in your résumé. If you do want to include it, judge your range carefully.

BASIC LISTING
•      Physical features and markings
Use the Résumé Worksheet to decide what unusual features (tattoos, pocked face, rapid hair growth, celebrity doubles, etc.) to put in. It is not important to include all the information, just anything which might affect your work or allow for special consideration. Be careful with celebrity double. I'm not talking about "You look just like Janis Joplin when you do that!" Celebrity doubles are winners of Elvis competitions, people who get mobbed by fans, anyone who can audition convincingly as the celebrity. If you've thought about doing a one-person show in the character, you may be a celebrity double.
•      Wardrobe and accessories
The Wardrobe Worksheet should contain a brief listing of the styles of outfits you have available for use. Now, you can condense the data for your résumé. You don't need to include every outfit. Simply classify what types you have. Be sure to include any special uniforms, formal attire, and unusual sets (nurse's uniform, tuxedo, psychedelic 60s, etc.). If you have a number of suits, state which kinds you have, e.g., Suits – Bus/Casual/Sport. If you have room, you may also include any bizarre or tacky accessories (or large collections). Don't go mad; keep your résumé wardrobe listing to what makes you unusual.
•      Driving and Vehicles available for set use
Look at the Résumé Worksheet to see some of the vehicles a production may be interested in. Unusual driving skills should go into SPECIAL SKILLS, but this is the place for your truck license and the 1956 Prairie Wagon. A regular driver's license and a nondescript suburban runabout, even a real clunker if it's not too noisy, are often useful assets.
•      Experience: A principal résumé would give first place to your film experience, but it's less important for extra work. You should only include it if your résumé appears a little blank. You can identify the specialty characters, but don't bother for generic Passers-by and Commuters, etc.

Like this:

| WAR OF THE WORLDS | (Alien) |
| --- | --- |
| ROBOCOP | (Police Officer) |

but FRIDAY 13th Passerby and F/X II's Bar Patron would appear as:
   Also appeared in FRIDAY 13th and F/X II.

Keep it to five or six lines: frankly, it's usually better to use the space to list your skills and talents.

## SPECIAL SKILLS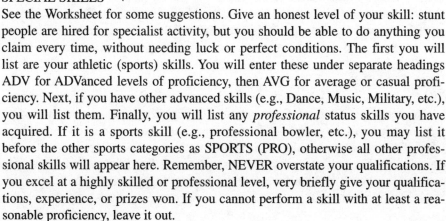
See the Worksheet for some suggestions. Give an honest level of your skill: stunt people are hired for specialist activity, but you should be able to do anything you claim every time, without needing luck or perfect conditions. The first you will list are your athletic (sports) skills. You will enter these under separate headings ADV for ADVanced levels of proficiency, then AVG for average or casual proficiency. Next, if you have other advanced skills (e.g., Dance, Music, Military, etc.), you will list them. Finally, you will list any *professional* status skills you have acquired. If it is a sports skill (e.g., professional bowler, etc.), you may list it before the other sports categories as SPORTS (PRO), otherwise all other professional skills will appear here. Remember, NEVER overstate your qualifications. If you excel at a highly skilled or professional level, very briefly give your qualifications, experience, or prizes won. If you cannot perform a skill with at least a reasonable proficiency, leave it out.

For the balance of the résumé we'll use the full width of the page and centre the last two headings. Make the information easy to get at quickly: keep linked subjects together.

## OTHER SKILLS
We all have something we can do that makes us unusual. We're looking for any odd skill you have seen people using on screen, but which isn't easily categorizable. The casting director may just be looking for someone who can pull extraordinary faces, and you could hardly put that under Sports. Reading is not an Other Skill: I can't tell you how many extra's résumés I've seen which boasted of reading. For extra work, it's easy to pretend that you're reading even if you actually can't.

## WORK RESTRICTIONS
In "Mirror, Mirror" and the Personal Limits Worksheet, you thought about the conditions under which you wouldn't be happy working. This is the place to be honest about the real no-no's. It seems odd to put in things that will be problems,

**123**

but the casting director should know right away if calling you would be a waste of time. For instance, if you don't wish to work around animals, or portray certain types of characters, say so. Having a specific area for such details draws the notice (and appreciation) of casting directors. It will save them a wasted call, and release you from having to find a polite way to turn them down.

## SPECIALTY CHARACTERS
This final section is perhaps the most difficult. Use the Casting Worksheet to see what types of character you are most suited to play. You're not limiting yourself to just these characters. By selecting a few specific character types, you'll receive priority booking when these spots are open. Choose eight to ten types from the Top Ten you created in the Assessment Worksheet. If you look like a member of an ethnic or racial group, you could get on a short list when a production is looking for a special crowd.

## DATE STAMP
The final detail to complete your résumé is the date it was most recently updated! It's the one piece of information most often forgotten by extras, yet the most valuable to your own sanity. Without dating your résumé, you could find yourself panicked if old versions should get mixed in with the new ones. Save yourself many future headaches and date stamp your résumé in very fine print at the bottom right corner. Now you'll be able to ensure the casting director always has your most recent stats close at hand.

## THE FINAL PRODUCT
After all your hard work and preparations, you now have enough material to prepare a promotional résumé you can be proud of for all your extra work ahead. Put all together, it will show what you have to offer, like this:

# JOHN SMITH

## ACTRA / EQUITY / SAG

(416) 555-1234 Pager (24 hrs)
Calls accepted at any hour!
Alternate Contact
Extras-R-Us Talent (416) 555-9876

| GENERAL: | | | | |
|---|---|---|---|---|
| | HEIGHT: | 6'4" | HAIR: | Brown |
| | WEIGHT: | 180 lbs. | EYES: | Hazel |
| | SHIRT: | 16 1/2 | WAIST: | 30-32 |
| | ARM: | 37 | LEG: | 34-35 |
| | JACKET: | 44 XT | SHOES: | 12-13 |

**MARKINGS:** Assorted Temporary Tattoos available
- Head/Face may be shaved as required
- Fast Hair Growth (2 wks growth rate)
Please call to confirm current status

**WARDROBE:** - Punk, Homeless, Suits (Bus/Casual/Sport)
- Biker Rings, Arm Bands, Bandannas, etc.
- Western Boots, Western Hat

**DRIVE:** - Automatic
- Motorcycle Licence
- Farm Tractors and Extensions
- Single Horse Carriage

**SPORTS (ADV):** - Horses (English/Jumping/Western/Gaming)
NOTE: 4 days req for full legs

**(AVG):** - Swimming, Diving, Rowing, Canoeing
- Baseball, Football, Tennis, Badminton
- Billiards, Darts, Cycling

## OTHER SKILLS

Cry on Cue. Comfortable around Firearms and Explosions. Basic Guitar and Electric Bass, Computers, Prosthetics Modelling, Stage/Stunt Fighting, Recording Engineer, Floor Directing, Voice (Impressions, Characterizations, Voice Over, ADR), French (Québécois). Work well in Prosthetics (Specialty).

## SPECIALTY CHARACTERS

Currently accepting roles as Actor/Background/Special Skills as Character Actor including all work requiring make-up/wardrobe involving Prosthetics. Specialty as Psycho, Loonie, Dullard, Demon, Biker, Gangster, Villain, Heavy, Punk, etc.

Nov '95

125

# DANGER ON SET

Union sets, and non-union sets run by sane people, take extraordinary care to avoid injury from weapons and explosives. ACTRA has collaborated on a set of regulations which provide elaborate control over the handling and storage of these materials on shoots within their jurisdiction. But no-one has found a way to control blind bad luck or stupidity. Don't relax in a scene using dangerous devices; be extra careful yourself and watch everyone around you. It's like driving on a busy highway: act defensively!

You're playing a SWAT officer, and the weapons handler gives you a pistol. Listen to what he is saying. It may feel like "Cops and Robbers," or "Cowboys and Indians," but playtime this is not! You may be tempted to giggle like a schoolkid with a new toy and wave that prop gun around. Don't. This is a serious, and potentially dangerous, business.

There are two sorts of guns on set: those that fire blanks and incredibly realistic fakes. Even if you're positive your weapon is only made of rubber, keep it secure. It will usually be heavy enough to hurt somebody if you swing it carelessly. Aiming a rubber gun at others often leads to careless mimicking by others who might not be sporting a phony weapon. It will never be necessary to point a loaded gun directly at anyone on set. That's what the editing room is for: this is make-believe, don't make the tragedy come true.

Firearms that really shoot on set are loaded with blanks, with special chemicals and reflective material to make the gunfire show up on screen. A light charge can shoot burning wadding twenty feet, and that can kill at close range. We've all heard the horror stories of accidents on sets where they have done just that, whether it was the tragic death of Brandon Lee or the nameless actor who put an unloaded gun to his head and pulled the trigger, not realising the prop had been loaded between takes. Both of us have seen someone injured by burning chemicals from a blank. It's disfiguring and horribly painful. Treat these weapons with the respect they deserve.

Even nonfiring guns are all too realistic and can raise tempers and fears on set. It's an accident waiting to happen: don't help cause it.

Pyrotechnics kill. Pay strict attention to all your instructions, where you have to be and where the pyrotechnics are. Do I have to tell you not to carry your smokes? The explosives will be well hidden, and detonated by remote control. When you're called to a set with explosives, turn off your pager, cell phone and radio, and leave them behind. A simple phone call can set the charges off. Tensions may be strained, so keep especially quiet while the scene is being prepared.

**126**

After the scene, stay in a safe place until you've been released. Then get off set. The danger isn't over yet. A few years ago, I was on a set rigged for major explosions and flames. After the shot, as the smoke cleared, everybody relaxed while the special effects people checked that all the pots had gone off. This is normally just a formality, but one of the handlers checked a live pot carelessly, a twenty-five foot flame shot up around her face and she was thrown fifteen feet away. She survived, but had severe burns and scars which required lengthy treatment. She was fortunate: she's alive.

Firearms and explosives handlers are responsible for handing out the weapons and setting the effects; when they are on set, they're God. Don't ignore any of their instructions simply because you've done it all before. When it comes to safety precautions, they overrule the director, even the producer. What they say goes. A firearms handler I will call François is typical: he takes his job with utmost seriousness and demands safety first at all times. I never feel as safe as I do when he's on set. Every crew member, all the Talent, feel much more than simple respect for him. I only hope you are lucky enough to work with handlers that are just as strict as he is about precautions. I owe him a lot of thanks and respect. I may owe him my life.

Proper sound-protection earplugs feel weird. You can hear what's going on around you, but it's a long way off. You can get used to them, however, and they do their job.

Even when the sound doesn't seem too bad, prolonged and repeated exposure can damage your hearing. If your ears are ringing, they've been damaged. Play it safe and don't be macho. Wear the damn plugs.

You don't want to learn your lesson the way I did. Trust me. I was playing a character on a cop show, who sat in the hero's car and shot him six times. They offered me earplugs, but when I saw the gun I was to use, I chuckled. It was only about three inches long and obviously couldn't fire through cardboard. "Who needs earplugs? I can handle it without them." Famous last words. Luckily for me, François was there, pulled me off to the side of the set and told me to try one test shot. My ears (and my nerves) were ringing for quite a while. I've never turned down the plugs since.

# PHOTOGRAPHS

You are your own product, you must sell your image to potential buyers, and a photograph is your means of showing your wares. Your résumé describes you, but your photo actually shows what they are buying.

You don't need to spend a lot of money on photographs, but you can't do without one completely, and an investment in good photographs is rarely wasted. Casting people may know what you look like – vaguely, among a thousand other extras – but they need that photo to bring your image to the forefront. The director, who may not know you at all, will choose the extra who has the good photo. If you are at all serious and you don't have a portfolio of good shots, you're at a big disadvantage.

You don't need a professional photo if you've never done extra work before. Don't spend a lot of money when you might try it once and quit. Agents and casting directors will need a small photo to remind them what you look like, but you can squeak by on a good home photograph for a little bit. Polaroid™ instant photos are generally only good enough for the agent's own use, but they are an easy way for an agent to get a standard photo of you for the agency's own book. Whether you have your own photo or not, the agent may take one and charge you a minimal amount: five dollars or less. If they use 35mm film, they may charge you ten bucks. If you have your own photograph you'll look like a better client, and the agent will have something better to show casting directors.

When I say you don't need a "professional" photo, that doesn't mean any old picture will do. The job of the picture is to make it easier for the agent to suggest you and the casting director to approve you. Here are a few guidelines for picking shots from your album, and for snapping your own:

**No crowd shots**! The picture should be of you, and you alone. Forget the picnic group: you want your agent to associate just one person with your name. Your photo should make the agent think of you, not your friends: if they want extra work, they should get their own pictures.

**Use a normal size picture** – a regular four by six inch print you would have made at your local photoshop for your own album. I got a lot of those tiny pictures from mall photo machines and discarded passport shots back in my agency days, and they end up at the bottom of the folder in a heap. Don't cut a picture of yourself out of a larger photo (I received a lot of those as well).

**A plain head-and-shoulders shot** or one taken about waist up is good: even better, offer both. Full body shots may seem like a good idea, but they often make your face too small to see properly. Unless you are 450 pounds or in a wheelchair, you want the agent to link your name to a face.

And here's advice on any publicity photograph:

**Use a recent photo**. We dream about how we looked in our younger days, but that doesn't help when the agent is casting you. The production expects to see your photo when you walk in, not someone ten years – and twenty hair-styles – older.

**Make-up shouldn't be visible**. A touch of blush is fine, but beware the Tammy Faye make-over. The picture is used to show you at your natural average, not at your painted best. If you've suffered from a temporary zit attack, you can use a bit of make-up to cover up the blemishes before taking the photo. If you have problem skin, or if you sport moles or other markings, leave the picture natural. We aren't models, we're regular people.

**Costumes don't help.** You must have at least one good normal picture to represent you. Simple, casual daily wear is the call of the day. And steer clear of props: will the teddy bear really make casting you easier?

**Wear moderate tones** against uncluttered backgrounds. This is publicity, not camouflage, so you want to be visible against the scenery. On the other hand, don't wear wild prints, bold stripes, or psychedelic patterns. You want them to cast you, not your clothes.

**Don't pose.** Those cutesy stances are distracting when the casting director is trying to imagine a casting possibility.

**Smile?** If you have one of those toothpaste fresh wonders, by all means use it. Keep the smile to the level you're honestly comfortable with, don't try forcing a "Cheese!" If you're like the pair of us, and a mild grin is about the most you can handle, don't worry: a pensive look, or even a harsh stare for certain character types, will do more to get you cast than a phoney smirk.

**Colour or B/W?** When you get your professional photos taken later, they'll be black and white. For the moment, use whichever is easier.

When you are sure this Extra thing is for you, you're ready to invest a little money in professional quality photographs. Professional 8 x 10 glossies are the way to say you're a serious professional. You've seen the juicy parts other people get: some people seem to be chosen out of the crowd to be individual characters for the scene before they even get to set. How come they are so lucky? More often than not, it's because they advertised themselves well, through their résumés and their glossies. Casting directors prefer to use proper black and white 8 x 10 photos for their own selection, and the agent supplying proper casting books with indus-try-standard glossies is more likely to be considered first.

The snapshot you started with helped your agent get you on set, but it's likely that nobody else in the industry ever saw it. Extras casting directors will rely on the agents' judgement for general characters, but are often more critical when selecting the look-specific characters. To help in their decision, they'll examine the 8 x 10 photos the agent supplied. Your little snapshot or the agent's instant photo wouldn't have been included, so you've missed out on a chance at the prime-cut pieces of work. If you're serious about the business, let's get you some real photos.

One of Uncle Bob's marvellous snapshots won't cut it. A department store or a mainstreet photographer are experts in different areas. Even a models' photographer produces material for a different market. An actor's 8 x 10 looks like an actor's 8 x 10. Actors' photos are a tool for Casting: it takes an experienced specialist to know what casting people are looking for.

Other photographers aim to make their subject look their very best; a performer's photographer captures the subject's quality and character, keeping the look as natural as possible. No floral backdrops or tricky angles for them, they realize that YOU need to be the focus of the photo. They're not trying to make "a pretty picture," they're concentrating on selling you. An otherwise good photographer might turn out a technically superb photograph which your family will love, but which will be worse than useless in the industry.

So how do you find a photographer specialising in performers? Your agent could be a good source of advice, but the in-house photographer may not be your best choice (see the caution in the "Agents" chapter). Check out the agent's suggestions, but don't stop there. Take a look in the trade magazines and the bulletin boards at your local union office and theatre organizations for advertisements.

You have access to one of the best sources of information about performer photographers: other extras. When next you're on set, ask to see other extras' photographs. Do any of them really catch your eye? Does a certain style appeal to you? When you see one that looks good, ask who took the shots. Ask for a contact number, what kind of rates were charged, what that bought, and get an idea of how the person enjoyed working with that photographer. If you have African or Asian colouring, look for one of those few photographers who understand how to light your skin tones.

Call the possibles to get the full details of cost and services offered. Check on the payment schedule. It's not unreasonable to pay something before the session, but be sure you keep back some of the fee, to be paid when you have a professional photograph acceptable to you. "To you," not to the photographer. This is quite normal, and without it you have no leverage if something goes wrong. A photo session can cost as little as fifty dollars, or as much as a few hundred. Shop around to get an idea of the going rate for your area. You can't guarantee quality by paying more, but don't choose a cheaper photographer when, for just a little extra, you could get someone you are really comfortable with. Use the rates simply as one factor in choosing.

Ask to meet with the photographer before you book the shoot. A photo session can be a very intimidating experience, and that unease will be captured on film. When you meet, look at the photographer's portfolio, to see more examples of actors' 8 x 10s, but mainly listen to your gut, to find out if the pair of you click. This photographer may be good, but you might get a better picture when you find someone you really see eye to eye with.

I had worked with some exceptional photographers, but something seemed to be missing until I found the photographer for me. The chemistry between the camera and me was strong, and suddenly the still shots I had feared were pure enjoyment. The ease I felt was captured in the final pictures, and later a major Toronto photographer who had seen the shots wanted to book me for his own promotion. It might have been prestigious for me, but I was so pleased with my own photographer that I turned the job down, out of loyalty.

Your ideal photographer, if you're lucky enough to find one, won't necessarily be the same one I use: personalities work in different ways between different people. If you find someone you feel good about, grab your chance right away.

Now you've booked your session: be certain to pack it in early the night before. At a pinch, you can go to set with baggy eyes – it may suit your character, they can hide it with make-up, or they can just keep you further from the camera – but a photo session will be featuring you, up close and personal. Maybe an afternoon booking would be better.

Some photo studios have a professional make-up artist on call, for an extra fee, but the less they do, the better. If you really don't feel well the day of the session, it's better to cancel. You may lose your deposit, but you want the shots to show you on a good day: rebook when you're feeling better.

You've hired an expert: take the advice you're given. I don't think anything here will contradict what the specialist will tell you.

Those of you with longer hair may want to have some shots with your hair hanging and some with it dressed back. Glasses? Take a couple of shots with, but leave them off for most, unless you simply can't work on set without specs. See the note in the "Mirror, Mirror" chapter.

Don't worry about making these publicity shots "interesting." These are meat-and-potatoes, run-of-the-mill pictures of the way you basically look. This is where your confidence in the photographer pays off. If you are relaxed, your shots will show the interesting and unusual person you know you are. You can choose to include some strong character shots, but these will only supplement your main headshots. The "Mirror, Mirror" chapter talks about offering a few specialist looks, but offering only character shots may get you restricted to character casting calls.

If you really want to add some character shots, you might be wise to book a second shoot. Your approach to the character shot will be so different from the easy, natural you in your regular 8 x 10s that you could end up with no usable natural shots. If you're creating a strong image, feel free to exaggerate your facial expression or your pose. We are not looking for Stratford subtleties here. A silly grin and bow tie works well for nerd specialties, and a stern stare from the side can gain you the bad guy work.

Those of you who have your ears pierced in a dozen places, or other facial perforation (ouch!), will want to show off your special appearance, without making it the only focus of the shot. If you have an interesting tattoo, it's worth featuring it, but remember this is a family show. Get a couple of medium shots, perhaps arms crossed enough to feature the tattoos while still emphasizing your look at the camera.

Do you need a swimsuit shot? If there are openings in your area for water lovers, and you're comfortable with your figure, it might not hurt to include swimwear in your portfolio. Body builders should include a photo showing off toned muscles, but, please, leave out the nude Atlas poses.

Normally, you'll only want to use one or two character glossies in your portfolio. Turn to the Casting Worksheet and look at the main character types you picked. Can you find a common theme? Rather than doing a separate shot of each character as an individual, try to catch the mood they share. Having many different photos in your file is not only costly, it means the agent and casting director will have to search through a pile of shots which are totally wrong for the call.

Your photographer or printing house may be able to piece together a number of shots into one composite picture. Don't cram too many shots on the sheet, and be sure they aren't just pictures of you wearing different hats. Certainly, do not use this as your main photo. Your headshot will be your main promotion: the composite shot combines your specialty characters into one easy-access picture for offbeat casting.

If you've decided to specialise beyond general extra work, then these character photos will be your main headshot. I rely solely on my specialty characters, so I use a number of character headshots, all following the "unusual and bizarre" theme. Here are two shots that cover my range: one photo for the loonier characters, and one for the dangerous roles.

Imre de Jonge      Imre de Jonge

About a week after the session, the photographer will give you the contact sheets, each containing miniature prints of the shots taken on a roll of film. The prints are only postage-stamp size, but with a good light and a magnifier you can decide which shots, if any, you want blown up. If you're lucky, the photographer may be using a film format that allows larger contact prints: this is an option worth taking, even if it costs a little more.

Don't worry about a photo being a little dark or light overall: this can usually be corrected in the final print. A photo that appears slightly off-center on the contact sheet can often be cropped by the photographer to centre the shot properly.

Get some small removable sticky notes. Cover up the shots that you really don't like. Go through again, narrowing the choice, to select the ones which can best represent you. This isn't the same as picking those that make you look the best. We all have distorted ideas of how others see us, so get opinions from others more experienced.

Photographers can help you, but they tend to like photos which show off their work. Extras agents will make suggestions, and of course they will be the ones using the shot most. A seasoned extra whose opinion you trust can advise you, based on having seen you work. Your best bet is to hope the casting director is on set and can spare a few moments to look at the contact sheet. Casting assistants will be easier to corner, and may be able to provide good input, but casting directors really know what they need from a photo.

If a lot of the photos have technical flaws – out of focus, dirty camera lens – try to get the photographer to shoot another session. You shouldn't have to pay for shoddy workmanship. If, however, you just aren't happy with how you look in any of the shots, you may be able to talk the photographer into a reshoot at a reduced rate, sometimes as low as the cost of materials. You may have to cut your losses, hang on to the last installment of your fee, and find another photographer.

If all went reasonably well, you can expect to end up with one or two good shots. Three or four good choices is a fantastic session. All you need from a session is one good headshot: get that and you're doing well.

Often the photographer will include one or two 8 x 10 prints in the session fee, with a small charge for additional prints. It's worth paying the extra money to have him print up one copy of each photo you're considering: the contact sheets are just too small to see all the minor details properly. See if it'll be cheaper to have these trial prints made 4 x 5. Ask for advice again on these larger prints.

Your photographer holds the copyright on the negatives of the pictures you have chosen, but you will be allowed to have reproductions made from the 8 x 10 prints

**133**

you were given. Identify these in light pencil on the back and NEVER give them away.

Reproduction houses (Galbraith and Graphic in Toronto accept orders from across Canada), and now some photographers, have machines to churn out acceptable prints from your master print, at about one tenth the cost of regular photofinishing, in about a week or ten days. The final product is a real photograph, and can be printed in either glossy or matte surface, either borderless or with a narrow white border. Which you choose is up to you, they are all professional and the cost difference, if any, will be small.

Have your name put on the photograph, either by the photographer or by the repro house. Photos easily get separated from résumés. The casting director might think you're perfect for a role, but if there's no name to go with the face, they won't know who to ask for.

I don't like the idea of including your agent's contact information on your photo, but you may have to make the best of it – check out the "Agents, Take Two" chapter, which should help you to do just that.

I suggest starting with at least 250 copies, and restocking when your supply gets low. That's a lot, but work it out. Each agent will want anywhere from twenty to fifty copies for their books and for casting distribution, and you'll want the casting directors to have a copy direct from you as well. Then there are the copies you give to potential agents, and those you'll take to go-sees. And don't forget the copies you should be ready to hand out to contacts on set. These prints will disappear faster than you think.

The more you order, the lower the cost per photo. However, if you order a truckload of copies, you may be stuck with photos which are too outdated to use. A new hairstyle and even normal aging means new photos: adults can probably get away with a new session every couple of years, but younger people, and especially children, will need new pictures more frequently.

An 8 x 10 print at a photofinisher costs around ten bucks, reproductions cost around two dollars, even in large quantities. Here are a couple of much cheaper routes that work:

**Computer generated prints**. Printing companies can accurately copy your master print into a digital computer-coded image and use the computer file to directly instruct their printing press to print the digitized image on a heavy 8 x 10 card stock, with a quality which closely rivals a real photograph – at under a dollar a copy, after the scanning fee. They look very professional, and you can usually get more in less than a week.

**Half-tone Screens** are the way to get good photocopies from photographs. And this is really cheap! I can get 100 publicity photos photocopied in under an hour, for about $15. Contact your local printing houses to see if they will make a PMT (Photo-Mechanical Transfer) half-tone screened copy of your 8 x 10 B/W master print. It'll cost about $25 to $35, and then you use the PMT as the master for your photocopies.

If you try to photocopy an original photo, the photocopy will look more like an ink spill than a picture. A screened print is made up of tiny dots. When you photocopy it, the copier just reproduces each dot. The dots are so close together that you can't really see them, but the copier can, and you get a clean copy.

Take your PMT around until you find a copy shop ready to work with you. This will probably be a place big enough to have good equipment and small enough to look after it. Have the photocopy made from the PMT on a heavy grade of semi-gloss paper. Enlarge the 8 x 10 to fill a regular 8½ x 11 inch page (105% to 108%). Get them to print out one copy and check it out. If you don't like the quality, pay the two-bits for the attempt and try another printer.

These photocopies are the only "photographs" I've ever used for my principal work. Not only have I never had a complaint about the quality, I've had many compliments about the shots from producers, directors and principal casting directors. The low cost means I can hand out a lot more photos, and if I run low, I can stock up again in an hour with a quick trip downtown. I've even used copies as scrap paper on set when writing messages, to remind people who it was sent the note. I've arrived at new sets to find my photos already plastered on the doors of the crew trucks. Use these less costly prints, and you gain the freedom to pass them around to any possible source of work. Because a fax machine works like a photocopier, you can fax screened copies perfectly, and casting directors really appreciate that.

Happy Happy – Joy Joy! You proudly strut around town with your new photos in hand. First stop – your agents. If they still have copies of the old version of your photo in your file, ask for them back. You don't need the old photos, but you don't want your agent to use them.

Agents don't update their roster books for the casting directors every week, and it may be a while before your photo gets changed. Get a couple of copies, and updated résumés, to each casting director. You can use the drop-off box at their office, or mail the copies in a stiffened envelope marked "Photos: Do Not Fold." It may be better simply to wait until you see them, or one of their assistants, on set. However you deliver the new photos, you should include a very short note, thanking the casting director ahead of time for accepting your new stats. With luck, they may update your photo in the roster book themselves.

Go-sees and auditions will use a lot of photos. It's always wise to leave a clean copy: you never know what state their copy is in. Take some with you whenever you're called to set: you never know when you'll make a new contact. Keep four or five promotion packets – pictures and résumés – in a durable folder: normal folders and envelopes don't protect photographs enough, especially in the deep dark forgotten reaches of your set sack.

Casting directors and agents send your photos out: that's why you gave them copies. Make sure they always have a stock. Handing over a stack is not a solution – they'll go straight into the blue box. Look for chances to give them a photo and résumé whenever you're on set or in the office.

Take the rest of the stock home and store it away safely, or better, stack each different shot flat on its own tray on your desk. That way you can easily see when it's time to restock. Avoid the panic that's guaranteed when you realize you're out of photos right before that big break casting chance. I speak from experience.

# PHONE EQUIPMENT

"If a man ... build a better mousetrap ... the world will make a beaten path to his door."

Oh no they won't, Ralph Waldo Emerson. Not unless they know about his mousetrap and where his door is. Even then, if his door is hard to reach, they are just as likely to buy a "good-enough" mousetrap from the nearest store.

The "Legwork" chapter helps you let casting people and agents know why they should hire you – this chapter is about making it easy for them to do so. The more serious you are about your extra work, the more you will try never to be out of touch. Regular people can take off for three weeks holiday and never think about their jobs until the trip back: not you. You're self-employed and that's with you all the time.

This business is run on the telephone. You must have a telephone number where you can be reached, and where messages can be left if you're away. The messages must be picked up and acted on quickly. That's a mess of problems already. What if you change apartments? What if other people use your phone? How do you get messages when you're at your day job?

Phone services, pagers, fax machines: they're complicated and they're expensive. Do you really need them? Yes. They're an investment; and they're tax deductible (generally). The investment pays off by making you easier to contact, so easier to cast.

It's hard to turn a personal phone into your professional number. If other people use the phone, you may not get your messages and the line may be tied up when the agent calls. You could get your own line into your home, but that's expensive. A business line is even more expensive and has no advantages for us. Your basic phone line is not tax deductible, but a second line would be.

So would a new service which gives you a second telephone number on the same line, with a special ring, so that other people can know it's your call, and leave it for the machine to pick up if you're not at home. This is much cheaper than another line.

In an office, there's someone whose job it is to take messages if you're not there. Unless you have someone who will always be home when you're not, and can always be trusted to answer and take messages efficiently, you need an answering machine, a service or a pager. Without one of them, you'll never know what calls you missed while you were out doing your legwork, on another set, or simply window shopping for such luxury items as food. With one, you can get some quality time away from the phone that never rings.

An answering machine is the most basic necessity for a performer. The machine picks up your phone after the number of rings you choose, plays your greeting, and records any message your caller wants to leave. You replay the tape to hear your messages, either when you come home, or by calling home and using the touch tone buttons or a beeper to command the machine from a distance.

Discount answering machines start at forty dollars. Whether this is the right choice for you deserves some thought: you don't want something that will break down inside the year, but neither do you need a bells-and-whistles monster you can't even understand. Choose the simplest machine that will cover your needs. Two-cassette and digital machines are most reliable, but any machine will record and play back messages satisfactorily: most of the difference in price is brand name and gizmos.

**Clarity:** This varies wildly, and not always according to price. A blurred message going out won't give a good picture of you, and an unrecognisable detail in a message coming in could cost you work. While in the store, ask to try recording your voice on the machine (nowadays, most machines have a built-in microphone). Speak in your regular voice and listen to the playback. If the sound is muffled or washed out, then pass on that model.

**Ease of use:** All you need is a machine to take your messages. Do you really need one that does your laundry and can be driven at Mach Five? Can others operate it for you in case you're not available? Will it be used strictly by yourself, or will it be used by your whole family? The simpler the machine, the more likely you are to use it religiously, and the less likely it is to break down.

**Remote:** Although you could simply check your messages when you get back home, you need some way to retrieve your messages if you are on a set, or away overnight. Most modern machines have some sort of beeper system, either through a credit-card-sized sound generator, or by using the phone keypad itself. My preference is a machine which doesn't require anything other than the touchtone phone itself. That way I don't need to worry about losing my little portable coder (they do disappear and, at about twenty to forty dollars for a replacement, that can add up to more than the cost of the answering machine itself). Of course, out in the boonies you may not find a touchtone phone.

Check your machine every couple of hours. You will come up blank a lot, but the most important casting calls are at short notice, where you can solve a big problem by being available. You want to make sure that you find out about job possibilities as soon as possible and return the call. If you don't, you'll miss that chance of work and you'll get the reputation of being constantly out and difficult to reach.

**Codes:** Some machines allow you to protect your incoming messages with security codes. Are your messages really that private? Stick to one number to press for your messages if you don't need the extra security, and save some money.

**Remote turn-on:** There's nothing worse than calling in and discovering that your machine isn't on. Even some low cost machines will turn the if you let the phone ring enough times. This is a very handy feature to someone has accidentally turned your machine off, or you had to rac house and didn't turn the machine on.

**Memo:** Another handy feature, in case someone at home wa... you a quick message before going out for the night or going to bed. The memo button will let them leave you a simple message among your phone calls, without having to phone in. It's great for reminding you that it's your turn to take out the trash tonight.

For about sixty bucks a year, your phone company will provide its own answering machine service. Callers can leave you a message if you don't answer their call – and also if you're on the line to someone else. You can retrieve the messages at home or away, from any Touchtone phone. This is more expensive than buying a machine, but they're easy, reliable and flexible, and the sound quality is excellent.

Please! Whatever machine you use, DO NOT create a star-spangled message to greet the caller. People say they hate talking to machines, but they hate listening to machines worse. When your callers are in a hurry they haven't got time for foolishness. Keep the message short: give your name (so that they know that they've phoned the right number), and ask them to leave their message. Your opening message should be no more than 10 seconds long:

*This is Bill... Please leave your message at the beep and I'll get back to you as*  *soon as I can... Thank you...*

When I was managing an extras agency, I used to make two or three hundred casting calls every day. I would often be greeted by machines with fully orchestrated pieces lasting 20-30 seconds before I even heard a voice. I would hear cute jokes that never seemed to end. I would hear from mom, dad, little sister Suzie, and Spot the goldfish. I wouldn't even know this was the right number, because I hadn't heard my client's name yet. I was in a hurry, so my solution was simple – I hung up! I simply called someone else for the shoot.

Your contact line is as important as your résumé – keep it businesslike.

Especially in their early years in the business, performers move around a lot. It is very frustrating to spend time making sure everyone has the latest number, only to hear that an agent has still been using the old résumé and is annoyed because you can't be reached. If you change apartments a lot, think about a phone service or a pager. You'll avoid wasted time and lost tempers. Yours and theirs.

Answering services are expensive, from five hundred dollars a year, but their phone number becomes your professional number. (You can have them pick up your home phone for you, but then you've just got an expensive answering machine.) Your callers get a human voice, but of course you are relying on the human taking down messages accurately. The most useful services will search for you if the message is urgent, and if you've told them where you may be.

 A pager is probably one of the best investments you can make in your career. Whether you purchase or rent, you need never miss a call for work again.

Pagers come in all flavours, but they are basically the same. Your caller has a telephone number for you which is answered by a machine. Some sort of message is then sent to a tiny receiver you are carrying, wherever you are. It can be just a signal to let you know you had a call, or the recorded message from your caller, or a written message on a little screen.

Because you use the pager company's number as your contact, it doesn't matter how often you move or how reliable other people are. Because the message is passed on immediately, your caller doesn't have to wait for a reply until you get around to calling your machine or service. A pager allows you the freedom to move about and still receive those urgent calls within seconds.

Use the pager number as your professional contact. If you are at home when the agent or casting director calls, you will call back in seconds; if not, you will still be in touch promptly, and it's only taken one call to contact you. If your home number is the first contact number, and you're away from the phone, a second call would be necessary. And there may be no chance to make it.

Your family or roommates will be pleased not to be woken by your early-morning emergency calls, and you will have a chance to wake up between the pager's beeper and talking to the agent or casting director.

Your pager number is for professional and emergency calls only. Don't pass it on to friends and family unless they can be trusted to use it only for urgent calls, and only after trying you at home. When your pager goes off, you need to be sure that you won't be struggling to a phone just to hear family gossip.

Get into the habit of carrying your pager everywhere. It does no harm to have it on the counter when you shower, or in the convenience store when you're buying milk, and one day the new habit will save your life. Or at least get you that plum job.

There's nothing worse than being in the middle of shooting a very intense and dramatic scene and suddenly, "BEEP-BEEP-BEEP." Your pager went off. Besides distracting everyone on set, the noise will mean reshooting the entire  scene (or your being thrown off the set). Look for the Vibrate feature, with which the pager replaces its beeping with a short, silent vibration which you will feel. If the unit is small enough, you can even hide it in your back pocket or socks and receive notification of calls while actually on set. At night, simply  switch the

pager back to regular Beep mode to wake you if someone calls
asleep.

Which brings us to a cunning plan: if your call time is ve
morning, arrange with a friend to call your pager when it's time t
way you can use the pager as a secondary alarm clock, and not w...
hold with the telephone bell.

You'll have to choose whether to buy or rent a pager. When you buy a
pager, the unit belongs to you and you pay for monthly air time, insurance, maintenance and repairs. When you rent, everything is included in the monthly rental
charges. Shop around for the best deal.

Pagers range from the most basic beeper, to phone number display, to the
sophisticated message display. Let's start with the fanciest (and most expensive):

**Message display:** As small as a credit card, these pagers have a miniature
screen to display your caller's message. They're great machines for use in the
industry as long as you don't mind the much higher costs involved.

**Phone number display:** When someone phones your pager, they use
their touchtone phone to key in their own phone number, which is displayed on a
tiny screen on your pager. The biggest drawback to this system is that, although
you know what phone number to call back, you don't necessarily know who's trying to call you. You'll recognise your agents' numbers, and those of casting directors' offices, but what if your caller is using the phone at a production office?
Since it can be very embarrassing to have to say you're phoning but you don't
know why, this is not a good paging system for this industry.

**Audible voice:** This type of pager is a disaster for us. When your pager
number is phoned, the caller leaves a voice message, which is then heard over a
built-in speaker in your unit. The unit is larger and the quality of the sound is
often very poor. If you are in a high noise area, chances are that the entire message won't be audible. If you are on set and the pager goes off in the middle of a
shoot, the production will not be very pleased. Stay away from this style, no matter what sort of bargain you're offered!

**Basic pagers:** No fancy displays, bells, whistles, or expensive gadgetry,
just the service you need. When someone calls your pager, they leave a short
voice message on the company's machine. You're warned, by the pager's beep
or vibration, that someone wants to get in touch. You call the pager number and
retrieve the message, then phone your caller if necessary. By hearing the voice,
you know who is calling, and they can tell you exactly where they can be
reached. Perhaps you are just waiting to get your call time and location, in
which case the details can be left on your pager without the need for a return
call. The greatest advantage of a basic system is the low cost. The disadvantage
is that it will take two calls (and two pay phone charges if you're on the road) to
retrieve the message and return the call, if the brief message isn't enough information.

The basic model has been my choice for many years and has served me well. Unless you find yourself on a lot of sets without nearby payphones, the higher cost of a display pager won't be worthwhile. If you're renting a pager, most companies willingly let you upgrade if you find the added features are really needed.

A few more things to think about before making your pager decision:

**Size:** Shop around: pagers of different makes vary in size, even for units with similar features. The smaller the unit, provided you're not paying a lot extra, the easier it is to carry around with you, and to conceal while on set.

**Batteries:** No pager is any good if the battery is dead. If your pager runs on standard AA or AAA batteries, you can easily carry a spare set, or dash to the nearest store to pick up replacements. If you use rechargeable batteries, you can constantly have a spare set recharging at home, so that your stand-bys will always be fresh. Some pagers have built-in rechargeable batteries, which can be a pain if you forget to recharge the unit and can't replace the built-in batteries with a stand-by set.

**Insurance:** If you are renting a pager, your insurance will be included in your monthly rental. If you buy, it's a good idea to insure against loss and theft.

Pagers are not that expensive to purchase, but they are small enough to be easily lost or stolen. Insurance will cost you annually about a quarter or a fifth of the cost of a replacement unit. I guarantee you will lose your unit in four to five years, by carelessness or theft. Over that length of time, you come out even in cost, and you will never be without a pager if yours disappears when you're short of cash.

With rental units, if your pager is lost or stolen, you may be required to pay a portion of the replacement fee, but it will still work out to be much less than if you had to cover the entire price yourself (and most companies will credit your account should the pager turn up).

It's very trendy to have a fax machine, but you're unlikely to get much return for its cost. While you can send your stats to a casting director in a minute, you're probably better off in most cases going to the office and maybe having a chat.

If you really need to fax material, you may find that the local printing shop has a fax service for a dollar a page or so. There are even pay phones with fax machines being installed in some cities.

If you do decide to purchase or rent a fax machine, be sure to get a unit with a good grey scale for sending photos. Without this feature, most of your photos will come out very dark and blotchy. Of course, a halftone screen copy of your photo (where the picture has been broken down into dots) will give you a much better fax copy than a standard photo, and the receiving party will be much more impressed. (See the details in the "Photographs" chapter.)

No matter how good your pager is, it won't help unless you've brought it along. No matter how reliable your service is, they can't pass on your messages in time if you don't call them regularly. Your answering machine won't answer unless you turn it on. Being constantly available is an attitude of mind, not a bunch of equipment. Consider this scenario:

You're a success! The casting directors love you and you're getting direct calls as well as specific requests through your agents. You've been working long days, with only random days off, for three months. Your friends laugh, your mate leaves therapists' cards around.

You've been broken early from the latest set and suddenly you see sense. You deserve a break. Half-scared, you take the phone off the hook, turn off your pager, don't set the alarm, and go to bed. And sleep. And sleep.

After you've had your first proper night's sleep since who-knows-when, you stretch ... relax ... Now, you've enjoyed your ten hour holiday, but it really is time to get back to work. You start to make your calls to see what's up next.

The first agent you call is furious. A casting director has been trying to track you down all night for a small role in an even smaller production. It's not much, but it would have been your first real chance in a residual role. Everyone has been trying to reach you, but you disappeared off the face of the earth, so the call went to someone else. You blew it. You now have one disappointed casting director and one ticked-off agent.

It may not have led to anything, it may only have been a nice fee for an Actor role, but it may have been the first link in a chain. You'll never know. But it will always haunt you. It happened. To me. And yes, I still think about it and wonder.

# OFFICE SYSTEMS

Being an extra is running a business, however much you enjoy it, and you need to keep some sort of records. I don't think you can run any sort of business without knowing what sells and who's buying it. Revenue Canada agrees, and will refuse to allow you to deduct your expenses if you can't show them the paperwork.

The more you take responsibility for your own career, the more organised you have to be. You are your own publicity and research department: if you set up a system, you can be better informed and better prepared than anyone around you. (Except me.) You'll see which shows have been doing well – several seasons, big budget, etc. – and how well you've been doing on them. You'll be able to track trends in the local industry, if the early publicity turns into actual shoots – which is why you include rumours – and what the production quality turned out to be. By tracking who is casting what and the types of characters they tend to use, you'll always be one step ahead of the competition when the hunt begins for the perfect extra.

How much you do, and how you organize things, is up to you. I suggest you start with more organisation, to see what works for you, and then pare it down as the novelty wears off, until you have a level you can maintain. It is an invest-ment that pays off: my office is very organised but still I backslide and let things get out of date. When I do, I eventually discover I don't have the one fact I need desperately, and I waste more time catching up than I saved by slacking off.

You don't need a whole room or a truckload of office stuff, you don't need to spend much money at all. As long as you have a phone and a flat surface, you're in business. I'll tell you about my office – use what sounds useful, adapt my ideas so they'll work for you.

I've got a worksurface. It's not full desk size, but it's got a light, it's not used for anything else, and it's big enough to lay out what I'm working on. There are a couple of In/Out trays to keep things tidy, and an ordinary telephone. There are two drawers, one for supplies and one for inactive files.

This is the way my file system works: I have my work diary, a tiny address book, a card index of productions in town, a card index of my profession-al contacts, a large calendar for my days on set and promotion activity, folders for stuff, a binder for my Call Sheets, an accordion file for my income and expenses, and a stout cardboard box in the basement for archives.

**I carry the work diary everywhere.** I don't bother with the expensive refillable type, I buy the cheapest durable one I can find, and then store it in the archive box at the end of the year. It's small enough to fit in a breast pocket, but with one day per page so there's plenty of room for notes.

**144**

I use the space to schedule days for doing the rounds (and make notes of the results), to jot down new contacts, and the air date of shows which need to be taped. When I get home, I transfer these notes to the appropriate files. When I'm going on set, I copy all the details of the shoot from my own Call Sheet into my diary, as well as onto an index card. It's belt and suspenders time. I write down my expenses (bus fare, pay phone calls, etc.), and leave a space for the date I got paid, how much it was, and how much commission. When the money actually arrives, I'll fill in the details and then I can easily see which payments are missing and need to be followed up.

**The mini address book lives in my wallet.** Small, under a buck from a variety store, this is a business contact book. It has my regular contacts: agents, casting, printers, unions, regular show contacts, etc. No research in here: this is the names and numbers of the fifty people my career is built around. In an emergency, I don't want to have to rely on memory.

**Production index cards** are 3 x 5 index cards in a box with a set of A-Z dividers. You could use the bigger size cards and box, but they're cumbersome. I use white, lined cards but you could use coloured cards for different categories (Features, TV Series, MOW, etc.). I file, alphabetically by name of the production, everything shot in my area, one show per card. When I hear rumours about an upcoming show, I make a card. I add more news as it turns up, and when the show is confirmed I'm right on the ball.

On the front of the card, I list the show name, the production company, address and phone number, type of show, shooting dates or season starts and ends, and the casting contact name for both principals and extras.

---

TV SERIES *(Jun–Sept '94) (Apr–Dec '95)*

**"AREN'T I GREAT"**
Big Time Prod. Inc.
9876 Downtown Blvd. Studio B
My Town, Ont. A1B 2C3

(416) 555-0000 (Bus)
(416) 555-1111 (Fax)

PRINCIPAL CASTING: SHIRLEY M.
EXTRAS CASTING : HIDDEN CASTING (416) 555-8989

---

The flipside is for the details: days worked on the set, characters, contacts, review or article references, problems, etc..

---

TV Series Lead: Johnny Wonderful

Period: Late 60's, lots of Hippie & psychedelic clothes

Some studio shooting, mostly outdoors

Worked: *June '95 (4 days) Beach Bum (continuity).*
*July 12 '95 (hobo), Aug '95-?? (regular: Ice Cream Man)*

Contacts: PJ (Sound) – hates sole platform shoes, bring sticky pads for bottoms
Barbie (Wardrobe) – loves my blue tie-dye poncho for each episode
Fred Trying (Extra) 416 555-2288 – bright red hair, called in often as cop. Also works a lot on "Bargain Basement" series

---

When a show is completely finished and won't be returning, for another season or more episodes, I take a highlighter and draw a diagonal line across the front of the card. Use a highlighter, not a marker, because you may still want some of the information for future reference and don't want to obliterate the details. You may want to shift these "complete" cards to the rear of the box to make finding current productions easier.

**Contact index cards** live in a second box with a set of blank dividers labelled Casting, Other Extras, Printing Houses, Agencies, etc. This doesn't duplicate the address book, because that's the place to find someone's number if you know their name. This index file is for contacts, both established and new introductions: your main contacts, but also anyone who might turn out to be useful. Use an Agency section for comments on agencies and what your agent(s) said when you called them, and one for which casting directors have used you, your impressions, and the word on the street.

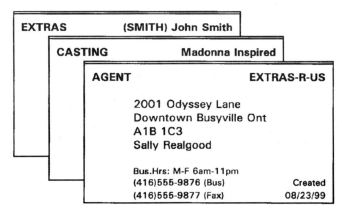

I usually limit the front o[...] he category, name of the person or company and specific contact per[...] nd phone numbers (including fax or other means of communication), and the date the card was first made.

The back is the place to make detailed notes (where and when you met, specific contacts within each company's entry, etc.) and to attach business cards.

**An appointment calendar** gives me the general picture, a month at a time. When I'm called for a shoot, I enter just the name of the show and call time: all the fiddly details are in the Work Diary and call sheets. If I can see the slow times for the month at a glance, it's easier to schedule days to do my legwork.

**Production schedule calendar** uses the start and end date information from the production index cards, and makes a visual listing of all the shoots in the area. This chart lives on the wall behind my desk to remind me what busy and slow periods are coming up. With this chart, you'll also be able to track shows about to end, which you haven't appeared on yet. It may be time to check in with your agents or with Casting to see if there's a spot for you before the show is finished.

| CAT | SHOW | Jan | Feb | Mar | Apr | May | Jun | Jul | Aug | Sep | Oct | Nov | Dec |
|---|---|---|---|---|---|---|---|---|---|---|---|---|---|
| F | Aren't I Great | 7... | ... | ...15 | | | | | | | | | |
| F | Keep On Tryin' | | | 16... | ......14 | | | | | | | | |
| TV | Risk Takers | 20... | ... | ... | ... | ... | ... | ... | | | | | |
| TV | The Extras | ... | ... | ... | ... | ... | ... | ... | ... | | | | |
| MOW | Pipe Dreams | | | | | 18... | ...12 | | | | | | |
| | | Rumoured Productions | | | | | | | | | | | |
| ⊦ | Do It Now | | ... | ... | ... | | | | | | | | |
| F | Big Budget | | | ...... | ...... | | | | | | | | |
| TV | The Taxpert | | ... | ... | ... | ... | | | | | | | |
| Category Legend | | | | | | | | | | | | | |
| **F** Feature - **TV** TV Series - **MOW** Movie of Week - **MS** Miniseries - **X** Other - **?** Unknown | | | | | | | | | | | | | |

**My tax files** are in a letter-size one-year accordion file. Each section holds the pay stubs and contract vouchers for a month, with the receipts of expenses incurred for each shoot attached to the actual vouchers. I find that's the best way to organize and track my yearly income, but you can file your vouchers by date and keep your receipts sorted by category in an accordion folder with blank divisions. (Look at the "Taxes" chapter and its Worksheets for the Taxpert's suggestions. He wants me to say the *Canadian Performers' Tax Kit* is nearly as cheap as an accordion file.) If you want to keep a Daily Journal of expenses and income, you can easily set up a cheap ledger with the help of a tax preparer who has experience with self-employed performers.

**A call sheet binder** keeps my call sheets filed in reverse chronological order (earliest first). Use whatever order seems logical: alphabetically by show name or grouped under production company or casting director. Until I've been paid, my call sheets go at the front of the binder; when the money comes in, I complete the call sheet, copy the final details to my work diary and refile the call sheet in its proper place by date. "Do you file your old gum wrappers?" I hear you say. Believe it or not, your schedule can be so busy that you'll lose track of what you've done. I've often had to go back through my old call sheets to see if I've been on a show or not.

**Letter size file folders** organize everything from newspaper clippings to the year's pay stubs. You will need a good supply of them: fortunately they recycle well.

**Blank videotapes** disappear. I try to keep plenty on hand for taping new shows, but I still dash around in a panic five minutes before a show airs to find a tape to record over. The hassle can be worthwhile: I recently received an audition call for a principal role on the series *Tekwars*. In the script, my character was to use the "VR set," so I pulled out my tape of two episodes I had recorded for future reference, and did a quick study of the VR effects and the way the actors used it. I was the only person auditioning who even knew what the Tekwar VR system was. I got the role, and was declared the first official "Tekie."

**Photo and résumé trays** are a better bet than keeping them in file folders. Storing your stock on the desktop makes for handier access, and helps you see when your stock is getting low.

The supplies drawer has all the stuff kids love to pinch from their parent's desk at work: stamps, paper, pens, paperclips, stapler and remover, large envelopes, letter-size envelopes, tape, ruler, memo and message pads, calculator, and in my case little paper dots from making binder paper, and a plastic lid of foreign coins.

And that's it.

What, no computer? Well, yes, I have a computer. Is it necessary? No. There is nothing you can do on a computer you can't do with a pencil and paper. A computer does things quickly, it does them neatly, and it can give you answers, if you know enough to ask the right questions. It will not write things down for you, or read them for you later on. It will not make decisions for you, it will not solve your problems. A used machine for about six or seven hundred bucks, with a good dot-matrix printer, is the most you need. If you want to pay more, you can play music and shoot down aliens in 64,000 colours. For much less, you can buy a typewriter to turn out the letters you want and a calculator to add up your tax deductions.

Here's your list for the stationer's. Or the thrift store.

2 (3x5) Index boxes
3x5 Index Cards – lined, white and coloured
Set of A-Z dividers, couple packs of blank dividers
Work diary
Monthly calendar
Personal address book
(Accounting ledger)
Letter-size file folders
One-year accordion file
3-ring binder
Blank videotapes
3 Trays
Paper, pens
Paperclips
Stapler and remover
Large and small envelopes
Tape, ruler
Memo and message pads
Calculator
Aspirin

# LEGWORK

Good agents will always be on the lookout for new productions so they can prepare themselves for coming casting demands. They make their commission by finding the work and getting you on set. You pay them to maintain contact with casting directors and submit you for suitable characters.

If you decide not to have an agent, to go freelance, you will have to search for your own film work. Casting directors won't usually have enough reason or time to contact you directly. Why should they, when with one call to an agent they can get twenty or thirty people for their shoot? Unless you've got something they really want, you'll find that freelancing is very difficult.

It's weird to spend more time researching than you do on set, and stupid to sit at home just waiting for the phone to ring. Fortunately, there's a lot of room between the two extremes. You can find your own way of working, but don't take the easy way out and rely on your agent to do all the legwork for you.

At the beginning, you may feel that it's sensible to depend on an agent. If you freelance, you will have to approach extras casting directors on your own, but most will not have time to deal with individuals, unless they know your work well. It would probably be wise to look for reliable extras agents, rather than have to hound casting personnel in search of work. With luck, the agents will get you enough work to keep you going for now. Their legwork will leave you more free time to concentrate on making a start on your own legwork, building your sources of information and becoming known and trusted.

Even at the beginning, your legwork will pay off. A good agent will appreciate it if you can update them on new sources of potential income. They'll likely be impressed that you can trace some work and save them time. (The lazier agents will just thank you and wait for casting directors to call them.)

Don't get discouraged. Legwork is hard, especially at the start, and it's unpopular with extras who feel they should being doing more but never get around to it. If you stick with it, it does get easier, and it does pay off. You'll always be a few steps ahead of those who have no idea about what is happening in the industry. Other extras will be much more ready to share their insights and dis-

coveries on set if you have valuable information to exchange.

TANSTAAFL – There Ain't No Such Thing As A Free Lunch: legwork requires organisation. Legwork requires a rigorous schedule. Legwork often requires running around to the point of exhaustion. Legwork is not always fun.

Legwork is an exercise in discipline. It's born of necessity; it keeps your career in shape, just as exercise keeps your body in peak health. With some help, you can work out a fitness program you can live with.

If you decide to work strictly as a freelance extra, you must have a stable network and a frame of mind that tracks possible work opportunities from any scrap of information you come across. You can train yourself to become not only your own agent, but also an indispensable reference source to other extras – and Casting itself.

Even if you use extras agents, you can't sit back and let them do all the work. The more you know about the industry you've chosen, the better prepared you'll be to get the jump on every available work call. If you want to be a professional, you need to know your craft, and part of the craft is getting the work. You can squeak by with just a minimum of legwork, but remember there are people willing to do much more than just the minimum. They will beat you out by keeping their careers just a little fitter. There's a lot of competition out there.

Let's look at your fitness regime. Basic information first: this is a daily chore, like a visit to the Y:

**Newspapers** are every researcher's starting point. Always check out the Entertainment section. Look for, clip out, label with the date and paper's name in the margin, and then file, anything remotely to do with the business. (Check the other side of the sheet before you cut: you may have to buy a second copy to get the clipping on the back.) Look for industry news, business happenings, show trends, reviews, public concerns about show contents, visiting celebrities, etc. You may even clip out ads for films which you know were shot in or near your city.

Next browse through the Business section. There are often articles about potential takeovers in sectors of the industry, and news of coming trends or new sophisticated technologies which might be used in our industry. Clip these out as well.

Finally, read the news and local news sections, for current events which could influence the business.

At the end of a week, you'll have an enormous and totally useless pile of odd-shaped clippings.

People have different ways of filing the material, and you will probably try a couple before you find one that works for you. Be warned that no method will save your knowing that there is a clipping that has the information you need, but it's not in the only place it could have been filed. Sort your clippings by current and future, by local and not, by film and television, by production companies, by type of programme, by casting director. Or by any combination that makes sense to you.

With this material, you will quickly have as much information as anybody you're likely to talk to, so you can keep your end up in informative discussions, and even start sensible discussion of areas where you feel ignorant.

Talk show hosts don't really know a lot about their guests: they have research teams who feed them the things that their guests are happy to talk about. If you know that a director was just honoured, or a casting director got the new series, you'll have the evidence that will persuade them you are fascinated by their career.

The material you collect will show you trends before they're common knowledge, and allow you to check on things you remember that other people deny. I'm amazed at how often I refer to articles I clipped three years ago.

**Television** is worth watching, if you treat it as part of the job. Unfortunately, most background performers watch only shows they enjoy or shows where they suspect they might turn up on screen. Don't stop watching for pleasure, but note the types of background characters used, and how they are used. Get the name of the extras casting director from the end credits.

Tape at least two episodes of any show filmed in your area, even if you don't like it. You may spot a trend in the looks the casting department uses the most. "Punk" for one casting director might mean people with shaved heads, another might look for colourful spiked hairdos, and still another might use average-looking unshaven people with leather jackets. That doesn't necessarily mean they're not using all three types, but you'll soon spot the looks they seem to prefer.

A change in extras casting director late in the season may mean a new way of using background performers. Tape two more episodes if that happens.

Taping the shows will give you a general feeling for the premise of the show, the main characters, and how over the top the show is willing to go with the looks for the extras. I've often reviewed my tapes before going out on actual auditions, and landed many roles thanks to knowing the show's format.

Other information is important but changes less quickly. Here is a weekly check list:

**Hotlines** are the trendy service from forward-looking government departments, performer organizations and unions. If you are a member, or if you come across a hotline number, use it. Check it regularly, and write down the names of all the shoots. Make an index card for each show and file it in your Production Index Box. Any information you hear about the show, especially on set, will go on the back of the card later.

**Doing the Rounds** used to be part of every actor's life. They would spend hours every day going to the offices of casting directors to see if there was any work. These days, we use the telephone. Call the office of the extras casting directors you know, once a week. Keep it brief! Leave a message saying you're simply checking in and you're free for work when needed. It's often best to call late in the afternoon or in the early evening, when they tend to be least busy.

Once a week will usually do unless they ask you to check in again that day or later in the week. If you speak to the casting director, rather than an assistant, keep conversation to a minimum. You want to become a visible part of the casting scene, not a blot on the landscape.

**Build your network.** If you have a day off set, touch base with one or two other extras. See if they've been working that week. If they have, collect any information you can about the show, the types of characters used, and the working atmosphere. Whether they have any information for you or not, fill them in on any shoots you've done, and any rumoured productions you've heard about coming in.

No, this isn't commercialising your friendship. What do hunters talk about over the campfire at night? Game trails and the newest ammunition.

Other legwork opportunities come up at longer intervals. Keep your eyes open for these:

**Magazines** will seldom have the latest news, but they often have stuff  you missed first time out, and informed discussion of interesting developments. Pick up the latest issues of the various general film and entertainment magazines. Read about the happenings everywhere, not just in your area. Look for specialty magazines as well, those geared to an specialized readership rather than general news and gossip. Publications like *Variety* will often include coverage of the main shows shot in each city. Background performers in Canada should check out how the Canadian shows are doing in the US ratings. When you see a show making an impact, pay attention. What kind of show is it, who cast it, is it or will it be shooting more episodes or sequels here? How can you become a useful character type for them? Who on your contacts list would be pleased to hear you've noted their success?

*Variety* often releases specialty issues. Grab these ASAP! They can pro-  vide a wealth of information, including occasional listings of every production shot world-wide, broken down by city, state or province, and country. See if you can spot the type of production a city specializes in, and how busy your neighbours are in comparison with your own territory.

**A workgroup** is a way of networking with your colleagues. If you feel comfortable with some of the other extras you meet on set, arrange a little workgroup to get together about once a month. An hour or two should do. Don't make it anything fancy, maybe just a little gathering at each other's houses in turn for discussion and encouragement, and sharing information. Keep the numbers small (from three to eight people): you don't want a big, formal meeting. If you prefer, arrange to meet at a local coffee shop. A bar is not such a great place: concentration may suffer, and the evening may turn into one long bitching session.

Just like networking chats with friends, this is people with si
ests talking over things that concern them all. You don't have tc
Discussion Group or a Working Seminar, just "Would you like to come over
Tuesday? I'm having a few friends in." It doesn't have to be presented as the first
of a regular series of professional work groups, but if you give it a chance, that
may grow out of the early get-togethers. Doing extra work can be very frustrating
at times, and these groups can keep everyone's spirits up, especially during the
slow times.

**Books** are still the most concentrated form of knowledge. You can never
learn enough about this industry: try to pick up a new book every month or so.
Highlight any areas that jump out at you, for later re-reading. You've made a good
start at building a library with this book. You may have to buy a second copy, if
you're in the habit of lending books. Do me a favour, give the other extras a brief
glance through it on set, then tell them to buy their own copy. *The Actor's Survival
Kit* is a good source of the how's and whys of principal work. I've had my copy
for a couple of years and still religiously read it every couple of months.

Don't limit yourself to books on acting. Pick up material on everything
from hair to lifestyles through the ages (for any shoots representing a specific year
or era) to a beginner's book on film lighting.

If you're fortunate enough to have a specialty bookstore in your city,
you're in for a real feast. Here in Toronto, I can spend an entire afternoon just
drooling over all the material at Theatrebooks. People in this sort of store, and certainly at Theatrebooks, really know their stock and are very helpful when you are
looking for good material on any facet of the industry. Note the publishers and
write for their catalogues.

Public libraries are buying fewer specialty books nowadays, but your
city's main library, if not your local branch, should have an Arts and Entertainment section. Look around 780 and 790 in the Dewey Decimal listings. Even
film biographies can give you some information, if you can sift out the useful
facts from the hype and hypocrisy. Remember, any branch can get you almost
any book, if you have the author and the correct title, through Inter-Library
Loan.

**Thrift stores** are the best source for the outdated fashions and bizarre
accessories we need for our wardrobe stock. Make it a habit (no pun intended) to
do the rounds of all the shops in your area. You never know when you'll come
across something perfect for the set.

**Industry organisations,** performer unions and clubs, are worth a monthly visit, if you're a member, just to check out the bulletin boards or to pick up the
latest brochures of classes. Schmooze with the staff while you're there: they know
more than you could imagine, and will share their information.

**Photos and résumés** need a careful examination every so often. You're
seeing more résumés now; does yours still look good? Is it up to date? Is yours a

**154**

good photo? Does it still look like you? Be sure you have plenty of stock, and be sure it reaches your contacts.

Be careful about handing out your material to someone you don't really know. Give your photos and résumés to people who can help, people respected by other extras and casting directors. It's expensive to distribute shots and stats to the world, because it's unlikely to pay off. And remember the crazies.

**Photo books and talent banks** may be worth joining, but they are not all useful, and maybe not all entirely legitimate. Let's just say some are heavily-promoted expensive failures.

ACTRA and other unions have directories of small photos of their members. Different versions feature extras, performers, and visible and audible minority performers. These aren't expensive to be in and, since they're distributed to producers and casting people, you're making at least a tiny contact with a whole lot of people. Other organisations have similar directories, which are also used regularly by casting people, but which have different qualifications for entry. Ask people what they subscribe to. It seems certain that casting people looking for a special type do flick through these directories, waiting for someone to pop off the page. You'll have to take them on trust to some extent: it's difficult to be sure that your entry in the book got you a piece of casting.

Normally, extras agents cover the cost of the regular casting books they supply to casting directors. If you are asked to pay more to be in a "private roster catalogue," you are allowed to wonder why. "International" photo publications, promising to display your photo to directors across Canada and the States, aren't likely to be useful to you. At best they are for main roles: it's not likely you'll be called in across the country for a day of extra work. Frankly, many are little more than get-rich-quick scams.

Computer casting services haven't taken off, despite serious and sincere efforts. Some agents and casting directors, realizing the time-saving features, try to maintain their own systems. I programmed my own system when I ran the agency, and learned how to express what I wanted in terms the database could handle. Up till now, computer systems can only narrow down selections. If the system is being used by casting departments and as long as the fee is reasonable, it's often worth signing on. It may put you on a short casting list.

Talent Banks are maintained by the CBC and other large producers. The banks are a larger version of the in-house casting department's performer files, made accessible to outsiders. Typically, performers are invited to update their own files, the records are occasionally used by in-house casting, and small producers are allowed to search the files when they're casting. Since they rarely charge anything, it's worth keeping your file up to date, however small the chance of a casting hit.

**Trend analysis** sounds like something a multinational corporation does. Well, it is: how do you think they got to be so big? You can get a start on what is going to happen, rather than joining the great majority, who are still catching up with what was true yesterday.

The best time to study new shows is at the start of the television season and when mid-season replacements air. Watch for minor shifts in the types of shows being produced. When one show becomes a hit, sure enough a dozen clones will follow. Individual shows will change style, the humour becoming broader, exteriors being dropped for studio work. The overall picture changes, too, from sitcoms to sci-fi to reality-based to prime time soaps. Watch the trend and figure out where you can fit into the picture.

Being able to talk about the things that agents and casting people deal with routinely makes you different from most actors, and makes you part of the in-group.

**Talk and listen.** We have talked about the networking you can be part of every working day. The group may be chatting and bitching and boasting, but you can also be tucking away facts for your files.

Listen to the crew. They often work on more than one set at a time, and obviously know about new productions way before the show begins filming. They can be your best source of inside information: I've received many leads from them that have been profitable. Another reason not to tick them off.

**A helping hand.** I'm often called by casting directors just to see if I can think of anyone good for a role. Sometimes I come up with a suggestion, sometimes I don't, but they respect my judgement and know I keep tabs on other extras. You won't be in this position for a while, but if the opportunity offers itself, recommend someone else for a job. Maybe you're calling by the casting director's office and get a couple of minutes to chat. Talk about other people, not just yourself. At the agency, if they're listing people for a category, tell a flattering story about someone you know who would be suitable. You're not auditioning for the directors' or agents' jobs, you're showing you have some of their skills, skills they admire in other people.

**The appointment calendar** will keep you on track. Plan when you're going to check out the union office, know when you last visited the casting director. If you get called to set, and have to put off a piece of legwork, mark in a new day for the event right away so you don't forget about it. Don't reschedule it too far in the future, or it'll never get done. Seeing the schedule in front of you will help you to get the work done when you know you should. Weekends are often days off for productions, so you can do some filing then, reserving your weekdays off for the casting director, agent, library, bookstore rounds.

**The production calendar** will give you the broad production picture, but only if you keep it up to date. It can help you see busy work periods coming up, so you can clear the decks ahead of time. It can force you to find out why you're not getting more work when there is more work out there.

If you're doing all that basic stuff, you're ready to start looking for d opportunities. First the casting directors:

**Be brief.** Their time is valuable. Don't ramble on about the your quest for stardom: they simply haven't got time for chit-chat. Cut to the chase. What have you got that will be useful to them? Use your files to see what they're working on, what they will be most interested in.

**Your résumé and photo** (8x10 B/W only) should be at hand every time you meet with them. Be sure your name and number is on both pieces. They receive a lot of unsolicited photos and have little time to sort them all into any real order. If your photo does become separated from the résumé, you want to be sure they still have a way to contact you. You may even want to include your stats right on the back.

**They aren't agents,** so they have very little reason to keep track of ten thousand photos and résumés. Your material will be filed in the garbage, sooner or later. Bring copies every time you visit, and leave them every time you meet.

In the normal run of casting, it is much easier for them to browse through the roster books provided by the agents, rather than search through a stack of loose sheets. You are hoping your material will still be on the desk, or at least fresh in the memory, when an unusual problem surfaces.

**Don't hound them!** They have important business to keep them occupied. Why should they worry about whether or not you're available for work? They don't even need you right now. It won't take long for them to get fed up with all the interruptions if you call them every day.

Say there are three thousand extras in your area (probably a very low figure). Ten percent of them (three hundred people) decide to phone in for work today. Each call takes at least thirty seconds, plus time for them to regain their train of thought before they were interrupted. With three hundred calls in a day, they lose over three hours answering calls from extras. Given their busy phone lines, that's three hours with someone else on hold, very possibly the production office itself.

**Read their voice** when they answer the phone. If they sound rushed, then you've called at a bad time. Make your call shorter than short!

**Call at a reasonable time.** I know a casting director who got a call from an extra on the weekend at 3 a.m. That extra even had the nerve to ramble on for a good ten minutes. Not improving his casting odds.

**If they work from home,** just leave your stats in their mailbox. They don't need a flock of people beating a trail to their door every day. Some casting directors detest extras disturbing them at home, so be sure that leaving your package is acceptable. You may have to mail your material to them, or to the production office for their attention.

**On sets,** you should always carry your photo and updated résumé, ready to give casting directors, to be sure they always have your most recent stats.

**Don't be pushy, don't be shy.** The casting director will know who you are, if you have a good agent and you're professional on set. They will take you seriously, if you behave as if you know your business and understand theirs.

You could approach the productions directly, but to what purpose? The whole reason they hired an extras casting director was to field all the background performers. Trying to bypass the casting people is like saying they don't know their job well enough or simply aren't important. If you don't know who is casting the extras, call the office and just ask for the name of the person you should submit your material to.

Most film and television production companies have an outside extras casting director come in to supply all the background talent. If the casting directors know you, there's no reason to make the rounds to each production. Any information you drop off at the production office will simply be sent to their extras casting director. There are usually only a few casting directors handling all the different productions, and no casting director wants a different set of your stats for each production they are handling.

One exception is productions running on a very low budget. They may not have hired the better-known casting directors you have been schmoozing, especially if they don't need much background talent. If this seems to be the case, from your research, then call and ask if you may stop by to leave your photo and résumé for the person in charge of booking background talent. If they insist there isn't any such person, thank them for their time and keep your ears open for changes.

# UNION MATTERS

When you sign performer union contracts, including extra vouchers, you are agreeing to obey the terms of the Agreement covering that sort of work. And so is your engager.

The Agreements the performer unions have negotiated with groups of engagers are enormously complicated, covering every turn of your professional life in detail. They're like the rules of baseball: everyone who plays should have a working knowledge of them, but when you get into trouble you need an umpire. In this case, the union. If the union makes a ruling and the engager disagrees, a grievance can be declared and judged by a committee of union and engager representatives.

Your obligations to your media performer union, on the other hand, are enormously simple. You may not perform for anyone, including theatre work, except under union rules. You may not work for a film or television engager who is not a signatory to a union Agreement (that is, who hasn't agreed to abide by the book of rules your contract refers to). You may not work for an engager the union has declared unfair, or who is being struck against.

The performer "unions" in Canada are moving toward full trade union status, from being professional associations, which do not have the legal powers granted trade unions. In Canada, the Status of the Artist legislation is making this possible, and will strengthen the performer's position in other ways. Work on film and television is regulated by ACTRA, ACTRA BC, UdA, and the newcomer UBCP, in Canada, and by SAG and AFTRA in the States. ACTRA has fought successfully for media artists in Canada, promoting Status of the Artist legislation, establishing minimum working conditions and rates, negotiating safety guidelines, etc. People are still treated unfairly, cheated of their due fees and worked dangerously hard and long, but that is very much the exception now, and not the rule.

This chapter is not a union primer – the best place to get up to date information and advice is your nearest performer union office. These paragraphs may give you a start; and you should look at the voucher and residual sections at the end.

Don't be in too much of a hurry to join any performer union: it may not be the right choice for you yet. You'll get the same advice from your local union office.

If you live in a small centre, with only occasional films coming through using the IPA, the productions will be set up to use local extras in simple crowd scenes, at rock-bottom cash rates. If you apply to join ACTRA, and become an

Apprentice, you'll be cut off from that work. Productions won't pay more money to hire you on an ACTRA voucher, and you aren't allowed by ACTRA to work as a cash extra once you have Apprentice membership.

If you are active in your local community theatre and join ACTRA to get better fees as an extra, you won't be able to work on stage except by joining Equity and working under an Equity contract, or by Equity's permission.

As a non-member, you can legitimately work as an extra on IPA sets, but once you're a performer union member, you may not perform for any non-union engager. Leaving a performer union isn't made easy. Being a member is like having a tattoo: it may seem like a good idea at the time, but it's the devil to get rid of if you decide it's not for you.

ACTRA is the oldest Canadian performer union, going back more than fifty years. It started as RATS (Radio Artists of Toronto Society) in the early 1940s and shortly after expanded to include Montreal, Winnipeg and Vancouver. In 1943, it became ACRA (the Association of Canadian Radio Artists), and later the Association of Canadian Radio and Television Artists, the Canadian Council of Authors and Artists, the Association of Canadian Television and Radio Artists, and in 1984, the Alliance of Canadian Cinema, Television and Radio Artists.

ACTRA is actually an alliance of Guilds. The Alliance itself is primarily concerned with lobbying and relations with performer organisations worldwide.

ACTRA Performers Guild (APG), which we call ACTRA in conversation, is a democratically organized, member-driven organization. There are ten autonomous branches located in major centres coast-to-coast. "Autonomous" means each branch runs its own affairs, including negotiating Agreements governing productions involving only its own members, for productions used only in its immediate area.

Members of each branch elect Branch Councillors, who handle local matters, and also Guild Councillors, who represent the branch on the National Council, which deals with policies affecting all members.

At all levels of ACTRA, members create policy and staff administers it. ACTRA continually negotiates collective Agreements with producers in all media performance areas. ACTRA staff, stewards and On-Site Liaison Officers (OSLOs) are available to enforce Agreements and resolve conflicts between performers and engagers.

The APG has reciprocal agreements with UdA, AEA, Canadian Equity, SAG and other performer unions, meaning they are pledged to co-operate on matters affecting each other's members. It also has formal and informal ties with other Canadian and international labour and arts organizations, and is affiliated with the Canadian Labour Congress (CLC) and the International Federation of Actors (FIA).

The ACTRA Fraternal Benefit Society administers a health insurance plan, funded by deductions from members' fees and contributions from engagers, to assist with medical and dental expenses, and life and injury insurance, and a Registered Retirement Savings Plan.

Membership in the ACTRA Performers Guild is open to any performer who has become an Apprentice Member and who:
- has six professional engagements (background work not included) under ACTRA jurisdiction, or
- for the disabled, and members of a visible, ethnic or audible minority, has three professional engagements (background work not included).

Performers who are members of performer unions, stage or screen, with reciprocal agreements, or who have assembled a recognized body of work, may also apply for membership based on professional reputation.

Here are the ACTRA Performers Guild offices and their areas of autonomy:

| | |
|---|---|
| **Vancouver**......... BC and Yukon | **Calgary** ............. Southern Alberta |
| **Edmonton**......... Southern Alberta | **Regina** ............... Saskatchewan |
| **Ottawa** .............. Eastern Ontario | **Toronto** ............. Southern Ontario |
| **Halifax** ............. Maritimes | **Montreal** .......... Quebec |
| **Winnipeg** .......... Manitoba, Northern Ontario | **St John's Nfld**... Newfoundland and Labrador |

The UdA (l'Union des Artistes) covers the francophone territory for film and stage work. Qualification for membership is very strict: you must prove you can function in French-speaking productions, and qualify with thirty work permits. The UdA holds reciprocal agreements with both ACTRA (for film and television productions) and Canadian Equity (for stage productions in Canada).

UBCP (The Union of British Columbia Performers) split off from ACTRA BC in 1990 and was supported partly as a protest against ACTRA's being based in, "and run by," Toronto. UBCP sat down with local and American engagers to work out a new Agreement, more attractive to them. With a higher session fee, but lower residual payments, it appealed to American producers. Solid information was hard to come by, but that didn't stop the rumour mill. The Teamsters were involved with the UBCP, which heated up the arguments. Battles started on many fronts for control of the region. Money in the high six figures was spent by both sides. Lawyers beamed.

As we write, immediately before this book's release, years of accusation, lawsuits, political twisting and turning, negotiation, voting and third party mediation have finally come to a plateau. We hope they have come to an end.

**161**

    UBCP has jurisdiction over the recorded media in BC and Yukon (score one for UBCP). If all goes as agreed, they will join the national ACTRA Performers Guild as another autonomous branch/local union (score one for ACTRA). This means they will have to use the ACTRA National Agreements (score another one for ACTRA). But UBCP's existing Agreements "must" legally run until they expire (score a big one for UBCP). UBCP would also have to break formal ties with the Teamsters (uh huh).

    And so it goes on. At the moment, if you're in BC, you're under UBCP. Whatever that means, as the two unions and various levels of law and government hack at each other. Frankly, if you're in BC and doing your research properly, you should know more than we do, relying on our network here in Toronto and three thousand miles away. Check with your local performer union branch to find out the latest.

Also at this time, SAG and AFTRA, the two American film and television performer unions, are in the late stages of joining together. This has been in process for some years, and the complications aren't worked out yet. When it will be finished, and what shape the new union will have, is just guesswork. Contact your closest office and ask for the latest official news.

The American Federation of Television and Radio Artists (AFTRA) covers performance in the taped media, including TV and radio commercials, drama and features. It has open membership – if you pay the initiation fee and annual dues, you're a member. Presumably, when SAG and AFTRA join, AFTRA members will automatically be full members of SAG, which is currently more difficult to join. The union is a national federation of "locals," each serving its own area. Here's a list of cities with AFTRA locals:

| | | |
|---|---|---|
| Albany | Fresno | Philadelphia |
| Atlanta | Hawaii | Phoenix |
| Bethesda | Houston | Pittsburgh |
| (Washington/Baltimore) | Kansas City | Portland OR |
| Boston | Los Angeles | Rochester |
| Buffalo | Miami | Sacramento |
| Chicago | Minneapolis | St Louis |
| Cincinnati (Tristate) | (Twin Cities) | San Diego |
| Cleveland | Nashville | San Francisco |
| Dallas | New Orleans | Schenectady |
| Denver | New York | Seattle |
| Detroit | Omaha | Stamford CT |
| | Peoria | |

The Screen Actors Guild (SAG) covers performance recorded on film, including features, filmed television, filmed commercials and industrial shows. You can join if you are offered a SAG principal contract, if you've worked three days as an extra under SAG jurisdiction, or if you are a member of a sister union in the States, or of ACTRA. The union is based in Hollywood, naturally, with branch offices across the country. Check these cities' phonebooks for the current address and phone number:

| | | |
|---|---|---|
| Atlanta | Irving (Dallas) | Nashville |
| Boston | Miami (Florida) | New York |
| Chevy Chase | Honolulu (Hawaii) | Philadelphia |
| (Washington, DC) | Houston | Phoenix (Arizona) |
| Chicago | Lathrup Village | San Diego |
| Cleveland | (Detroit) | San Francisco |
| Denver | Minneapolis/St Paul | Seattle |

The Screen Extras Guild (SEG) has given up its jurisdiction to SAG. Apparently, the complex state laws governing extra work made its locals uneconomical to run. SAG has extras built into its Agreements, and its local branch will give you the details for your area.

RESIDUALS

Extras don't get residuals; the release on the back of your voucher allows the engager to use your piece of film for anything, forever. When you are upgraded to Actor or Principal categories, or to do a Stunt, you get residuals.

When you act on stage, the theatre pays the cast for its time, the audience pays for its ticket, and at the end of the run there's nothing left but to balance the books. In film and television, engagers pay for actors' time and end up with a filmed or taped product to sell around the world, again and again, sometimes for years. Residuals are fees paid for the right to use the product the actors helped make.

Residuals were first put in place, in Canada in the fifties, by ACTRA negotiators, when many production companies argued, "Why should we pay actors again for work they've already done?" It's an old, old song, heard in the States in 1960, when SAG won residual payments for feature films, and still heard in negotiations now.

In fact, residuals are simply compensation for the low pay initially received, if the production makes money. The actors are betting that the production will be a success by accepting lower pay with the understanding that, if the show is successful, they will receive a little additional payment.

## CONTRACTS

As Sam Goldwyn said, "A verbal contract ain't worth the paper it's w
verbal contract is in fact legally binding, but you'll never win a case based on anything but a written contract. Which in our case, except on television commercial
productions, is the extra voucher.

At some point during the day, usually when they arrive on set, non-union
extras are told whether they are on cash or voucher: union members are always on
voucher. In Canada on ACTRA Independent Production (IPA) sets, there are four
sorts of Extra contracts: blue ACTRA vouchers used for ACTRA members, green
Apprentice vouchers for people who have committed to the union, but who
haven't yet done enough work to qualify for full membership, yellow Permittee
vouchers, which entitle non-members to ACTRA rates when ACTRA quotas
aren't being filled with members, and Cash, which is what it sounds like.

The CBC uses cute pink forms, and commercials will hire you on a regular Commercials Agreement contract in various Extra performance categories, but
since the majority of our work is on Independent Productions, I'll concentrate on
those.

In Canada, ACTRA has agreed with the engagers that non-member extras
can work on ACTRA sets as Permittees with a yellow voucher and union rates,
less a permit fee. There is a quota of ACTRA members (including apprentices)
first in line for each day of Extra work on each production. The figures differ from
place to place, but let's take Toronto as an example. If a production hires fifteen
member and apprentice extras (on blue and green vouchers) for tomorrow's crowd
scene, they can hire as many non-members as they need that day, as cash extras
with no voucher. If there aren't fifteen ACTRA people available, the first twenty-
five extras must be made up of blue and green, plus yellow, permittee, vouchers.
Anyone after that can be a cash extra.

The extras casting director must give voucher priority to ACTRA members. Any permittee vouchers to make up the quota will then be distributed to non-
union extras. In Toronto, if a crowd scene has thirty extras, there might be ten
ACTRA members cast; then fifteen more extras will get yellow permittee vouchers and the larger union fee, and the final five get cash at the end of the day.

Sometimes the casting department will allow an agent to decide who gets
some of the vouchers. Since having a yellow voucher means you make more
money, extras are very keen to get one. The casting director rewards good agents
with more vouchers, and the good agents reward their favourite clients. If you're a
non-member, check with your agent when you're officially booked whether you'll
be on cash or voucher. Don't assume you'll be on voucher just because you were
last time: if there aren't enough for everyone, you'll have to settle for whatever
you get.

If you were promised a voucher by your agent, but are told on set that
you're on cash, don't make a scene. There's nothing the AD or casting person on

set can do about a misunderstanding between you and your agent. C
agent and pass the problem on: it was probably just a slip. If you l
problem like a grown-up, and don't whinge and accuse your agent of
off, you'll probably get first dibs on the next available voucher.

If you feel slighted by the idea of union members always ge
ers while you have settle for the lower cash call fee, remember union rules promo-
it members from accepting cash calls, even if they'd be welcome. This means if
there are no vouchers available, they can't accept the work. Productions don't hire
any more expensive member extras than they have to: if a day requires a hundred
or even a thousand extras, there may still only be fifteen blue and green vouchers.
All the rest of the roles are available for non-members, which means more work
opportunities, more opportunities for being featured.

Some non-member extras will not work on anything but voucher calls.
Fine, it's their loss. They may get a couple more vouchers in the long run, but
they'll also have lost a lot of chances for work and upgrades. Being a permittee
gets you a bigger fee, although you do have to wait for your cheque, and you do
have ACTRA Fraternal's deductions and your Work Permit to pay for (see the
"Taxes" chapter). Casting and agents know who is flexible, and who is greedy. A
cash call is not the end of the world. The union fought for better on-set conditions
for performers but by and large they are applied to everyone, including cash
extras.

Here's a member voucher to look at. Green and yellow vouchers aren't
that much different. You get the voucher at the start of the day, and you hang on to
it through thick and thin. At the end of the day you hand over the filled-in form to
the AD or casting person in charge of signing out. They countersign it, you leave
with your copy.

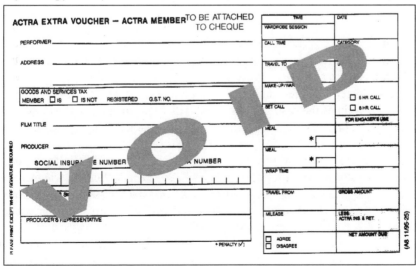

R    Simple: print your name here.

Where you want the cheque mailed (your own address or c/o your agent, etc.).

Your GST number here. If you aren't registered yet, check off the "is not" box.

FILM TITLE    The name of the show you're on. You can include the episode number if you know it offhand, but it's not a necessity. It makes it easier to track the fee.

PRODUCER    The name of the Production Company (e.g., Big Time Prod. Inc.)

S.I.N.    If you don't have your Social Insurance Number on hand, you had better make sure you phone it into the production's payroll service first thing in the morning. If they don't have your number, you won't be paid.

MEMBERSHIP NUMBER    Your ACTRA or Apprentice number here.

PERFORMER SIGNATURE    Sign your name here.

PRODUCER'S REPRESENTATIVE:    This is where the AD or casting person will sign.

NOTE: If substantials were provided (see the "On Set" chapter), write a large S/P at the bottom of the voucher. If none was brought in, but it was due, write "No Substantial Provided" with short explanation if required, e.g., "S/P in holding area, but didn't receive because I was on set. AD notified at time."

**Right hand column**

DATE    The date you started this session. If it's two in the morning, but you started last night at nine, you would put in last night's date.

CATEGORY    Either leave blank (for the person signing you out to fill in) or insert the proper category initials: GE (General Extra), SSE (Special Skills Extra), SI (Stand-In), PD (Photo Double). For wardrobe calls only, put WARD.

UPGRADE    This space is used to note any bumps or pay perks due, e.g. $5 for clothing changes over the requirement, and for upgrades to higher extra category, e.g. Special Skills. Upgrade to residual category means a new contract. Be sure any bumps or upgrades you expect are initialed by the production on your voucher.

RATE    For wardrobe calls, leave blank. Stand-Ins (SI) check off 8-hr box, all other extra categories check off the six hour box. The rate per hours doesn't change, just the minimum number of hours which must be paid. Your actual rate depends on Category. Check with the local union representative for the current rates.

FOR PRODUCER'S USE    Leave the rest of this column blank.

**Left hand column**

NOTE: You can use the 12-hour clock format, but the 24-hour clock (military time) is clearer and recommended (Midnight = 0000, 7:00 a.m. = 0700, Noon = 1200, 7:00 p.m. = 1900).

WARDROBE SESSION  For Wardrobe Session days only! Leave blank on regular shooting days.

CALL TIME  The time you were told to arrive.

TRAVEL TO  Used only for travel to distant locations. Check with the AD, casting, or union rep if you are to shoot beyond the city limits and are unsure if travel time is due.

MAKE-UP/WARDROBE CALL  Start and end time of your make-up and wardrobe call today. Either leave blank for the AD/Casting to fill out, or add up the time (including travel to and from their trailer, and time to change into and out of wardrobe) in 15-minute increments up to a one hour maximum. No matter when the process took place, list it as starting at your call time.

SET CALL  Leave blank for AD/Casting to fill, or insert the end time of the Make-Up/Wardrobe Call.

MEAL (first box)  Start and end time of the first meal break. Meal breaks must be within five hours of your call time if no substantial was available, or by the sixth hour after your call time if a substantial was provided. If you were broken for lunch later, check off the box marked "*" to indicate a meal penalty.

MEAL (second box)  Start and end time for second meal break. You will only need to fill in this box on really long shooting days. Check with the AD/Casting/Union rep on set if you think it's due.

WRAP  The time you are being signed out (usually in fifteen minute increments, but not always). Do not sign out until after you have changed, returned props and wardrobe, and removed the set make-up (if you don't intend to leave it on for your trip home).

TRAVEL FROM  Return travel time from distant location.

MILEAGE  Leave blank. Production fills it in when using TRAVEL TO/FROM.

AGREE/DISAGREE  Double check all the information has been filled out properly by both you and the AD. If it all is correct, check off and initial the "Agree" box. If something appears wrong, check with the person signing you out. If you still don't agree with them, simply check off the "Disagree" box. Don't start an argument with them. If either of you initialed the "Disagree" box, call your local ACTRA office in the morning and ask to speak to the Steward of that production. Fill them in on the situation so they have the information on file. Have the voucher handy when you call.

The person signing you out will give you one copy of the voucher, and the rest go to the production accounting office.

Your cheque should be mailed to you within fifteen calendar days. If you receive your pay and the information on the voucher was changed, call the ACTRA office. If the pay is simply wrong, call the production office and ask for Artist Payroll. If the cheque is late by more than a couple of days, contact your agent: it may have been sent there. If not, call Artist Payroll. Don't wait a month: the production may have closed its office by then. Tell them you did some extra work on such-a-such day, and you're calling to find out when the cheques were mailed out. These people are usually very friendly and supportive; they've helped me many times. If you seem to be spinning your wheels, contact your local ACTRA office, and speak to the Steward for that show. Voucher in hand, fill them in on the details.

One final note: did you ever read the back of your voucher? You've signed a small contract. Check it out. Scary stuff. And you're now one of the six people who have ever read it.

Cash sign-out sheets vary from production to production. The sheet will have a clause about the rights you've granted the production (read it before signing), and a place for your name, contact info, Social Insurance Number, how much you were paid, etc. The production keeps the copy, you get cash in hand at the end of the day.

# PRODUCTION PERSONNEL

This is a partial listing of production departments – actual production departments and positions may vary. You can see you're a small fish on a big pond.

| DEPARTMENT | POSITION |
|---|---|
| ACCOUNTING | PRODUCTION ACCOUNTANT<br>ASSISTANT ACCOUNTANT<br>ARTIST PAYROLL |
| ADs | 1st ASSISTANT DIRECTOR<br>2nd ASSISTANT DIRECTOR<br>3rd ASSISTANT DIRECTOR<br>TRAINEE ASSISTANT DIRECTOR (TAD) |
| ART DEPARTMENT | PRODUCTION DESIGNER<br>ART DIRECTOR<br>ASSISTANT ART DIRECTOR<br>ART DEPARTMENT TRAINEE |
| CAMERA | DIRECTOR OF PHOTOGRAPHY (DOP)<br>CAMERA OPERATOR<br>1st ASSISTANT CAMERA<br>2nd ASSISTANT CAMERA<br>CAMERA TRAINEE – CLAPPER LOADER<br>STILLS PHOTOGRAPHER |
| CASTING | PRINCIPAL CASTING DIRECTOR<br>EXTRAS CASTING DIRECTOR<br>CASTING AGENCY (Both of Above) |
| CRAFT SERVICE | CATERER<br>SUBSTANTIALS<br>HONEY WAGON |
| CONSTRUCTION | CONSTRUCTION COORDINATOR<br>HEAD CARPENTER<br>ASSISTANT HEAD CARPENTER<br>SET CONSTRUCTION TRAINEE<br>SCENIC PAINTER |
| CONTINUITY | CONTINUITY<br>SCRIPT SUPERVISOR |

**169**

| | |
|---|---|
| DIRECTORS | DIRECTOR |
| | DIRECTORS' PERSONAL ASSISTANT |
| | (DOP) DIRECTOR OF PHOTOGRAPHY |
| | 1st AD |
| | 2nd AD |
| | 3rd AD |
| | Trainee AD (TAD) |
| | |
| EFFECTS | DIRECTOR OF VISUAL EFFECTS |
| | VISUAL EFFECTS ARTIST |
| | EFFECTS ARTIST ASSISTANT |
| | SPECIAL EFFECTS |
| | PROSTHETICS |
| | SPFX WATER |
| | SPFX SMOKE |
| | |
| ELECTRICS | GAFFER |
| | BEST BOY |
| | ELECTRICIAN |
| | GENERATOR OPERATOR |
| | |
| GRIPS | KEY GRIP |
| | 2nd GRIP |
| | DOLLY GRIP |
| | CRANE GRIP |
| | GRIP |
| | |
| HAIR | HAIR STYLIST |
| | ASSISTANT HAIR STYLIST |
| | |
| LEGAL | DIRECTOR OF BUSINESS AFFAIRS and LEGAL |
| | ATTORNEY OF LEGAL AFFAIRS |
| | MANAGER MUSIC CLEARANCE |
| | |
| LOCATIONS | LOCATION MANAGER |
| | ASSISTANT LOCATION MANAGER |
| | LOCATIONS ASSISTANT |
| | LOCATIONS SCOUT |
| | STUDIO MANAGER |
| | SECURITY |
| | |
| MAKE-UP | MAKE-UP ARTIST |
| | ASSISTANT MAKE-UP ARTIST |
| | |
| MUSIC | COMPOSER |
| | ARRANGER |
| | STUDIO MUSICIANS |

**170**

| | |
|---|---|
| POST PRODUCTION | POST PRODUCTION SUPERVISOR |
| | POST PRODUCTION COORDINATOR |
| | POST PRODUCTION ASSISTANT |
| | SUPERVISING EDITOR |
| | EDITOR |
| | ASSISTANT EDITOR |
| | SOUND MIXER/RE-RECORDER |
| | SOUND SUPERVISING EDITOR |
| | SOUND EFFECTS RECORDER |
| | SOUND STUDIO MANAGER |
| | SOUND SCHEDULING |
| | |
| PRODUCERS | EXECUTIVE PRODUCER |
| | PRODUCER |
| | SUPERVISING PRODUCER |
| | |
| PRODUCTION DEPT. | LINE PRODUCER |
| | UNIT PRODUCTION MANAGER |
| | ASSISTANT PRODUCTION MANAGER |
| | PRODUCTION SUPERVISOR |
| | PRODUCTION COORDINATOR |
| | ASSISTANT COORDINATOR |
| | |
| PRODUCTION OFFICE | OFFICE PRODUCTION ASSISTANT |
| | RECEPTION |
| | |
| PROMOTIONS | DIRECTOR OF PUBLICITY |
| | DIRECTOR OF ADVERTISING and PROMOTION |
| | UNIT PUBLICITY |
| | |
| PROPS | PROPERTY MASTER |
| | ASSISTANT PROPERTY MASTER |
| | PROPS BUYER |
| | LEAD PROPS |
| | PROPS ASSISTANT |
| | |
| SAFETY | HEALTH and SAFETY OFFICERS |
| | ACTRA STEWARD |
| | ACTRA OSLO |
| | ETF |
| | PARAMEDICS |
| | AMBULANCE |
| | POLICE |
| | FIREMAN |
| | |
| SET DECORATING | SET DESIGNER |
| | HEAD SET BUYER |
| | SET BUYER |
| | SET DECORATOR |

|  |  |  |
|---|---|---|
| | LEAD SET DRESSER | |
| | SET DRESSER | |
| | TRAINEE SET DRESSER | |

SOUND          MIXER
                          BOOM OPERATOR
                          CABLE PULLER
                          PLAYBACK OPERATOR

SPECIAL:

| • AIRCRAFT | PILOT | • ANIMALS | TRAINER |
|---|---|---|---|
| | GROUND CREW | | WRANGLER |
| | FUEL TRUCK | | |
| | AIRCRAFT | | |
| | | | |
| • BOATS | OPERATORS | • HANDLERS | ANIMAL TRAINER |
| | CAM BOAT | | EXPLOSIVES |
| | SAFETY BOAT | | FIREARMS |
| | PICTURE BOATS | | |
| | DIVERS | | |

STORY                STORY COORDINATOR
                          WRITER
                          EXECUTIVE STORY EDITOR
                          STORY EDITOR
                          ASSISTANT TO STORY

STUNTS              STUNT COORDINATOR

TALENT              LEAD PRINCIPALS
                          GUEST STAR
                          PRINCIPALS
                          ACTORS
                          ANNOUNCER
                          HOST
                          CO-HOST
                          STUNT PERFORMER
                          STAND-INS (2nd Team)
                          VOCAL OR DIALOGUE COACH
                          SINGER
                          GROUP SINGER
                          CHOREOGRAPHER
                          DANCER
                          GROUP DANCER
                          CHORUS PERFORMER
                          PUPPETEER
                          SPECIALTY ACT

MODEL
BODY DOUBLE
PROSTHETICS MODEL
SPECIAL SKILLS EXTRA (SSE)
PHOTO DOUBLE (PD)
GENERAL EXTRA (GE)

TRANSPORT

TRANSPORT COORDINATOR
DRIVER CAPTAIN
HEAD DRIVER
PICTURE VEHICLE COORDINATOR
PICTURE VEHICLE DRIVER
DRIVERS:
INSERT CAR
CAMERA/SOUND TRUCK
CHAPMAN CRANE
FORKLIFT/CONDOR
PRODUCTION VAN
PROPERTY TRUCK
UTILITY TRUCK
SPECIAL F/X TRUCK
STATION WAGONS
MAXI VANS
CREW CABS
GAS TRUCK
MAKE-UP TRAILER
STAR WAGON
WARDROBE TRAILER
CAR TRAILER
WATER TRUCK
HONEY WAGON
ADDITIONAL GENERATOR
SCHOOL TRAILER
MOTOR HOMES
CAST TRAILER
AMBULANCE
PICTURE CARS

# TAXES

Like all the information in this book, this chapter is the result of experience and careful research. This chapter will help you with your tax return, but if you have any concerns, hire a professional tax preparer who has experience with self-employed performers.

This is advice for Canadians: the IRS has different rules. If you are filing a return in the States, call your union office to see if they have a VITA group.

In Canada everyone plays by the same rules for federal tax, but different provinces, Quebec particularly, have different provincial tax details.

When you work as an extra, even if you are paid in cash at the end of each day, you are a self-employed performer and you should declare your fees as professional income. You are not excused from paying tax and CPP, although lots of people remain uncaught for years. Certainly if you take extra work seriously, and if you are being paid on union vouchers, as a member or a permittee, you have no choice. It's not complicated, it needn't be expensive, and if you face up to it you won't have the ghostly fingers of "The Auditor" round your neck.

A regular store-front tax service will know little, if anything, about a performer's tax. They'll fill the form in with the information you give them: it will be cheap, and you may be perfectly satisfied. Their advice may not be accurate, they won't be able to advise you about missing deductions, and their assumptions may be wrong, so you should know a bit before you go in. If you know just a little bit, you may think it's worthwhile doing your own tax, getting the best deal you can, and not paying anyone else to fill in your form for you.

In a regular job, your employer deducts income tax, Unemployment Insurance and Canada Pension Plan contributions off your wages before you see them, and adds his own CPP contribution. The income tax is based on your gross income, with some tiny deductible expenses. Your employer reports your income to Revenue Canada (and to you) on a T4 in March. You settle up with the tax people by filing a return. Often you've had too much tax deducted, and get a refund after you file. You use a T1 General form, or a T1 Special if your return is really straightforward.

When you are self-employed, your engagers don't deduct UI premiums and you can't claim benefits based on your self-employed income. You have to pay your CPP premiums when you pay your tax – plus the other half, the employer's portion that's paid for you when you're employed. Engagers report your income on T4As – even if you don't get a T4A, the engager may have sent Revenue Canada their copy, so 'fess up, declare the income.

**174**

When you're self-employed, you're running a business, and you're taxed on your profit. Losses are allowed, and even expected in the early years. The important thing is that you are running a business with a reasonable expectation of profit, and that the expenses you claim come from carrying out the business.

You have to keep clear evidence of income and expenses, but formal bookkeeping isn't needed. Keep your paystubs, and ask your agent to give you a summary of the commission you paid at the end of the year. A work diary is a good idea, to note down things like pay phone costs, for which you can't get a receipt, and to show your level of professional activity.

It's best to keep all your receipts, to maximise your deductions, and to show you're only taking a proportion of something that is part business and part personal (like your transit passes). Store them in an accordion folder or a bunch of envelopes: whatever works for you. Break them down into subjects that make sense for you, such as those that follow, and add up the subject totals at tax time. The Canadian Performers' Tax Kit was specially designed to help performers make the most of their expenses. Ask your local bookstore or call The Taxpert at (416) 960-1785.

Receipts of fifty dollars or more should have your name and the store's, and a description of what you bought. Add the details: who you were treating, what you discussed. The more information, the safer you'll be. If you just get a till receipt, at least write on it what you bought.

Keep each year's tax return, and receipts, for six years after your file them.

There's nothing to stop you being both employed and self-employed, and all you have to do to be treated as self-employed is to say you are. After you first file a self-employed tax return, Revenue Canada should automatically send you the Business and Professional Income guide each year. This contains a Statement of Professional Activities form T2032(E), which you must complete. If they don't send the guide, you can get it from any tax office, or look in the Blue Pages under Revenue Canada and get them to send you a copy. The Tax Worksheets will help you to list your professional fees and your expenses.

On Page 1 of the regular T1 General tax form, under the information section at the top, is the slot where you're used to putting your employed income. Three-quarters down the page, at line 164, is where you put the total of your fees. Right beside it is line 137, where you put your profits, that is your fees less your professional expenses. Add this net professional income (or loss), your employed income, and the other income on page 1 to get your Total Income, on Line 150 at the bottom.

You can deduct from your gross professional income "reasonable" amounts spent in connection with carrying on your business, provided you have written evidence of what you spent.

•     ADVERTISING, PROMOTION     Deduct anything you buy to get people to hire you: résumés, photographs, directory entries, letters.

•     CAR     Running costs, including insurance, maintenance, registration, license, motor club, gas, oil, should be claimed – to the extent the car is used for business. Keep a mileage log as evidence and work out the ratio of business use to total use. (Sorry, you can't claim parking fines!)

•     COACHING / HOME STUDY     As well as training for a specific job, deduct the professional coaching that keeps you generally tuned as a performer. Unfortunately, you can't claim a health club.

•     ENTERTAINMENT     Business meals, whether you are entertaining other people or eating between auditions, are partially deductible. Note on the receipt the reason for the meal. As of March 1994, you can deduct only 50% of the bill, including gratuities. Before that you could deduct 80% of the bill. (Don't ask.)

•     HAIR / MAKE-UP     If you have paid for a hair style or cut for a specific job, then you may claim 100%. You may claim a "reasonable" amount of general styling and maintenance. Your appearance is part of the job, so some expense is allowable. This is being challenged, though.

•     LOCAL TRANSPORTATION     One way of receipting bus travel is to pick up an extra transfer on every trip. If it turns out that you do business on the trip, make a note on the transfer and you've got a ready-made receipt. If you forget to ask for a transfer, mark the trip in your work diary.

•     BUSINESS USE OF HOME     This need not be a whole room, but should be clearly for business use, not the corner of a table where you write letters. It needn't be used solely for business purposes, but all your business work should be done there. Take a proportion of the entire cost of accommodation – mortgage interest, rent, upkeep and maintenance, taxes, utilities, insurance, cleaning. Work out the proportion for business use, as opposed to personal use, by square footage or number of rooms.

You can only use this expense to reduce your professional income to zero: follow the T2032 instructions. Anything left over can be carried forward and added to next year's Business Use deduction, and so on into the future.

•     OFFICE SUPPLIES AND EQUIPMENT     Expensive equipment such as instruments or word processors will be entered under Capital Cost. Put postage and stationery bits and pieces here, as well as the office's own maintenance and insurance costs.

•     PROFESSIONAL JOURNALS     You may deduct 100% of a work-related periodical. You may deduct a reasonable part of the cost of magazines and newspapers that are not wholly related to your career but have a Performing Arts or Entertainment section.

•     TELEPHONE     Unless you have a business line, you may not claim monthly rental of line or equipment. Answering services, pagers, cell phones, and Call Answer are deductible; Revenue Canada has made no decision on the other extras like Call Forwarding and Call Waiting, but they are probably not claimable.

- TRAVEL     You may not claim any trip your engager should pay for. Claim whatever fraction you can defend of a mixed business and pleasure trip.
- WARDROBE     You may claim only the proportion that is used for work. Don't forget that pursuing work is a business activity, so that you will claim a proportion of the cost of the outfit used for auditions. Any hefty item should go in Capital Cost.
- CAPITAL COST     Capital Cost Allowance (CCA) is often called "depreciation." Revenue Canada says if something is going to be around for more than a year, you should take the deduction over the life of the article. CCA is only insisted on for big ticket items. You need not take any CCA in a year, just carry it forward until you need it: see the form in the Business and Professional Guide, obtainable from your local tax office.
- NON-RECEIPTABLE EXPENSES     Meter parking, street food, single transit fares, and so on are accepted if backed by diary entries, giving details of business use.
- UNIONS     Basic and working dues are deducted on Line 212, NOT as regular expenses. You can't deduct the initiation fee (although everyone does). The initiation fee is claimed over a number of years, like CCA. Read about Eligible Capital Expenditure in the Business and Professional Guide. Enter the allowance on Line 8246 on the T2032.

    If you're not a member, claim Permit fees as an ordinary expense.

### PENALTIES and INTEREST
Revenue Canada charges these on money you owe. There's no cash penalty on late returns if no tax is due, but you're likely to lose tax credits if you wait too long, and you're greatly increasing the odds of an audit.

### TAX AUDIT
Don't lie awake worrying about The Audit. Most audits are either research to find out what's normal behaviour for, say, NWT deerhunters, or requests for more information about something that seems odd about your particular return. Lower your chance of being audited by filing on time and including a note with the tax return, explaining any big changes. Lower the pain of being audited by relying on your receipts, rather than lying through your teeth.

### ACTRA FRATERNAL
If you are a non-member working on ACTRA shoots on Work Permits, write ACTRA Frat for a claim form for the 3% insurance and RRSP contributions deducted from your fees. There's no charge if you're claiming less than $150 of  refund. If you are an ACTRA member, ask for a receipt for the medical premium part of the ACTRA Frat deductions from your year's fees. This is a medical expense and could push your total of receipts for medical services over the 3% of your net income that is deducted before you get a Medical Expense deduction from tax.

177

# TOOLKIT

# QUESTIONNAIRE – TELL ME ABOUT MYSELF

## (SEE "MIRROR, MIRROR.")

If you don't know where you're going, how will you know when you've got there? Work on this questionnaire now, in a month, after three months, six months, and in a year's time. Mark the dates in your diary.

Take the time to complete the questionnaire even if you've been in the industry for a while. You can't run a business without examining the market and your product; this is a business, and you are the product you are selling. You are selling yourself as well as your skills. Your difficulties make you human and give you your uniqueness and strength.

Be honest. Don't try to work out the "proper" response. Answer the questions openly, and thoughtfully, but don't try to second guess yourself. If a question doesn't apply, don't answer it, but be sure you're not just ducking something you don't want to face.

Once we see our own strengths and weaknesses, we can start dealing with external problems. The simple truth is that we are sometimes too close to the worst problem: ourselves.

Copyright laws cover the material in this book, but please photocopy this questionnaire for each step in the project. (Leave the original blank, to copy as you need for stocktaking in the future.) Fold the copies in sets, keep them handy. Answer each follow-up questionnaire and only then compare your current answers with what you used to think.

Don't worry about finding some of your old answers comical once you've gained more experience. This is for your eyes only. Motives and goals have a way of changing as time goes by, and we have a way of rewriting history if it doesn't suit us. What seems obvious today may seem stupid tomorrow: be honest now and you can be smarter in future.

Stay with the process: these questionnaires will help you find out where you are and, more important, where you are going. Don't get stuck in an old way of thinking because that's the way you've always thought. This is a new game, or a new approach to a game you're already playing, and if you give yourself a chance, you can get better at it.

What goes around, comes around, but if you can't remember what it was, how will you recognise it when it turns up again?

**180**

## BEFORE YOU START

We lose sight of why we start things, so we never know why we sometimes feel disappointed. If you're just coming into the Extra world, think about why. There are near-duplicate answers – check as many as apply.

I want to work as an Extra because:

___ it's exciting work
___ it's a good way to get into show business
___ I want to see how films are made
___ I want to meet some stars
___ I want to see myself on TV or in films
___ I want a hobby
___ it's a good place to meet people
___ I might get discovered
___ it's an easy job
___ it might be fun
___ my friends will be impressed when they see me
___ I'll have something to look back on when I'm older
___ I want people to recognise me
___ I need the money
___ I know I have to pay my dues before my big break
___ it's good training
___ it's a chance to get invited to some big parties
___ I can socialize
___ I enjoy watching movies and TV
___ my friends told me to try it
___ I can make a lot of money
___ I can see how shows are really made
___ an agent told me I would be great
___ it's a good way to study the crew's job
___ I need the experience
___ I can tell people I'm an actor
___ I'm ambitious and will become famous someday
___ it's the only way to break into the business
___ I just need a director to see me perform
___ there are free meals
___ the experience will get me a principal agent
___ I'm very talented
___ I haven't got anything to lose
___ it's been a lifelong dream to work in the movies
___ it will help my modelling career

**181**

YOUR FIRST QUESTIONNAIRE

You'll want to look at your progress as time goes by. Make *four* copies of the questionnaire, and label them: START, ONE MONTH, SIX MONTHS, and ONE YEAR. Keep them filed together, and answer the new questionnaire when each time rolls around (mark the dates on your calendar or in your work diary now.)

**QUESTIONNAIRE # ___**

Fill in the number before you start on this copy.

Go through the questions carefully, but trust your instinctive first answer: don't try to second-guess yourself. Try to answer every question that applies to you now.

An extra's job is to:

My biggest dream in the film industry is to:

Compared with other extras, on a scale of 1-10 (1=well below average, 10=well above average), I would describe myself as being:

| | | | | | | | | | | |
|---|---|---|---|---|---|---|---|---|---|---|
| hard-working | 1 | 2 | 3 | 4 | 5 | 6 | 7 | 8 | 9 | 10 |
| ambitious | 1 | 2 | 3 | 4 | 5 | 6 | 7 | 8 | 9 | 10 |
| honest | 1 | 2 | 3 | 4 | 5 | 6 | 7 | 8 | 9 | 10 |
| career oriented | 1 | 2 | 3 | 4 | 5 | 6 | 7 | 8 | 9 | 10 |
| energetic | 1 | 2 | 3 | 4 | 5 | 6 | 7 | 8 | 9 | 10 |
| punctual | 1 | 2 | 3 | 4 | 5 | 6 | 7 | 8 | 9 | 10 |
| studious | 1 | 2 | 3 | 4 | 5 | 6 | 7 | 8 | 9 | 10 |
| successful | 1 | 2 | 3 | 4 | 5 | 6 | 7 | 8 | 9 | 10 |
| talented | 1 | 2 | 3 | 4 | 5 | 6 | 7 | 8 | 9 | 10 |
| healthy | 1 | 2 | 3 | 4 | 5 | 6 | 7 | 8 | 9 | 10 |
| available | 1 | 2 | 3 | 4 | 5 | 6 | 7 | 8 | 9 | 10 |
| modest | 1 | 2 | 3 | 4 | 5 | 6 | 7 | 8 | 9 | 10 |
| financially sound | 1 | 2 | 3 | 4 | 5 | 6 | 7 | 8 | 9 | 10 |
| a team player | 1 | 2 | 3 | 4 | 5 | 6 | 7 | 8 | 9 | 10 |
| business minded | 1 | 2 | 3 | 4 | 5 | 6 | 7 | 8 | 9 | 10 |
| spontaneous | 1 | 2 | 3 | 4 | 5 | 6 | 7 | 8 | 9 | 10 |
| a perfectionist | 1 | 2 | 3 | 4 | 5 | 6 | 7 | 8 | 9 | 10 |
| a workaholic | 1 | 2 | 3 | 4 | 5 | 6 | 7 | 8 | 9 | 10 |
| a procrastinator | 1 | 2 | 3 | 4 | 5 | 6 | 7 | 8 | 9 | 10 |
| introverted | 1 | 2 | 3 | 4 | 5 | 6 | 7 | 8 | 9 | 10 |
| extroverted | 1 | 2 | 3 | 4 | 5 | 6 | 7 | 8 | 9 | 10 |
| full of drive | 1 | 2 | 3 | 4 | 5 | 6 | 7 | 8 | 9 | 10 |
| moody | 1 | 2 | 3 | 4 | 5 | 6 | 7 | 8 | 9 | 10 |

| friendly | 1 | 2 | 3 | 4 | 5 | 6 | 7 | 8 | 9 | 10 |
|---|---|---|---|---|---|---|---|---|---|---|
| egotistical | 1 | 2 | 3 | 4 | 5 | 6 | 7 | 8 | 9 | 10 |
| confident | 1 | 2 | 3 | 4 | 5 | 6 | 7 | 8 | 9 | 10 |

On the same scale, I think I have:

| stardom potential | 1 | 2 | 3 | 4 | 5 | 6 | 7 | 8 | 9 | 10 |
|---|---|---|---|---|---|---|---|---|---|---|
| good self-esteem | 1 | 2 | 3 | 4 | 5 | 6 | 7 | 8 | 9 | 10 |
| leadership skills | 1 | 2 | 3 | 4 | 5 | 6 | 7 | 8 | 9 | 10 |
| good concentration | 1 | 2 | 3 | 4 | 5 | 6 | 7 | 8 | 9 | 10 |
| attention to detail | 1 | 2 | 3 | 4 | 5 | 6 | 7 | 8 | 9 | 10 |
| physical appearance | 1 | 2 | 3 | 4 | 5 | 6 | 7 | 8 | 9 | 10 |
| general education | 1 | 2 | 3 | 4 | 5 | 6 | 7 | 8 | 9 | 10 |
| performance training | 1 | 2 | 3 | 4 | 5 | 6 | 7 | 8 | 9 | 10 |
| improvisation skills | 1 | 2 | 3 | 4 | 5 | 6 | 7 | 8 | 9 | 10 |
| long attention span | 1 | 2 | 3 | 4 | 5 | 6 | 7 | 8 | 9 | 10 |
| good imagination | 1 | 2 | 3 | 4 | 5 | 6 | 7 | 8 | 9 | 10 |

## STRENGTHS AND WEAKNESSES

MY FIVE WORST weaknesses are (in no special order):

1 ................................................................
2 ................................................................
3 ................................................................
4 ................................................................
5 ................................................................

How can I work on weakness # 1?

How can I work on weakness # 2?

How can I work on weakness # 3?

How can I work on weakness # 4?

How can I work on weakness # 5?

Looking back, I have had most success in dealing with these weaknesses:

I am still dealing with these weaknesses:

The next things I am going to try to solve are:

MY FIVE BEST physical features and strongest qualities are (in no special order):

1 ..............................................................
2 ..............................................................
3 ..............................................................
4 ..............................................................
5 ..............................................................

How can I cash in on quality # 1?

How can I cash in on quality # 2?

How can I cash in on quality # 3?

How can I cash in on quality # 4?

How can I cash in on quality # 5?

CHARACTER TYPES

I have played these character types:

I was surprised to be called to play these character types:

I was surprised to be told I wasn't right for these character types:

This is why I think I wasn't considered, and this is what I intend to do about it:

The characters I enjoyed playing the most were:

And this is why:

## TIMETABLES

How many hours a week (off-set) *should* I be dedicating to my craft (Legwork, promotion, classes)?

\_\_\_Hours

How many hours have I actually been dedicating to my craft?

\_\_\_Hours

What is the minimum time per week I will spend with my mate and/or children, even if I have be unavailable for work?

\_\_\_Hours

## RELATIONSHIPS

Industry-related facts have affected my relationships in the following ways, good and bad. Have relations improved or worsened lately? What made them better, or worse? How can I make things better?

SPOUSE/MATE:

CHILDREN:

FAMILY:

FRIENDS:

WORK/BOSS:

## INCOME

Working as an extra, I can realistically expect to earn:

In my first month          $
In my third month          $
In my sixth month          $

In my first full year      $
In my third year           $
In my fifth year           $

What will I do to supplement my film income?


## SUCCESS

What does being successful in the industry mean to me?

How long will it take me to become successful in the industry?

I would rate my progress towards "success" so far as:
(1=well below average, 10=well above average)

     1    2    3    4    5    6    7    8    9    10

What will I do if I don't do well in the industry?


## AVAILABILITY

On a scale of 1-10 (1=well below average, 10=well above average),
I would describe my availability when called when called for work on set as being:

     1    2    3    4    5    6    7    8    9    10

Recently I had to turn down extra work for the following reasons:
(e.g., already booked on another show, transportation, regular job)


How can I make myself more available for extra work?

## CONTACTS

I have made these new contacts and friends in the industry:

**NAME, POSITION, HOW CONTACTED. (FILED YET?)**

..........................................................................................
..........................................................................................
..........................................................................................
..........................................................................................
..........................................................................................
..........................................................................................
..........................................................................................
..........................................................................................
..........................................................................................

## THE INDUSTRY

So far, I have found extra work to be:

My *biggest* complaint or disappointment about the industry so far is:

This is what I think needs to be done:

This is what I have done, or could do, to improve the situation:

When did I last update my résumé?

## NOTES FOR LATER QUESTIONNAIRES:

### ONE MONTH

There will be changes in your answers since the first questionnaire, if you're being honest. Don't let your new knowledge of the workings of the industry replace your optimism with self-doubt. Smile grimly, and try to work out what has changed, whether you're glad about the difference, and what you should do now.

### THREE MONTHS

Go back and look at your first two questionnaires. You're not the same person you were. How have your answers changed? What have you done about the problems you identified earlier?

### SIX MONTHS

Welcome back! You're already ahead of the pack, still active in the business, still taking it seriously. When you're finished, lay out your previous questionnaires and compare your answers, question by question. Some answers are unchanged. Is this a good thing, or are you looking at continuing problems? Are you fighting against something that you haven't changed much yet, or have you decided to give up and live with it? That can sometimes be the only sensible choice.

### ONE YEAR

Congratulations! You've survived where others have given up. The average new business lasts three years before folding, so you're on the way. In fact, most extras don't last nearly this long, which is why agents charge registration fees. You're a veteran already!

Don't worry if your success, in terms of work done and money made, is disappointing. Maybe you aren't promoting yourself in the right way, maybe you really are as useless as you think you are in your most depressed moments.

It's also possible that no-one in your casting slot has been getting much work. Film fashions change: first every film has short fat extras, now every film has beanpoles. If you're not this season's style, you don't get cast.

It's possible you set unrealistic goals back then. Don't be too proud to change your target.

### AND ON, AND ON

If you're looking at this some time down the road, wondering what problems the questionnaire can solve at this point, the answer is: none at all. Using the questionnaire to look at yourself coolly, however, might help if you're ready to do something about what you see.

There's no penalty for having been wrong in the past, only for going on lashing yourself with it.

# WORKSHEETs

## (SEE "MIRROR, MIRROR.")

## CASTING WORKSHEETS

This worksheet is about what you look like, not what you are. It is about the casting categories used on breakdowns, not any sort of description of the real world. In the real world, we can't sum people up in a word or two: everyone is a mixture of appearances and behaviour. Your job or appearance or sexual habits don't define you: there are weedy-looking bouncers and college professors built like the Sasquatch. We are talking about TV and film stereotypes of characters.

Casting is about what the producer wants for the screen: it's not about your feelings about your body, your physical abilities, your heritage or your race. The following categories are not meant to be limiting, insulting, or degrading. They don't try to be Politically Correct. Nationalities are only used as a referencing "look" or features which may be required by a production.

Do not allow any physical limitations to disqualify you from casting where it makes no difference. You may not get called to play many marathon runners (who wants to? it's exhausting), but you've got an advantage at being featured where others can't even try out for the role.

Use this section to decide what your appearance will allow you to play. Photocopy it before you fill it in: you'll need a clean copy for later.

Circle your best playable screen age range. Choose one only:

| | | |
|---|---|---|
| Under 2 | 15-20 | 40-50 |
| 2-5 | 15-25 | 45-55 |
| 4-7 | 20-30 | 50-60 |
| 5-10 | 25-35 | 55-65 |
| 10-15 | 30-40 | 65-75 |
| | 35-45 | |

North American laws against discrimination on the grounds of sex, race, and so on allow otherwise unlawful choices to be made when the job requires special abilities. Nowadays, casting people are extraordinarily careful to avoid giving offence by using the wrong words to describe racial and ethnic backgrounds, and physical differences. They make mistakes. Be courteous, and point out calmly that your group dislikes the term being used.

Which racial types can you pass as?

| | | |
|---|---|---|
| ARAB | KOREAN | AFRICAN |
| CAUCASIAN | HAWAIIAN | JEWISH |
| ASIAN | JAPANESE | AFRICAN-AMERICAN |
| EUROPEAN | HISPANIC | NATIVE INDIAN |
| CHINESE | LATINO BLACK | JAMAICAN |
| EAST INDIAN | ITALIAN | MULATTO |

"Gee, he's a brain surgeon? He sure doesn't look the type." You couldn't describe what a brain surgeon should look like, but you know the type. What types do you match? What characters would you be picked out of the crowd to play? They're sorted into rough groups, just for this exercise.

| CAREER | BEHAVR/APP'RANCE | Nervous |
|---|---|---|
| Bartender | Aristocrat | Passive |
| Business Person | Beach Dude | Psycho |
| Business Exec. | Beach Bunny | Rugged |
| Caretaker | Caveman | Sexy |
| Chauffeur | College Student | Sickly |
| Craftsperson | Colonial | Trashy |
| Doctor/Dentist | Country Bumpkin | Wild |
| Labourer | Drunkard | |
| Lawyer | Exotic | UNIFORMED |
| Monk | Farmer | Bodyguard |
| Nun | Gigolo | Cop |
| Nurse | Glamour Girl | Detective |
| Personal Servant | Group Leader | Military (low) |
| Priest | Homeless | Military (high) |
| Professor | Hooker | Security Guard |
| Scientist | Intellectual | SWAT Team member |
| Secretary | Mental Patient | |
| Shop Keeper | Nerd | TRENDS |
| Teacher | Parent | Avant Garde |
| Technician | Redneck | Beatnik |
| TV Reporter | Snob | Flower Child |
| Wait staff | Socialite | Hip Hop |
| | | Hippie |
| ORIENTATION | PHYSICAL | New Wave |
| Don Juan | Athletic | Psychedelic 60s |
| Gay | Average (Plain) | Punker |
| Lesbian | Bimbo | Rocker |
| Prude | Body Builder | Skinhead |
| Sexpot | Bouncer | Stoner |
| Transvestite | Boxer | Trendy |
| | Heavy Set | |
| FICTIONAL | Marlboro Man | LOW LIFE |
| Dead | Martial Arts | Biker |
| Demon | Runway Model | Bum |
| Dwarf | Weakling | Criminal |
| Elf | Western Cowpoke | Drug Addict |
| Santa | | Gangster |
| Sprite | EMOTIONAL | Hooker |
| Zombie | Goofy | Pimp |
| | Hysterical | |

190

Of course, we all know we could play any of these, but be realistic: go back and highlight no more than *ten* types you know you are perfect to play, characters which strangers might guess you were from seeing you at a party.

It's up to you to learn how to make these characters your own. These will become your specialty characters, to be listed at the bottom of your résumé. If you succeed, you'll be at the top of the list whenever these character types are needed.

Other people's reactions may be more useful than your own opinions, however honest you are with yourself: give a copy of the list to some friends and ask what they think. Better still, do this in a group. Make photocopies, have everyone assess everyone else. Use the columns at the side to check off each friend's most likely casting, swap the sheets around to hide who said what, and read out the results. I guarantee you'll be surprised.


## HEALTH WORKSHEET

How is your general health?
    (Describe)


Do you suffer from colds, dizziness, or headaches easily?
    (Describe)


Do you suffer from any allergies?
    (List and Describe)


Are you on any special medication or do you have any medical conditions of which the production should be made aware in an emergency?
    (List and Describe)


Do you have any special dietary requirements (not simply food preferences) which will make eating in the scene a problem?

## PERSONAL LIMITATIONS

For various reasons, different people have trouble performing under certain conditions. This is about how you react, physically and mentally, to the setting and content of the scene you might be working in. Read the chapter, see why it can be stupid to be brave.

Rate the following work conditions as to how able or willing you are to work in them:

| | NO! | | NEUTRAL | | SURE |
|---|---|---|---|---|---|
| LARGE CROWDS | 1 | 2 | 3 | 4 | 5 |
| HEIGHTS | 1 | 2 | 3 | 4 | 5 |
| CLOSED-IN PLACES | 1 | 2 | 3 | 4 | 5 |
| WIDE OPEN AREAS | 1 | 2 | 3 | 4 | 5 |
| AROUND FIREARMS | 1 | 2 | 3 | 4 | 5 |
| AROUND EXPLOSIVES | 1 | 2 | 3 | 4 | 5 |
| PROSTHETIC MAKE-UP | 1 | 2 | 3 | 4 | 5 |
| FIRE | 1 | 2 | 3 | 4 | 5 |
| WATER (e.g., lakes) | 1 | 2 | 3 | 4 | 5 |
| SMOKE (natural) | 1 | 2 | 3 | 4 | 5 |
| SMOKE (artificial) | 1 | 2 | 3 | 4 | 5 |
| WATER (e.g., pools) | 1 | 2 | 3 | 4 | 5 |
| SNAKES/REPTILES/RODENTS | 1 | 2 | 3 | 4 | 5 |
| DOMESTIC PETS | 1 | 2 | 3 | 4 | 5 |
| LIVESTOCK (e.g., horses) | 1 | 2 | 3 | 4 | 5 |
| WILD ANIMALS (e.g., tigers) | 1 | 2 | 3 | 4 | 5 |
| OTHER ANIMALS | 1 | 2 | 3 | 4 | 5 |
| LATE NIGHTS | 1 | 2 | 3 | 4 | 5 |
| EXTREME HEAT | 1 | 2 | 3 | 4 | 5 |
| EXTREME COLD | 1 | 2 | 3 | 4 | 5 |
| SNOW | 1 | 2 | 3 | 4 | 5 |
| RAIN | 1 | 2 | 3 | 4 | 5 |
| NUDITY – others | 1 | 2 | 3 | 4 | 5 |
| NUDITY – skimpy | 1 | 2 | 3 | 4 | 5 |
| NUDITY – partial | 1 | 2 | 3 | 4 | 5 |
| NUDITY – full | 1 | 2 | 3 | 4 | 5 |
| RACIALIST CONTENT | 1 | 2 | 3 | 4 | 5 |
| VIOLENT CONTENT | 1 | 2 | 3 | 4 | 5 |
| STRENUOUS ACTION | 1 | 2 | 3 | 4 | 5 |

Any other working conditions which may prohibit you from accepting work:

## SCHEDULING WORKSHEET

Rate your availability for work in these situations:

|  | NEVER |  |  |  | ALWAYS |
|---|---|---|---|---|---|
| Weeknights | 1 | 2 | 3 | 4 | 5 |
| Weekdays | 1 | 2 | 3 | 4 | 5 |
| Weekends | 1 | 2 | 3 | 4 | 5 |
| All Night Shoots | 1 | 2 | 3 | 4 | 5 |
| Late Night Calls | 1 | 2 | 3 | 4 | 5 |
| Short Notice Calls | 1 | 2 | 3 | 4 | 5 |

Shoot locations are often widely scattered. A reliable source of reliable transportation is essential. Rate the reliability of your possible methods of transportation. Keep in mind variable weather conditions, mechanical breakdowns, and off-hour travelling.

|  | VERY UNRELIABLE |  |  |  | VERY RELIABLE |
|---|---|---|---|---|---|
| Car | 1 | 2 | 3 | 4 | 5 |
| Motorcycle | 1 | 2 | 3 | 4 | 5 |
| Public Transit | 1 | 2 | 3 | 4 | 5 |
| Bicycle | 1 | 2 | 3 | 4 | 5 |
| Walking (Distance) | 1 | 2 | 3 | 4 | 5 |
| Family and Friends | 1 | 2 | 3 | 4 | 5 |
| Other......... | 1 | 2 | 3 | 4 | 5 |

How long, travelling at an average rate, would it take you to reach:

LOCAL AREA (Under five miles), by:

Car .........
Motorcycle.........
Public Transit.........
Bicycle.........
Walking.........
Family and Friends (inc. contact time).........
Other.........

How long, travelling at an average rate, would it take you to reach:

OTHER END OF CITY

                                                Car .........
                                        Motorcycle.........
                                    Public Transit.........
                                            Bicycle.........
                                            Walking.........
                Family and Friends (inc. contact time).........
                                              Other.........

NEIGHBOURING CITY

                                                Car .........
                                        Motorcycle.........
                                    Public Transit.........
                                            Bicycle.........
                                  Walking (Distant).........
                Family and Friends (inc. contact time).........
                                              Other.........

OUT-OF-TOWN/DISTANT LOCATION

                                                Car .........
                                        Motorcycle.........
                                    Public Transit.........
                                            Bicycle.........
                Family and Friends (inc. contact time).........
                                              Other.........

If you should receive a last minute call to set, how quickly can you be prepared and on your way (take into account any arrangements for sitters, gathering wardrobe and supplies, etc.)?

                                            Minutes.........

Add the average travel time expected for each distance (which you've just worked out) and the time it would take you to be ready to hit the road, and then add safety margins to allow for these unforeseen circumstances, such as heavy traffic, mechanical breakdowns, or being unable to find the set.

SAFE TRAVEL TIME

            LOCAL AREA ____ + 1 hour   =

    OTHER END OF CITY ____ + 1 hour   =

    NEIGHBOURING CITY ____ + 1 ½ hours =

    OUT-OF-TOWN/DISTANT ____ + 2 hours   =

## FINANCES WORKSHEETs

Take stock. Look at your credit, the amount you make and the amount you've saved, and your debits, the amount you spend and the amount you owe.
You may be surprised by the result. I hope pleasantly.

### FINANCES WORKSHEET 1
CREDIT

What is your current financial status? Don't kid yourself: how much have you got, how much do you really make, now?

SAVINGS

Locked-in (GIC's, RRSPs, Term deposits, etc.): $.................
Money owed to you: $.................

TOTAL $_____

READY CASH

Chequing Accounts: $.................
Cash On Hand: $.................
Liquid Assets (CSB's, RRSP funds): $.................

TOTAL $_____

INCOME

Monthly Income (worst-case minimum from films, TV): $.................
Monthly Income (other, Joe jobs): $.................

TOTAL MONTHLY INCOME $_____

## FINANCES WORKSHEET 2
### EXPENSES

How much does it cost you to live for a month?
(Estimate if necessary, keep all your receipts for a month to be sure.)

| | |
|---|---|
| Rent/Mortgage | $................. |
| Food | $................. |
| Phone/Pager | $................. |
| Utilities | $................. |
| Credit payments | $................. |
| Travel | $................. |
| Entertainment | $................. |
| Other | $................. |

TOTAL MONTHLY EXPENSES      $_____

About how much do you expect to have to invest in the near future in:

| | |
|---|---|
| Agency Initiation Fees | $................. |
| Wardrobe | $................. |
| Photographs | $................. |
| Training | $................. |
| Trade Magazines/Books | $................. |
| Travel Supplies and Equipment | $................. |
| Pagers/Answering Machine | $................. |
| Other | $................. |

TOTAL      $_____

CONCLUSION
How much, at a minimum do you need to earn through your film work each month, to add to your other sources of income, to cover your running expenses?

FILM INCOME NEEDED      $.................

Remember, your savings won't last forever. Draw on them to help you over an emergency, but plan to live on your income as soon as you can. Aim at building up a cushion of savings, even if you have to miss out on some nice things in the short term.

## RELATIONSHIPS WORKSHEET

I know you know the answers to these questions. Filling them in, putting your feelings into words, will help you look at your situation more logically, see it more clearly, and deal with it more effectively.

MARITAL STATUS (single, married, boy/girlfriend, etc)?

ANY OTHER PERSONAL DEPENDENTS:

How do the following people feel about your getting into the film industry (N/A if Not Applicable):

SPOUSE/MATE:

CHILDREN:

OTHER FAMILY:

FRIENDS:

COWORKERS/BOSS:

What do you see as the biggest strain, due to your work in the industry, in your relationship with your:

        SPOUSE/MATE:


        CHILDREN:


        OTHER FAMILY:


        FRIENDS:


        COWORKERS/BOSS:


How flexible will your employer be when you want time off to work on set? There could be absences with little notice, for go-sees and regular gigs, and successive days on set when you are made a continuity extra.

How accepting is your mate of your time away on set?



What other social and personal commitments (involving children, clubs, activities, etc.) do you have? How will these commitments be affected?



How many hours will you need to dedicate (off-set) per week to your craft?

           …………Hours


How will this allow you enough time for your mate, children, work, friends, social life and activities?

## CONTACTS WORKSHEET

Read Background on the Background about using your contacts. If you are polite and sincere, most people will do what they can to help. Don't be shy about contacting star Names, even if you only have their agents to write to. Don't bother with fan clubs.

| Hot / Backlist / Name | | | | |
|---|---|---|---|---|
| Contact | | What they do | Your link | What to do now |
| | | | | |
| | | | | |
| | | | | |
| | | | | |

• **Contact**: Enter here your contact names, but be careful. What name would you use if you met them again now? What did you call them in the past? What name would you would use in a letter or phone call? Decide if you should use a nickname, if you know it; be cautious.

• **Hot/Backlist/Name**: Get in touch with your Hot prospects, but don't let "Backlist" equal "Garbage." Again, don't be shy about contacting star Names.

• **What they do**: Get it right before you talk about it.

• **Your link**: This will structure your whole approach. If you are linked through another person, talk to your contact before you start work on the prospect.

• **What to do next**: What do you want from them? How can you get it? Just the first step for now. See the "Office Systems" chapter for keeping this going.

# CALL SHEET

DATE: _____

FILM: _____   TIME: _____

PROD: _____

LOCATION: _____   INTERSECTION: _____
_____   BUS ROUTE: _____
_____   PARKING: _____

CONTACT: _____   MAP REF.: _____

===============================================

ROLE: _____   WARDROBE: _____
_____                  _____
_____                  _____

HOW PAID: _____

===============================================

CALL _____ Hours          AGENT: _____

PAID _____ (Cash/Chq/Contract)
_____

SPECIAL: _____
_____

===============================================

PAY RECEIVED: $_____   PAID BY: _____
            DATE: _____
   COMMISSION: $_____
      DATE PAID: _____
      RECEIPT #: _____

===============================================

ON SET

ROLE: _____   WARDROBE: _____
                                          _____
USED: _____                     _____
    (Seen/Background/Etc)
HOURS: _____   BREAKDOWN: _____
                                          _____
SPECIAL: _____
    (Upgrade/Lines/Etc.)
LOGGED?: _____

## EXPENSES

**TRANSPORTATION:** _____     **PHONE:** _____

**ACCOMMODATIONS:** _____     **FOOD:** _____

**CLOTHING:** _____     **MISC:** _____

## COMMENTS

.......................................................................................................................
.......................................................................................................................
.......................................................................................................................
.......................................................................................................................
.......................................................................................................................
.......................................................................................................................
.......................................................................................................................

## TRAVEL CHECKLIST

| | |
|---|---|
| _____ Wardrobe | _____ Umbrella |
| _____ Rings, Gloves, etc. | _____ Toiletries |
| _____ Accessories | |
| _____ Windbreaker | |
| | _____ Book |
| _____ Callsheet Details | _____ Crosswords |
| _____ Map | _____ Cards |
| | |
| _____ Meal Money | _____ Pens and paper |
| _____ Change (bus, phones) | _____ Pocket fan |
| | _____ Batteries |
| _____ Work Diary | |
| _____ Address Book | _____ Photos/Résumés |

# AGENT CHECKLISTS

### (see "Agents" and "Agents, Take Two.")

(☞ Caution area. 📹 )

### PHONE CONTACT

AGENCY:
ADDRESS:

PHONE:          (   )
FAX:             (   )

Contact Name:

CONTRACT?                    Y / N

Exclusive?                      Y 📹/ N

REGISTRATION FEE
                    Non-union              Union
                    $                      $      📹

One-time/Yearly/Other

COMMISSION RATE    Non-union              Union
                   %                      %

Of Gross or Net?
Plus GST on commission?        Y / N

INTERVIEW DATE:

TIME:

TO SEE:

INTERSECTION, OTHER GEOGRAPHY:

## OFFICE INTERVIEW

CONTRACT?                  Y / N
Exclusive?                   Y ☛/ N
REGISTRATION FEE
        One-time/Yearly/Other/Payable as you go

| | Non-union | Union |
|---|---|---|
| | $ | $ ☛ |

COMMISSION RATE  Non-union          Union
                     %                     %
Of Gross or Net?
Plus GST on commission?    Y / N

ADDITIONAL COSTS/FEES?  Y ☛ / N
(List):

OFFER COURSES?         Y ☛/ N
Make videos here?       Y ☛/ N
Photograph needed?     Y / ☛ N    What Kind?     How many?
Use their photographer?  Y ☛/ N

CASTING BOOK?         Y / N     Your impressions?

OFFICE
        Business Hours
        Hours On Call / On Duty
        Okay to call in (Y/N)      Best time to call
Phones busy?            Y / N
Modern? (Computer/Fax)    Y / N
Office Condition:         Dump ☛ / OK / ☛Extravagant
Well staffed?             Y / N
Knowledgeable?          Y / N
Answered questions?      Y / N
Negative gut feelings?     Y ☛ / N

NOTES

Your personal rating _____

**☛IF THEY INSIST THAT YOU COMPLETE AND SIGN ALL FORMS ☛
IMMEDIATELY DURING INITIAL INTERVIEW, WALK OUT!**

# RÉSUMÉs

## (SEE "RÉSUMÉS")

## RÉSUMÉ WORKSHEET 1

### GENERAL STATS

Get a friend to help you fill in this next page, someone who knows where your hip measurement should be taken.

Don't let pride get in the way of accuracy. If you know you won't be losing the 30 pounds you gained after the holiday festivities (it was a really big turkey), don't lie about your sizes. It won't be a very pleasant experience to be fired because you gave sizes from ten years ago.

Wardrobe measurements are almost always still taken in inches.

HEIGHT: _____ (nearest inch)    WEIGHT: _____ lbs. (nearest five pounds)

### SIZES

___ HAT    ___ GLOVES    ___ SHOES

| FEMALE SIZES | | MALE SIZES | |
|---|---|---|---|
| ___ BUST | ___ INSEAM | ___ CHEST | ___ WAIST |
| ___ WAIST | ___ SLEEVE | ___ SHIRT | ___ SLEEVE |
| ___ HIPS | ___ DRESS | ___ JACKET | ___ INSEAM |
| | | ___ DRESS LEFT/RIGHT | |

# HAIR (check as many as apply)

| LENGTH | | FACIAL | |
|---|---|---|---|
| __ VERY LONG | __ BRUSHCUT | __ FULL BEARD | __ CLEANSHAVEN |
| __ LONG | __ SHAVED | __ SHORT BEARD | __ SHADOWED |
| __ MEDIUM | __ BALDING | __ MOUSTACHE | __ SCRAGGLY |
| __ SHORT | __ BALD | __ GOATEE | __ ZZ TOP'ish |

## USUAL HAIR COLOUR (check one)

| | | |
|---|---|---|
| __ BLACK | __ BROWN | __ LIGHT GREY |
| __ LIGHT BLONDE | __ DARK BROWN | __ GREY |
| __ BLONDE | __ AUBURN | __ DARK GREY |
| __ DARK BLONDE | __ RED | __ SALT/PEPPER |
| __ STRWBRY BLONDE | __ OTHER | __ WHITE |
| __ LIGHT BROWN | | |

## EYES

| COLOUR | | OTHER | |
|---|---|---|---|
| __ BLUE | __ GREY | __ GLASSES | __ EYE PATCH |
| __ BROWN | __ HAZEL | __ CONTACTS (Clear) | __ GLASS EYE |
| __ GREEN | __ VIOLET | __ CONTACTS (Coloured) | |

# RÉSUMÉ WORKSHEET 2
## BASIC LISTING

## SKIN TONE

<u>COMPLEXION</u>
___ VERY LIGHT
___ LIGHT
___ MEDIUM
___ DARK
___ VERY DARK

___ _____

<u>MARKINGS</u>
___ MOLE
___ BLEMISHED
___ TATTOOED
___ PIERCED
___ SCAR

___ _____

## HAIR STYLES (check usual style, and wigs if applicable)

___ TRENDY
___ PUNK
___ 50s
___ BEEHIVE
___ WILD
___ AFRO
___ FLAT-TOP
___ SHAVED EMBLEMS

___ MILITARY CUT
___ CLEAN CUT  (Businessman)
___ WAVY
___ CURLY
___ STRAIGHT (Body)
___ STRAIGHT (No Body)
___ WIGS (list)

## DRIVING

List any driving skills you have. For a regular licence, simply list Automatic/Standard (as applicable). You may also include details of any actual vehicle(s) which you are willing to use on the actual set.

___ AUTOMATIC
___ STANDARD
___ MOTORCYCLE
___ ATV
___ LIMOUSINE
___ BUS
___ PICKUP TRUCK/VAN
___ CUBE VAN

___ _____

___ CAR WITH TRAILER
___ FARM MACHINERY
___ GO CART
___ FACTORY FORKLIFT
___ HEAVY MACHINERY
___ MOTORHOME
___ TRACTOR TRAILER
___ STUNT DRIVING

___ _____

# RÉSUMÉ WORKSHEET 3
## SPECIAL SKILLS

If you excel at a highly skilled or professional level, highlight or circle the entry. NEVER overstate your qualifications. If you cannot perform a skill with at least a reasonable proficiency, don't put it on the résumé.
Check as many as apply:

## SPECIALTY SKILLS

| | | |
|---|---|---|
| Baton twirling | Magician | Stunt person |
| Clown | Mime | Firearms |
| Fire eater | Prosthetics model | Trapeze |
| High wire | Stilt walking | Unicycle |
| Improv. comedy | Stunt falls | |
| Juggler | Stunt fighting | |

## MUSICAL SKILLS

The instruments you play with confidence. Don't leave out the spoons or the ocarina because you can't find a group to include them in. Do put in your level of competence (**Pro**fessional, **Good**, **Fair**), your style of music, and any qualifications you've won. Think about these suggestions and list your instruments in detail.

| | | |
|---|---|---|
| Accordion | Piano | Brass |
| Drums | Strings | Percussion |
| Guitar | Woodwind | Other |

## DANCE SKILLS

| | | |
|---|---|---|
| Ballet | Flamenco | Line dance |
| Ballroom | Folk/ethnic | Modern |
| Belly | Go-go | Square dance |
| Break | Hip hop | Tap |
| Charleston | Jazz | |

## ATHLETIC SKILLS

Give your precise area of skill – Horseriding (Western and English), Skiing (Downhill), as well as your level of competence, and type of awards you've won.

| | | | |
|---|---|---|---|
| Archery | Diving | Martial arts | Surfing |
| Baseball | Fencing | Mountaineering | Swimming |
| Basketball | Football | Racquet ball | Table Tennis |
| Body-building | Frisbee | Roller blading | Tennis |
| Bowling | Golf | Roller skating | Track and field |
| Boxing | Gymnastics | Sailing | Volleyball |
| Canoeing | Hang gliding | Scuba diving | Water skiing |
| Cricket | Hockey | Skateboarding | Weight lifting |
| Curling | Horse-riding | Skiing | Wind surfing |
| Cycling | Ice skating | Sky diving | Wrestling |
| Darts | Lacrosse | Soccer | |

**207**

# TAX WORKSHEETS

## (SEE "TAXES")

### INCOME
### TAX WORKSHEET 1

I am assuming you are a regular unincorporated Canadian resident: get expert help if you're not sure.

Make up a page like the one below, and send it with your return.

On a T4A, your fees should be in Box 28. The figure may be higher than you expected, because RRSP and medical deductions are taxable.

If the production or payroll service didn't send you a T4A, ask them nicely. If they still won't help, work out the amount from your payslips, or the vouchers, or your agent's commission receipts. That's safer than under-declaring your income, because the engager may have sent the T4A details to Revenue Canada, and not to you.

If you are registered for the GST, show your GST number. However little you make, registering is a good idea. You have to register if your world self-employed income is over $30,000 (fat chance), but anyone may register, and since you'll gain around 6% of your expenses each year, why not? (The Quick Method would be a good choice if your expenses are less than a quarter of your self-employed income and you never show a loss.) The arithmetic at tax time is easy. Check out the leaflets, and get help, at the local GST office, or the Business Number counter at the Tax Office (see your local blue pages).

If you are registered, remember not to include as income the GST that was added to your fees. If you are paid a fee with no GST added, you have to pay the GST anyway. That's what happened with Slitely Dodgy, below. The fee was $450, but it had to be declared as $420.56 plus $29.44 GST.

| Your Name | PROFESSIONAL INCOME | | |
|---|---|---|---|
| SIN 123 456 789 | | TAX YEAR 19XX | |
| GST# 111 222 333 | | | |
| T4A | $ | GST on income | |
| Performer Payroll | 1538.51 | 107.70 | |
| No T4A | | | |
| Jimbo Films | 107.89 | 7.55 | |
| Slitely Dodgy Inc | 420.56 | 29.44 | |
| TOTAL INCOME | 2066.96 | | |

**EXPENSES**
TAX WORKSHEET 2

**For your own calculations – DO NOT FILE THIS FORM.**

Use this form to collect the totals from your sorted receipts.
If you're not registered for the GST, just use the first column of totals. If you are, use both columns and claim the deduction totals in the second column.

|  | With GST | Without GST |
|---|---|---|
| Advertising and Promotion . . . . . . . . . . . . . . . | | . . . . . . . . |
| Agent Commission . . . . . . . . . . . . . . . . . . . . | | . . . . . . . . |
| Car . . . . . . . . . . . . . . . . . . . . . . . . . . . . . . . . . . | | . . . . . . . . |
| Dressing Room Supplies . . . . . . . . . . . . . . . . | | . . . . . . . . |
| Entertainment before 1 Mar '94, @ 80% . . . . | | . . . . . . . . |
| Entertainment from 1 Mar '94, @ 50% . . . . . . | | . . . . . . . . |
| Hair / Make-up. . . . . . . . . . . . . . . . . . . . . . . . | | . . . . . . . . |
| Local Transportation . . . . . . . . . . . . . . . . . . . | | . . . . . . . . |
| Office Space. . . . . . . . . . . . . . . . . . . . . . . . . . | | . . . . . . . . |
| Office Supplies and Equipment. . . . . . . . . . . . | | . . . . . . . . |
| Out of Town. . . . . . . . . . . . . . . . . . . . . . . . . . | | . . . . . . . . |
| Postage and Stationery. . . . . . . . . . . . . . . . . . | | . . . . . . . . |
| Professional Development. . . . . . . . . . . . . . . . | | . . . . . . . . |
| Professional Gifts . . . . . . . . . . . . . . . . . . . . . | | . . . . . . . . |
| Professional Journals. . . . . . . . . . . . . . . . . . . | | . . . . . . . . |
| Professional Tickets. . . . . . . . . . . . . . . . . . . . | | . . . . . . . . |
| Telephone. . . . . . . . . . . . . . . . . . . . . . . . . . . . | | . . . . . . . . |
| Travel. . . . . . . . . . . . . . . . . . . . . . . . . . . . . . . | | . . . . . . . . |
| Wardrobe . . . . . . . . . . . . . . . . . . . . . . . . . . . . | | . . . . . . . . |
| . . . . . . . . . . . . . . . . . . . . . . . . . . . . . . . . . . . . | | . . . . . . . . |
| . . . . . . . . . . . . . . . . . . . . . . . . . . . . . . . . . . . . | | . . . . . . . . |
| . . . . . . . . . . . . . . . . . . . . . . . . . . . . . . . . . . . . | | . . . . . . . . |
| . . . . . . . . . . . . . . . . . . . . . . . . . . . . . . . . . . . . | | . . . . . . . . |
| Total. . . . . . . . . . . . . . . . . . . . . . . . . . . . . . . . | | . . . . . . . . |

## TAX WORKSHEET 3 – CONVERSION TO T2032 FORMAT

### DO NOT FILE THIS FORM.

Take these totals from the previous page, Professional Expenses

Advertising and Promotion ................................................. 8204 ........

Entertainment before 1 March '94, at 80% plus

   Entertainment from 1 March '94, at 50% .......................... 8217 ........

Car ...................................................................................... 8218 ........

Office Supplies and Equipment, Postage and Stationery ....... 8219 ........

Professional fees — Agent Commission .............................. 8220 ........

Travel ................................................................................. 8224 ........

Telephone ........................................................................... 8225 ........

OTHER EXPENSES

   Dressing Room Supplies....................................................

   Hair / Make-up .................................................................

   Local Transportation .........................................................

   Out of Town.......................................................................

   Professional Development..................................................

   Professional Gifts ..............................................................

   Professional Journals.........................................................

   Professional Tickets ..........................................................

   Wardrobe ..........................................................................

   Work Permits.....................................................................

TOTAL "OTHER EXPENSES"............................................

Put this total on T2032 as "OTHER EXPENSES."

Transfer the Other Expenses list to a sheet laid out like the next page, and send it with your return.

**Your Name**

# OTHER EXPENSES
details of total filed on T2032

SIN  123 456 789 ..................................................TAX YEAR 19XX
GST# 111 222 333

Tote-bag Supplies ....................................

Hair / Make-up .......................................

Local Transportation ...............................

Out of Town ...........................................

Professional Development ........................

Professional Gifts ...................................

Professional Journals .............................

Professional Tickets ...............................

Travel .....................................................

Wardrobe ...............................................

Other .....................................................

...............................................

...............................................

...............................................

...............................................

...............................................

_____

TOTAL                                    _____

COMMENTS ON CLAIMED EXPENSES:

## Preparing the T2032(E) / TAX WORKSHEET 4

Form T2032(E) is in the Business and Professional Income guide from Revenue Canada. It's best to use it to declare your income and expenses. Don't get formophobia: you won't need to worry about a lot of it, which is meant to cover every sort of straight business possible. The following advice should make sense if you match it up with the form. Look at T2032(E) now:

- The first box is your details:

| This is the name attached to your SIN | SIN |
|---|---|
| The tax year will usually be from January 1st to December 31st | Enter YES if you are no longer looking for acting work |
| Put your professional name here (this may be the same as the name above) | "Performer," "performer/writer," — whatever you do professionaly |
| Your regular mailing address here | The best code available is 9933 |
| You don't need to fill the preparer's name in | You won't have a partnership number |
| | ... nor a tax shelter number |
| You won't have a Business number | ... and you don't have a partnership |
| But you may have a GST number | |

- The large box starts with your professional income. Not your employed income, investments, pension or other government benefits.

    (a) is your gross income, from the Income Statement Worksheet

    ... and so is (b)

    ... and 8123

    ... and 8124

Use the Expenses Worksheet and the T2032 Worksheet, to sort out your deductions. Put the expenses in the first section on their appropriate lines and list the rest on a separate sheet, with their total on an "Other expenses" line on the T2032.

You are now at the Subtotal of your expenses.

- Capital Cost Allowance, on the second sheet of T2032, is the "depreciation" you should take on large-ticket items instead of claiming the whole cost as a deduction. Use the Equipment Additions and Disposals sections for the computer, car, fur coat, and so on. Look in the Business and Professional Guide for instructions on filling in this page. Put the Total CCA Claim on line 8207.
- On the second page of the T2032, skip down to "Calculation of Business-use-of-home expenses," discussed in the "Taxes" chapter. Put the result of your calculations over the page as your last deduction from your professional income.

# GLOSSARY

**4 A's Union**
- American performer union, within the Associated Actors and Artistes of America, affiliated with the American Federation of Labor.

**Actor**
- Person who portrays a character in a production.
- Under the ACTRA IPA, a performer engaged to speak or mime ten or fewer lines of dialogue, or whose performance constitutes an individual characterization without dialogue.
  (See also **Principal**)

**ACTRA**
- Alliance of Canadian Cinema, Television and Radio Artists.

**ACTRA Fraternal**
- The ACTRA Fraternal Benefit Society administers health insurance plans, life insurance plans, and Registered Retirement Savings Plans (RRSPs) for ACTRA members.

**AD**
- Assistant Director.
  (See crew chart in "On Set" chapter)

**ADR**
- Automatic Dialogue Replacement.
  (See **Looping**)

**AEA**
- Actors Equity Association (US stage performers union).

**AFTRA**
- American Federation of Television and Radio Artists.
  (See "Union Matters" chapter)

**Agent**
- Person or company who has been authorized by a performer to seek to gain them employment in the industry.

213

**Agreement**
- The negotiated conditions forming the basis of the contract under which members of a union, e.g. ACTRA, work for a given group of engagers.

**Amateur**
- Person who approaches an activity as a hobby without any intention of developing it as a career.
- (uncomplimentary) One who performs without exhibiting trained or professional skills.

**Ambience**
- Background sound and acoustics of a space.
- Chemical smoke in the air for effect.

**Apple**
- Wooden box nine inches high (about the size of a small apple crate), for performers to stand on to raise their height in a shot.

**Apprentice Member**
- Performer working with probationary membership status in a union, until union criteria for full membership status are satisfied.

**Audit**
- Attend a class without being allowed to participate in actual class activities.
- Revenue Canada examining your tax records.

**Audition**
- Performance for casting and production personnel, in which performers demonstrate their suitability for a role in Actor or Principal categories in the production.

**Availability Check**
- Agent's or Casting's call to the performer to determine performers' availability for work if cast.

**B/W**
- Black and white. Of a monitor, monochrome.

**Background**
- That part of a scene behind the main performers.
- Extras, background performers.

**Background Performer**
- Extra, a performer with business, but no scripted dialogue, in a scene to give the scene realism or atmosphere.

**Back To Firsts**
**Back To First Positions**
**Back To Number Ones**
- Return to your starting place and stance used at the beginning of the shot or scene.

**Back to Holding** • Return to the Extras Holding Area.

**Barn Door** • Movable hinged panels at the side of lighting instruments, which can be adjusted to block the edge of the light from side areas (they look like the swinging doors on old barn haylofts).

**Bell** • Warning buzzer (which may be synced with start and end of flashing red warning lights) to signal preparation for, and end of, actual shooting.

**Best Boy** • First assistant to the gaffer (chief electrician), does the electrical tie-ins, sets the lights, etc. Should be qualified to fill in for the gaffer in an emergency. (See crew chart in "On Set" chapter)

**BG** • Background (which see).

**BGP** • Background Performers (which see).

**Blackballed Blacklisted** • Prevented from getting further work on set as punishment, revenge, or vindication, by someone in power. No reliable evidence of this in Canada. This is not the same as a production refusing to hire a performer on the basis of real or perceived trouble or unsuitability.

**Blanks** • Gun cartridges with less explosive charge than a regular cartridge, and no bullet, but sometimes with extra flash and smoke ingredients.

**Blocking** • Setting up placement and determining movement of performers, scenery, props, and camera for a scene or shot.

**Body Double** • Performer, all or part of whose body will replace that of another member of the cast, e.g., for a nude scene.

**Booking** • Engagement. A verbal contract to perform.

**Boom** • Long pole used to hold the microphone above the performers.

215

**Boom Operator**
- Person holding the mike boom in a scene, normally the audio department second in command, responsible to the mixer.
(See "Production Personnel")

**Breakdown**
- Report listing scenes, performers, and special considerations required for a day of shooting.

**Bump**
- Small increase in pay as a usage fee or for special performance provisions, e.g., additional money for use of a vehicle in a scene, or for allowing an extensive haircut by the production or providing a tuxedo or other specialty clothing.

**Business**
- Entertainment industry.
- Series of actions, often with a prop ("Give her some business with the anchor").

**By the Numbers**
- Exactly as instructed.

**Cable Puller**
- Audio trainee, assisting the boom operator by feeding or taking up slack in the mike cable as the boom operator moves around on set.
(See "Production Personnel")

**Calling Service**
- Phone service responsible for taking performers' messages from casting and agents, acting as a middleman or go-between to make calls in search of work for the performer (mostly available in the US).

**Call Sheet**
- List of performer requirements and roles, along with pertinent information, e.g., call time, shoot location, wardrobe needs, and other special requirements.

**Call Time**
- When you are contractually obliged to be at the location or set, your start time for the day.

**Camera Left**
- Move to the right (the camera operator's left).

**Camera Right**
- Move to the left (the camera operator's right).

**Casting**
- Assign the various roles in a production.

- Department or person(s) in charge of casting.
- Holding a viewing session (audition, go-see, look-see, cattle call, or interview) for performers, to consider their suitability for roles.

**Casting Agency**
**Casting Agent**
- Company or person in a small centre, acting as both casting department and agent when casting performers (extras and principals). Paid by the production and receives no commissions from the performers.

**Casting Couch**
- Sexual harassment. Originally derived from sexual favours demanded by persons of power in exchange for film work, often taking place in their private office (on couch).

**Casting Director**
- Head of the casting department, or casting executive.
- Principal Casting Director: responsible for screening potential main performers, arranging auditions and booking contracted players.
- Extras Casting Director: responsible for finding and booking suitable background performers, arranging Go-Sees if requested by production, and sometimes supervising extras in the holding area.

**Cattle Call**
- Call for a large number of performers to attend an audition or go-see.

**CBC**
- Canadian Broadcasting Corporation.

**Character**
- Any role in a production.
- Specifically, a role or performance that emphasizes strong characteristics or personalities of a person or group, which may be very different than those of the performer concerned.

**Character Shot**
- Headshot or photo taken of a performer in character.

**Cheat the Shot**
- Move position slightly to the left or right, shift timing, path, or action from what was done in a previous shot.

**Checking the Gate**
- Checking the focal plane of the camera to be sure no slivers of film stock fell across it.

| | |
|---|---|
| **Chew the Scenery** | • Overact, ham it up. |
| **Clapper** <br> **Clapper Board** | • Slate (which see). The board with a swinging arm on top used to identify the scenes, shots, take number and assorted information, recorded on camera to identify the portions of developed film to be considered in editing. From the sound the board makes when the top is slammed down, allowing the editor to synchronise the audio and video signals by the "clap" sound made when the moving arm stops. |
| **Clip** | • Recording of a small portion of the scene or project. |
| **Commercial** | • Short production intended to sell a product, service, or message. |
| **Commission** | • Agent's fee. A percentage of the amount earned by the performer for work procured by the agent, or for any work as a performer, if the agent has exclusivity. |
| **Continuity** | • Repetition of all dialogue, actions, and placements in scenes shot earlier. |
| **Continuity Character** | • Character which has been established and is required for additional shooting later. <br> • Character established as a **Regular** throughout a series. |
| **Continuity Person** | • Person responsible for taking note of all dialogue, actions and placements in order to maintain continuity between shots. <br> (See "Production Personnel") |
| **Contract** | • Agreement, especially a formal, enforceable agreement in writing, between two parties, e.g., contract between performer and agent or production. |
| **Course** | • Training which combines seminar (theory) and workshop (practical) instruction. Usually a fairly long period of study, possibly full-time. |

218

**Craft**
- Trade requiring special skills.
- Craft service department. Food people on set.

**Craft Service**
- Food people on set: caterers, substantials, snack table.

**Crane**
- Machine with (usually) a horizontal arm swinging on a vertical axis, used to raise the camera and its operators to shoot above a scene or from an otherwise awkward location, e.g., over a creek.

**Crew**
- Group of people working as a team on the technical side of a production.
(See "Production Personnel")

**Crossover**
- Move through a scene past the camera.

**C.U.**
- Close-Up. A close view of an object or performer, e.g., a head and shoulder shot.

**Cue**
- Audible or visual signal to commence, change, or end an action.

**Cut**
- Stop shooting this take of the scene or sequence.

**Demo**
**Demo Reel**
**Demo Tape**
- Video tape displaying recorded clips of a performer's work, mostly used for long-distance auditions or to provide potential principal agents with examples of the performer's work on camera.

**Dialogue**
- Scripted words spoken by an actor. Not necessarily a conversation.

**Director**
- Person who interprets the script, plans the scenes, stages (and sometimes guides) the performers' presentation of the characters.
(See "Production Personnel")

**Dolly**
- Frame on wheels used to move the camera during filming.
- To move the camera during the filming of a scene or sequence, typically toward or away from the action.
(See also **Track**)

| | |
|---|---|
| **Dolly Grip** | • Technician responsible for camera stabilization and movement on dolly, platform, and scaffold. (See "Production Personnel") |
| **Dolly Tracks** | • See **Track**. |
| **DOP** | • Director Of Photography. Works with the directors' vision of the production to create the look of the film, controls all camera, lighting and electrical supplies, and the crew needed. (See crew chart in "On Set" chapter) |
| **Double Speed** | • Recording the film at twice normal speed to create a slow motion effect when played back at regular speed. |
| **DP** | • DOP (which see) in the States. |
| **Drama School** | • (More or less) established college offering a specialised training in performance arts. |
| **Dub** | • A copy, or to make a copy of, all or part of a recording of a production. |
| **ECU** | • Extreme Close-Up: a very tight shot of the face only, or less. |
| **Edge Of Frame** | • Outer boundaries of what the camera can see. |
| **Edit** | • Revise or create a sequence of shots, scenes, or sound by means of cutting and splicing sections of tape or film. |
| **Editor** | • Person who edits the recorded material to create the final show. <br> • Machine used to make the edits. |
| **Effects** | • (FX) Technical tricks, including visual and sound edits. |
| **Eighty-Six** | • Get rid of. (Just count the different explanations of this!) |

**Employed**
- Working under the detailed instructions of the person who pays you. Most performers are self-employed, hired out to various engagers to carry out a task in a creative way.

**Engager**
- Production company.

**Entertainment Industry**
- Business of creating artistic works that interest, please or amuse the public, e.g., a movie, television show, live performance.

**Episode**
- One program or production, complete in itself but forming part of a series.

**Equity**
- Canadian (CAEA) or American (AEA) stage performers' union.

**Exclusive**
- (Of an agent) Having sole authority to act as your representative for specific areas of the industry (e.g., extra or principal work).

**Executive Producer**
- Person above the producer, sometimes the main financial backer for the production.

**Explosives**
- Chemicals which explode (TNT) or give the effect of an explosion (flash powder plus black gunpowder).

**Extra**
- See **Background Performer.**

**Extras Agent**
- Agent who represents performers for background work.

**Extras Casting**
- Person or people responsible for choosing and providing background performers for a production.

**Extras Casting Director**
- Head of the Extras Casting department.

**Extras Holding**
- Waiting room or area where extras are kept between shots on set.

**Eye Line**
- Point or object you are to look towards.

**Feature**
- Film made to be shown in theatrical or direct to video release.

**Featured**
- Seen promininently on camera as a definite focus within a scene.

**Feedback**
- Information about one's actions.
- Howl when a microphone is too close to a speaker.

**Film**
- Record a performance on light-sensitive strip.
- Motion picture, the finished production so recorded.

**Final Positions**
- Your position and stance at the end of the shot or scene.

**Final Touch-Ups**
- Adjust hair or wardrobe for scene continuity, repair or refresh performers' make-up, etc. immediately before shooting the scene.

**Firearms**
- Weapons such as pistols, guns or rifles, either live (with a charge) or props.

**First AD**
- First Assistant Director, second to the director. (See "Production Personnel")

**First Team**
- Main cast.

**First Unit**
- (Also **Main Unit**) The principal crew team, responsible for recording the main scenes. (See also **Unit, Second Unit**)

**Firsts**
**First Positions**
- See Final Positions

**Flag**
- Hand-held or mounted panel, translucent to soften the light or opaque to cut the spread of the light. (See also **Barn Door**)

**Flash**
- Warning that a flash camera is about to go off, so that the Gaffer won't look for the lighting instrument that he assumes has burned out.

**Flash Pot**
- Metal container filled with charge and material to create an explosive flash.

**Focus Puller**
- Person responsible for keeping camera shots in focus, should be able to substitute for the DOP in an emergency.

**Frame**
- Outside edges of the cameras' viewing area.

**Freelance**
- A performer who seeks work independently, without using an agent.

**From the Top**
- From the beginning of the scene or shot.

**F/X**
- Effects.

**Gaffer**
- Chief electrician, determines electrical supply needed and technical requirements, and helps maintain continuity lighting when shooting.

**Gate Is Clean**
**Gate Is Clear**
- See **Checking the Gate**

**GE**
- General Extra.

**Gig**
- Job as a performer.

**Glossy**
- Promotional photograph of performer.
  (See also **Character Shot, Headshot**)

**Go-See**
**Look-See**
- Like an audition, but set up for viewing background talent, for appearance and behaviour, not acting skill.
  (See also **Audition, Cattle Call**)

**Green Room**
- Extras Holding Area.

**Grievance**
- First stage of arbitration in a formal complaint filed through the performer union against an engager.

**Grip**
- Technician who loads, unloads, moves and places equipment and scenery.

**Guild**
- A trade union, or a professional association, or a section of either serving a group within the whole membership.

| | |
|---|---|
| **Hair** | • The people in the Hair Department, or the department itself. |
| **Half-Apple** | • Half the height of a full **Apple.** |
| **Half-Speed** | • Record or film at half normal speed to create a fast forward effect when played back at normal speed. |
| **Handler** | • Person responsible for handling and controlling the use of animals, or of special equipment and effects, such as firearms or explosives. |
| **Headshot** | • Performers' main promotional 8x10 inch B/W photo, usually of head and face in close-up. |
| **Hiatus** | • Temporary break in the usual shooting schedule before the production resumes normal operations. |
| **Hit Your Mark** | • Move to a specific predetermined position and arrive at a specified time during the scene. The mark may be set with tape, or determined by using the props and scenery as points of reference, using your peripheral vision.<br>(See **Mark**) |
| **Holding**<br>**Holding Area** | • Waiting room or area where the extras are kept between takes. |
| **Hold the Roll** | • Cancel the warning that the scene is about to be shot. |
| **Honey Wagon** | • Trucks and trailers for crew departments, cast rooms, changing rooms – and restrooms, whence the name. |
| **Hot** | • Doing well, good performance.<br>• In the shot: something, or an area, which will be seen on camera. |
| **Hot Set** | • Extreme caution needed: explosives or fire hazards are present (usually hidden) in the scene. |
| **Improv**<br>**Improvisation** | • Creating a performance without script or rehearsal. |

| | |
|---|---|
| **Industrial** | • Video production not meant to be broadcast or shown publicly, for in-house company training use, for training or education, or to promote the image of a company, at a convention, for example. |
| **Industry** | • The acting business. (See **Entertainment Industry**) |
| **In-House** | • Done within the company's own premises or under the company's direct control. |
| **Initiation Fee** | • Fee paid upon admission into a performer union. |
| **In the Wings** | • In the area beside the set, off camera. From theatre jargon. |
| **IPA** | • ACTRA's Independent Production Agreement. |
| **Jurisdiction** | • Range of work or geographical territory over which a union's authority extends. |
| **Key Grip** | • The Head Grip, master stagehand. |
| **Key Light** | • Main light on an actor. |
| **Lavalier** | • Small condenser microphone pinned or hung around the performer's neck, usually hidden. |
| **Lighting** | • Department in charge of lights.<br>• Various types of lighting instruments and the way in which they are arranged on set. The effect of the lights in action. (See also **Key Light, Flag, Gaffer, Best Bo**y) |
| **Lines** | • Scripted words spoken by the actor. |
| **Live** | • Of a production, broadcast as it is being performed, rather than from a previously-recorded tape of a performance.<br>• Active or present.<br>• Carrying an electrical charge, burning or glowing, charged with explosives, or (of a firearm) containing unfired cartridges. |

**Live To Tape**     •   Recorded and shown without editing.

**Location**     •   Where the production is shooting, not in the studio. (See also **On Location**)

**Locations**     •   Department in charge of production location, permits, scouting, parking, preparations, etc.

**Look-See**     •   See **Go-See**

**Looping**     •   In **post-production** (which see), taping lines, new or previously recorded, to insert and match to visuals.

**Lose**     •   Get rid of.

**LS**     •   Long Shot: filmed at a distance, showing the full length of the performers, up to wide landscape shots.

**Lunch**     •   Meal break, regardless of time of day. Or night.

**Main Unit**     •   See **First Unit.**

**Make-Up**     •   The department and the crew, and the cosmetics they use.

**Mark**     •   Positions, and angles to be facing, at specific times in a scene, usually indicated by strips of tape or chalk lines on the floor (out of camera view) marking the position where the actor's feet should be. Also, a reference point to aim at when making a move. (See **Hit Your Mark**)

**Master**     •   Original version or copy from which all reproductions are taken, as in "master tape." The reference version of a scene, as in "master shot."

**Master Shot**     •   Overall view of a sequence, into which all other shots of the same scene from different angles are edited.

**Meal Penalty**     •   Penalty or compensation paid by the production to performers and crew for continuing work when meal break is contractually due.

**Mime**
- Perform, appearing to speak but using movement and gestures but no audible words.
- Perform, pretending to use an article which doesn't exist.

**Mini-Series**
- Production intended for broadcast in segments, with a single essential storyline beginning in the first segment and concluding in the last.

**Mixer**
- Head of the sound department, the person with the earphones and movable cart of recording equipment.
- Equipment used to adjust audio recording levels.

**Monitor**
- Television screen, usually B/W, usually on a cart, used to view scenes on set as seen by the camera.

**MOS**
- "Mit-out Sound." Scene shot without any audio recording. From supposed Mittel European accent of early film directors.

**Moving On**
- Current scene is done, continue on to next scheduled scene.

**MOW**
- Movie of the Week.

**MS**
- Mid-Shot. Performers from the waist up.

**Non-Member
Non-Union**
- Performer who does not belong to a professional performers union, alliance, association, guild, or organization.
- Production which has not agreed to meet the minimum requirements of a performer union, and there fore may not employ union performers. Also a production, often a commercial, over which individual crew unions are not exercising jurisdiction, allowing members of different crew unions to work together.

**Number Ones**
- Return to your starting place and stance at the beginning of the shot or scene.

**On Location**
- Shooting at a place away from the studio.

**Over the Top**
- Perform the character in an exaggerated or extreme manner, e.g., at a frenzied level of energy.

**Pager**
- Portable receiver to notify you of messages waiting or to signal someone is trying to reach you.

**Pan**
- To rotate the camera on its mounting across the viewing area so as to take in a whole scene or to follow a moving character or object.

**Pancake**
- Water-based make-up. An old-fashioned term.
- (Crab-apple) Wooden platform, just over an inch high, an eighth-apple, for performers to stand on.

**PD**
- Photo Double (which see).

**Performer Union**
- In Canada: ACTRA, EQUITY, UdA, UBCP.
- In US: the 4 As, including AEA, AFTRA, SAG.
  (See also **Guild**)

**Period**
- Characteristic of a certain period of time, such as medieval kingdoms, Old West, psychedelic 60s, futuristic, etc..

**Permit**
- Permission (a "work permit," extra "permittee voucher") for non-members to work on a union production at the same pay scale and working conditions as members, but without membership status.

**Permittee**
- Non-member performer allowed same rights of protection and pay scale, and bound by the same regulations, as performer union members on a union production, on a temporary basis through a permit.
  (See also **Permit**)

**Personal Manager**
- Person who manages and guides the business side of the performer's career, including high end promotion, interview bookings, and sometimes agent work as well, administering to long-term career development.
  (See also **Agent**)

**Photo Double**
- (PD) Background performer who resembles another performer and is used to replace that person at a dis-

tance or from a view in which it is not obvious they are doing so, e.g., in the back of a car driving by, or seen from behind in a large crowd.

**Pick-Up**

- To record a portion of the shot again, not the entire scene.

**Picture's Up**

- We're ready to shoot the scene: everybody quiet, hold the work, performers to their first positions, sound the warning bell/buzzer (if available), stand by ready to roll.

**PMT**

- Photo-mechanical Transfer. Method of producing a printed copy from a photograph.

**Post-Production**

- Period after all shooting is over, when the film or video raw footage will be edited into proper order, with additional soundtracks, effects, and credits to turn it into a completed saleable product.

**Pots**

- See **Flash Pot**

**POV**

- Point Of View. The camera replaces a character, and records the action as the character would see it.

**Principal**

- Major scripted character.
- Performer who does non-extra work (Actor category and higher).
  (See **Actor**)
- Technically, under the IPA, a performer engaged to speak or mime eleven or more lines of dialogue, or engaged to perform a sufficiently major role without dialogue.

**Principal Agent**

- Agent who represents the performer for principal work.
  (See also **Agent, Talent Agent, Casting Agent, Principal, Extras Agent**)

**Principal Casting**

- Person, company or department responsible for screening potential main performers, arranging auditions, and booking contracted players.

(See also **Casting, Casting Agent, Casting Director, Principal**)

**Print**
- Copy of your personal promotional photo or head shot.
- On set, "that's a print," "print it," or "print," means the scene is acceptable for consideration to be used in the edited film.

**Producer**
- Person or company in charge of presenting a show or production, putting together the major elements of the production, arranging finances including crew and cast payments.
(See also **Executive Producer**)

**Production**
- Project to be filmed or taped.
- Company and its personnel making and carrying out the producer's decisions.

**Production Company**
- Producer's employer or own corporation.

**Profession**
- People involved in an occupation, or the occupation itself, requiring special skills, training, or talents, e.g., the acting business.

**Professional**
- Making a business or trade of something others may do for pleasure.
- Approaching work with proficiency, dedication, precision, and pride.
(See also **Amateur**)

**Promotion**
- Process of furthering the development, growth or acceptance of one's career.
- Publicity and advertising, e.g., distribution of one's photos and résumés.

**Props**
- Properties: Portable objects (fake or real) used by the performers on set.
- The production department and person(s) in charge of creating, distributing, and maintaining the props.

| | |
|---|---|
| **Prop Buyer** | • Person in charge of purchasing props for a production. |
| **Props Master** | • Head of the props department. |
| **Quarter Apple** | • One quarter of the height of a full **Apple.** |
| **Reciprocal Agreement** | • Legal agreement between two or more unions pledging to co-operate on matters affecting each other's members. |
| **Reel** | • See **Demo** |
| **Registration Fee** | • Money charged (by an agent) in return for being included on the agent's roster. |
| **Regular** | • Established as a character recurring in a series, e.g., regular desk cop in a police station, bartenders and servers in a restaurant scene frequented by the main cast. |
| **Rehearsal** | • Performance before actual filming for technicians to see the blocking (which see).<br>• Rarely, and usually only for stars, practising and developing the performance which will be recorded. |
| **Residual** | • Fee, not paid to performers in extra categories, licensing the use of the performer's recorded work beyond the period bought in the original fee, or as transferred to another medium. |
| **Residual Character**<br>**Residual Performer** | • Character in SOC, Actor, Stunt or Principal categories, contractually entitled to receive residuals (excludes those performing in an extras category). (See also **Residual**) |
| **Résumé** | • Short (one-page) summary of a performer's physical statistics, skills, talent, training, etc. |
| **Retake** | • Shoot it again. |
| **Risk Performance** | • One in which more than day-to-day danger is present. |

ACTRA does not allow performers to be put in danger, demanding that Stunt performers be hired, advance notice be given, and Stunt fees be paid.

**Roll Camera**
- Direction to start filming or taping.

**Roll Sound**
- Direction to mixer to start audio equipment recording to bring audio tape to full recording speed.

**Rolling**
- Acknowledgement that camera has started recording in response to "Roll Camera" directive.

**Room Tone**
- Nature of "silence" in a space, due to air currents, equipment within the room, reflective or dampening surfaces, etc. May differ from spot to spot within a room.

**Roster**
- List of the performers represented by an agency.

**Rounds**
- Process of performing business management or promotion.
(See "Legwork" chapter)

**Run-Through**
- Attempt to rehearse a full scene without stopping.

**Rushes**
- Unedited prints from the previous days of shooting, to view or review the look, continuity, performances, and technical aspects of the recorded scenes.

**Safety**
- "Shoot a safety" or "print a safety": do another take of the scene or shot just to be sure of a backup for editing.

**SAG**
- Screen Actors Guild (US performer union).
(See "Union Matters")

**Scene**
- Time, place of circumstances of a story.
- Portion of the scripted story.
- Set (walls, room, etc.) where the action takes place.

**Script**
- Written text of a production.

**Season**
- Period in which a series of episodes is scheduled to be filmed or taped.
- Period in which a series is scheduled to be aired.

**Second AD**
- Second Assistant Director, usually responsible for directing extras' placements, movements, and actions on set. (Compare **Third AD**)

**Second Team**
- Stand-Ins (which see).

**Second Unit**
- Team of set personnel used to film atmosphere shots, crowds, stunts and special effects, etc. while the main unit is filming the main scenes elsewhere.

**SEG**
- Screen Extras Guild (US union no longer in existence).

**Self-Employed**
- Working for oneself, running a personal business with reasonable expectation of profit.

**Seminar**
- Specialized conference or short intensive course of study.

**Series**
- A number of episodes produced as a group to be presented in a regular pattern.

**Set**
- Physical setting where the acting takes place. (See **Scene**)

**Shoot**
- To film or tape.
- Part of the process of recording a production ("a film shoot"), defined by being in one location, or by taking place in a set period of time.

**Shooting**
- Filming or taping is taking place.

**Shot**
- Part of the action, to be recorded continuously as a unit.
- What the camera sees.

**SI**
- Stand-In (which see).

| | |
|---|---|
| **Sides** | • Script, especially a performer's own scenes. |
| | • Miniature copy of the part of the script for the current day of shooting, for handy reference by the actors. Small enough to be hidden in a pocket during shooting. |
| **Sign-Out** | • Complete voucher or time sheet at the end of the shooting day, agreeing (or registering disagreement) with the time recorded as worked. The voucher "contract" is countersigned, and the cash extra's fee is paid by the authorized production or extras casting representative. |
| **Silent on Camera** | • See **SOC** |
| **Slate** | • **Clapper Board** (which see). From the chalk board or slate upon which the production and shot information is written. |
| | • Before a taped audition performance: identify yourself and your agent. |
| **SOC** | • Silent On Camera: In Canada, appearing recognizably in a commercial, but performing without dialogue. A residual category under ACTRA. |
| **Smoke, Smoke It Up** | • Use a smoke machine to create an subdued atmosphere when seen through the camera. |
| **Special Skills Extra (SSE)** | • Performer required to perform silent business with a level of proficiency or other physical skills superior to that of the average person, but not amounting to Stunt work (which see). Is paid a little more than basic extra rate. |
| **SPFX** | • Special Effects. Trickery added in **Post-Production** (which see) to make a shot more effective. |
| **Standby** **On Standby** | • On hold. Awaiting confirmation or instructions. |
| **Stand-In** | • (SI) Person used to replace or represent a member of the cast during the set-up or blocking of a scene. |

**Stats**
- Statistics. Your physical measurements, appearance, skills, and experience.

**Status of the Artist**
- In Canada, federal legislation which allows and administers collective bargaining, and recognises artists' continuing rights in their performances (which rights had until 1995 only been negotiated and agreed between engagers and performer "unions"). Quebec has its Bill 90, and in BC there is Status of the Artist legislation, but ACTRA-BC and UBCP are registered trade unions. Apart from these, provincial legislation has yet to be enacted.

**Statutory Holiday**
- Ain't no such thing in the film industry (except maybe for Christmas Day). A legal statutory holiday for others is just another regular work day for people in show business. No break, no special holiday overtime.

**Steadicam™**
- Patented camera mount, on a harness on the camera operator, giving hand-held manoeuvrability with close to studio smoothness in movement.

**Steward**
- ACTRA employee responsible for administering the terms of one or more Agreements.

**Story Board**
- Series of drawings showing the types of shot and viewpoints to be used in a sequence.

**Strike**
- Get rid of, often short for "strike the set."
- Withdrawal of services, to go on strike. Not yet legal for most performers, who can only refuse to sign new contracts.

**Studio**
- Building devoted to production recording and broadcasting. The space within that, or any, building where recording or filming takes place.

**Stunt**
- Feat or act showing boldness or skill, which may entail a high degree of risk, intended to thrill an audience.

**Stunt Double**
- Stunt performer hired to photographically and physically resemble and replace another performer during the filming of stunts or dangerous scenes.

| | |
|---|---|
| **Stunt Performer** | • Trained or experienced performer who carries out risk and stunt performances in a production. |
| **Substantial** | • Snack provided by an IPA production to the cast and crew, to allow an extended (six-hour instead of five-hour) period of work before a meal break without incurring a meal penalty. |
| **T4** | • Annual total income and deductions information slip provided to an employee – and to Revenue Canada. |
| **T4A** | • Annual total income and deductions information slip often provided to a self-employed person – and to Revenue Canada – by an engager. |
| **TAD** | • Trainee Assistant Director (below the 3rd AD). |
| **Take** | • Attempt (successful or not) to record a sequence. |
| **Talent** | • Performer(s). |
| **Talent Agent** | • Principal Agent (which see). (See also **Agent, Extras Agent, Principal Agent, Casting Agent**) |
| **Tape** | • Record a performance electronically on videotape. |
| **TBA** | • To Be Announced. |
| **Third AD** | • Third Assistant Director, often responsible for supervising background performers in holding area, and assisting in directing crossovers on set. (Compare **Second AD**) |
| **Tracking** | • Moving the camera, typically parallel to the action, typically on tracks (which see). |
| **Tracks** | • Little choo-choo train trestles allowing the dolly to move in a straight smooth line. |
| **Trades** **Trade Books** **Trade Magazines** | • Periodicals or publications dealing with various aspects of the entertainment industry and with those involved or working in the industry. |

**Trailer**
- Short film made up of selected scenes from a show, used to advertise or promote the production.
- Vehicle equipped for use as temporary dressing rooms, offices, hair and make-up rooms, etc. while on location.

**Type**
- The qualities or appearance of a particular class or group. The kind of stereotyped characters you look like.

**Typecast**
- Cast a performer in a role or as a character to fit their appearance, personality, etc., or to cast the performer repeatedly for the same type of character.

**UBCP**
- Union of British Columbia Performers. Recently given jurisdiction (which see) over recorded media in British Columbia, Canada.

**UdA**
- l'Union des Artistes. Performer union based in Montreal, Canada, with a branch in Toronto, having jurisdiction over stage and media francophone work.

**Unemployed**
- (Of actors) Regardless of work status, not currently under an acting contract.

**Union**
- See **Performer Union**

**Unit**
- Group formed by the cast and crew, and their equipment.
(See also **First Unit, Second Unit**)

**Upgrade**
- Promotion to a higher performance category with an increase in pay.

**Video**
- Electronic transmission and reception of a visual signal.
- Video (tape): reusable magnetic tape for recording video (and audio) signals.

**Voice-Over**
- Voice of an unseen commentator or narrator, heard over action on screen.

| | |
|---|---|
| **Voucher** | • Extra's contract: written evidence of work done and payment due. |
| **Waiver** | • Written statement giving up a right, claim, etc. Found on extras' contracts and vouchers, and cash extras' sign-out sheets. |
| **Walkie** | • Walkie-talkie. Radio transceivers used by the crew (especially ADs). |
| **Walk-Through** | • Slow version of a Run-Through, performers slowly working through stages of blocking. |
| **Wannabee** | • "Want To Be" (a star, etc.). |
| **Wardrobe** | • Costumes worn on set, the crew working in the wardrobe department, and the department itself. |
| **Wild Line** **Wild Track** | • Dialogue recorded without filming or videotaping. (Compare **MOS**) |
| **Window Shot** | • Next-to-final shot of the day. From "Win do we go home?" |
| **Wings** | • Area beside the set, out of camera view. |
| **Workshop** | • Training covering a specific skill, usually with a hands-on approach. |
| **Wrangler** | • Person(s) in charge of the animals, or, jokingly, anything else ("the doughnut wrangler"). |
| **Wrap** | • Finish or be done for the day.<br>• End of a production. |
| **Wrap Party** | • Celebration (by invitation if not a crew member) after a production is finished shooting; the production's way of thanking the cast and crew for their work during shooting. |
| **X-it** | • Get rid of it. |